The War for Muslim Minds

The War for Muslim Minds

ISLAM AND THE WEST

GILLES KEPEL

TRANSLATED BY PASCALE GHAZALEH

THE BELKNAP PRESS OF
HARVARD UNIVERSITY PRESS
Cambridge, Massachusetts, and London, England
2004

Library of Congress Cataloging-in-Publication Data
Kepel, Gilles.
The war for Muslim minds : Islam and the West / Gilles Kepel;
translated by Pascale Ghazaleh.
p.   cm.
Includes bibliographical references and index.
ISBN 0-674-01575-4 (alk. paper)
1. East and West.   2. Islam—21st century.   3. War on
Terrorism, 2001-   I. Title.
CB251.K38   2004
909'.09767083—dc22   2004050474

TO THE MEMORY OF
MAXIME RODINSON

الصديق
ماص سارق

JANUARY 25,1915
MAY 23, 2004

Contents

Introduction

In December 2001, in an online manifesto written in Arabic, one of the chief instigators of the attacks on New York and Washington provided a political rationalization for the events of September 11. The text, entitled *Knights under the Prophet's Banner*, was signed by the Egyptian physician Ayman al-Zawahiri, Al Qaeda's principal ideologue and Osama bin Laden's mentor. This remarkable document purported to explain why Islamic jihadists had attacked the United States—the "faraway enemy"—and to outline the benefits they expected to reap from that cataclysm.

Dr. Zawahiri began his text with a somber diagnosis of the movement's failures in the 1990s, measured against the hopes that were raised by its triumph over the Red Army in Afghanistan in 1989. From Egypt to Bosnia, Saudi Arabia to Algeria—everywhere in the Muslim world—jihad activists had failed to mobilize the "masses" in the effort to overthrow their corrupt rulers, the "nearby enemy." To reverse the course of this decline, a radical change of strategy was necessary. The sheer audacity and magnitude of the massive blow struck against the United States was designed to galvanize un-decided Muslims by convincing them that the Islamist militants were irresistibly powerful and that the United States, the arrogant protector of apostate regimes in the Middle East and North Africa, was abhorrently weak. But terrorism on Western territory would not distract the militants from their primary task: waging a war for the hearts and minds of Muslims. Al Qaeda's long-term strategy was to strengthen its grip on co-religionists and to enlist them in establishing an "Islamic state" through armed struggle.

The setbacks of the 1990s, Zawahiri wrote, were due to the absence of a great rallying cause that could unify the Muslim world behind its activist vanguard. But suddenly, at the turn of the twenty-first century, Palestine provided just such a cause. The termination of the Oslo peace process, the eruption of the second intifada in the fall of 2000, and the repressive campaign waged by Ariel Sharon's government made armed struggle in Palestine seem legitimate to viewers of Al Jazeera and other Arab satellite television networks. In the summer of 2001, suicide attacks on Israeli civilians, organized by Palestinian Islamists and described as "martyrdom operations" by preachers in the Muslim world, were seen as a practical answer to the crushing superiority of Israel's military arsenal.

The deadly downward spiral in Palestine provided the opportunity that the masterminds of September 11 had been waiting for. They conceived of the carnage in New York and Washington as an extension of the Palestinian suicide bombings, whose popularity Bin Laden sought to channel for his own purposes. In a videotape broadcast on October 7, Bin Laden sat with Zawahiri in front of an Afghan cave and swore to his television viewers that, "by Allah who raised the heavens without pillars, America [will] never know peace" as long as the Palestinian people continued to suffer.

In the 1990s, as Islamist militants turned to global terrorism to advance their agenda in the Muslim world, the Middle East was caught in a political maelstrom following the Soviet Union's collapse. The resurgence of the Israeli–Palestinian conflict in 2000 was the most striking symptom, but an underlying cause of unrest in the region went much deeper. It originated in a worldview—neoconservatism—that acquired influence in Washington long before the election of President George W. Bush. After the attacks on the World Trade Center and the Pentagon, it would become predominant.

The neoconservatives made their own diagnosis of the 1990s, and it was just as devastating as Zawahiri's—but for diametrically opposed reasons. The neocons, self-declared champions of Israel as a predominantly "Jewish state," saw the Oslo peace process as a trap. It created an illusion of security for Israel, whose existence the Arabs accepted because of their circumstantial weakness. But as soon as they had the means to do so, the Arab states would resume their campaign of eradication, according to the neocons. In addition, the Oslo peace process reinforced a deplorable status quo in the Middle East by granting authoritarian, corrupt Arab governments a seal of approval from the White House. As long as these regimes went along with Oslo and supported the United States' other primary interest—a reliable supply of oil at a reasonable price—neither the administration of George H. W. Bush nor that of Bill Clinton challenged these antidemocratic regimes in any forceful way.

In the mid-1990s, neoconservatives at think tanks, in the media, and on university campuses started to lobby for a general reshuffling of the deck in the Middle East. Their program called for military intervention aimed at breaking the back of those states considered a menace to Israel: Baathist Syria, Iran under the mullahs, but especially Saddam Hussein's Iraq. A civilian extension of this campaign would encourage political reform that would put democratically elected representatives of civil society—preferably people well integrated into the global economy under U.S. hegemony—in control.

Though the ultimate goals of jihadists and neoconservatives diverged, their proximate goals were remarkably aligned: ousting the region's regimes, whose authoritarianism and corruption they both abhorred. The coincidence has more than anecdotal value: it demonstrates that the balance of political power on which the Middle East was poised just prior to and immediately following 9/11 was considered illegitimate by actors on both sides, and they were willing, indeed eager, to use force in order to modify it—terrorism in the case of jihadists seeking to establish an Islamic state, and military action in the case of neoconservatives seeking to advance democracy.

On both sides of this conflict, a complicating source of friction was the presence of massive oil reserves, which provide a major portion of the planet's total energy supply. When barrel prices were high, the petro-monarchies accumulated enormous cash reserves which allowed them to influence the course of international events—by financing movements, such as the Afghan jihad, that advanced their interests, and on occasion by strong-arming their clients, especially the United States. But these oil revenues were unevenly distributed throughout the population, and as a consequence basic economic indicators for the region were low. As the U.N. Development Program report on the Arab world made clear, the region suffered from a disastrous combination of overpopulation, low employment and low pay, and deficient access to education and modern communications. This situation created fertile conditions for conflict, particularly over control of the dominant ideological system that maintained the region's political and social balance: Islam.

Thus, the September 2001 attacks represented a crossroads for two diametrically opposed ways of thinking. Each group responded by formulating a project for the radical transformation of the Middle East. The jihadists endeavored to capitalize on the "triumph" of September 11 to attract sympathizers to their cause. Their goal was to become the spokesmen and defenders of the faith against President Bush's war on terror. They sought to manipulate a classic political cycle: their aggression triggered repression, which inevitably produced casualties, which allowed them to express solidarity with the victims—women, children, the dead and wounded, and abused prisoners, whose Muslim identity the militants emphasized. The purpose of this exercise was to swell the ranks of recruits for martyrdom.

The neocons, on the other hand, saw September 11 as a tragic opportunity to sell their radical new deal for the Middle East to the shell-shocked Bush administration. Still reeling from an attack they did not foresee, George Bush and his advisers, with the approval of Congress, adopted most of the neoconservatives' agenda. Before 9/11, over the course of several decades and administrations, Washington had been careful to maintain equilibrium between two imperatives: Israel's security and a guaranteed oil supply. The war on terror upset this traditional balance in America's Middle Eastern policy by putting support for Israel first and downplaying relations with the world's paramount oil producer, Saudi Arabia.

Prior to September 11, the Saudi royal family had collaborated closely with the Bush clan, in business and in politics, and since the Second World War the kingdom had proven to be a trustworthy ally of the United States. The seething resentments and rhetoric that had poured out of mosques, religious schools, television broadcasts, and websites for many years were not the Bush administration's concern—until it discovered that fifteen of the nine-teen hijackers on September 11 were from Saudi Arabia.

The war on terror declared by the Bush administration had three goals: liquidating Al Qaeda and its Taliban hosts; pressuring Saudi Arabia for political reform; and overthrowing Saddam Hussein in Iraq. The hunt for Al Qaeda turned Afghanistan into a testing ground for a formidable arsenal of "smart" weapons that had been developed to strike down the USSR. But GPS-guided missiles and unmanned drones proved unsuitable against an elusive, intangible enemy. Al Qaeda was less a military base of operations than a data-base that connected jihadists all over the world via the Internet. The U.S. attack on Afghanistan and the elimination of the Taliban mistook a shadow for the prey. Even as Bin Laden disappeared into the valleys and caves of the Afghan-Pakistani border, he reappeared in cyberspace to claim responsibility for deadly attacks as far away as Indonesia. The sponsor of global jihad was at once everywhere and nowhere.

The war against Iraq attempted to complete—and, in large part, to make up for—America's inconclusive hunt for the source of Islamist terrorism. The new message of the Bush administration seemed to be that the failure to capture Bin Laden was no longer important, because he was merely the poster boy for a much more threatening target. The true sponsor of international terror was the Bush family's nemesis, Saddam Hussein. By toppling the Iraqi dic-tator, the neoconservatives in the Bush administration hoped to kill two birds with one stone. First, the removal of Saddam Hussein would allow democracy to spring forth in Iraq and civil society to flourish throughout the region, as predicted by the example of Eastern Europe after the fall of the Berlin Wall. The political frustration that bred terrorism would evaporate, and, most important, Israel would be welcomed into the fold of a now-reconciled "New Middle East."

Second, the fall of Saddam Hussein's regime would end a decade of embargo and sanctions that had kept Iraqi oil from flowing freely to the marketplace. Once Iraqi oil fields were operating at full capacity, the Saudi royal family, weakened by the competition in barrel price, would give in to demands for reform, and the country would cease to function as an incubator for terrorists. Any temporary destabilization within America's old ally would not have catastrophic consequences on the global energy supply, now that Iraq's petroleum resources could be tapped.

The American invasion of Iraq, assisted by the British, resulted in a stunning military victory over a conventional Third World army. But the occupation rapidly hit a wall. When Saddam's weapons of mass destruction—used to justify rushing the invasion without U.N. support—could not be found, governments in the United States and Britain were undermined. In Iraq itself, the occupation opened up a Pandora's box of ethnic strife, out of which sprang Kurdish, Shiite, and Sunni separatists, along with other armed resisters. Jihadists from neighboring countries were not far behind.

With the occupation of Iraq, the war for Muslim minds entered the global jungle of the Internet. Photographs of Iraqi prisoners being tortured or sexually humiliated by their American guards circulated freely, along with videos of hostages being mistreated by their terrorist captors. One video showed the decapitation of an American civilian contractor, to cries of "Allahu akbar!" ("God is great!"). Through its coverage on the Internet, the Iraq War erased the geographical boundaries of Dar al-Islam (the domain of Islam) and Dar al-Harb (the domain of war) that had structured Muslim geopolitics for fourteen centuries.

Exactly two and a half years after the attacks on New York and Washington, on March 11, 2004, Islamist terrorists simultaneously killed 191 people on four commuter trains in Madrid. The choice of this European target was not random. Spain was both part of the U.S.-led coalition occupying Iraq and, in the jihadists' imagination, part of Andalusia, a Muslim land usurped by infidels. With the Madrid bombings, Spain joined Israel, Kashmir, and Bosnia on the list of countries that jihadists must conquer anew.

But Spain is also a country that hundreds of thousands of Muslim immigrants—mostly from Morocco—now call home. Like their co-religionists from North Africa, the Middle East, Turkey, or the Indian subcontinent who have settled in France, Britain, Germany, and the other countries of the European Union since the 1970s, this population is riven with contradictions and confused loyalties. At one extreme are Islamist websites in every language that condemn Europe as a "land of unbelief" and call upon the faithful to defy the laws and practices of their adopted countries in order to follow Islamic law (sharia). At the other extreme are young second-generation Muslim immigrants who have never lived in a predominantly Islamic country and who have experienced the personal freedom, liberal education, and economic opportunity of democratic societies.

The most important battle in the war for Muslim minds during the next decade will be fought not in Palestine or Iraq but in these communities of believers on the outskirts of London, Paris, and other European cities, where Islam is already a growing part of the West. If European societies are able to integrate these Muslim populations, handicapped as they are by dispossession, and steer them toward prosperity, this new generation of Muslims may become the Islamic vanguard of the next decade, offering their co-religionists a new vision of the faith and a way out of the dead-end politics that has paralyzed their countries of origin.

1

The Failure of the Oslo Peace

On September 28, 2000, the Arab–Israeli peace process suddenly fell into violent death throes, after a decade when it had seemed to embody the very breath of life for the Middle East. On that day, Ariel Sharon, the aspiring Likud candidate for the post of Israel's prime minister, took a provocative walk in Jerusalem on the city's most contested piece of holy ground. To Jews, it was the Temple Mount, where first the Babylonians in the sixth century BCE and later the Romans in 70 CE had left Judaism's most sacred site in ruins. For Muslims, it was the Haram Sharif, or noble sanctuary, whose dome, mosque, and fountains—dating to the seventh century CE—proclaimed the ascendancy of Islam. By going for his walk on the esplanade of the Haram Sharif, Sharon symbolically reaffirmed the Jews' ancient claim to Jerusalem, and took the first step in a deliberate strategy to undermine the logic of peace that had been built into the 1993 Oslo Peace Accords.

The following day, Yasir Arafat, president of the Palestinian Authority, did his part to destabilize the peace process further. By instigating protests among Palestinians, which Israel repressed in a bloodbath on September 29, Arafat triggered the Al Aqsa intifada—a violent movement named in reference both to Haram Sharif's principal mosque, Al Aqsa, and to the first Palestinian uprising against Israel in 1987. Thus began a vicious game of one-upmanship between Arafat and Sharon.

Each man felt extreme pressure from members of his own camp to escalate the level of aggression. As 2001 approached, a growing portion of both the Israeli and Palestinian populations saw the peace negotiations as a ruse, albeit for opposite reasons. President Bill Clinton, who had been personally committed to the peace process, was leaving office, and his successor in the White House, George W. Bush, would not offer the disputing parties comparable political guarantees. The moment seemed opportune for a power struggle. Through a show of political strength at home, both adversaries hoped to exploit the transition in Washington and turn the United States against their rival.

But as the two septuagenarians rolled up their sleeves to settle an old quarrel at the cost of thousands of Palestinian and Israeli lives, they were not playing the same game. Arafat's strategy was the more naive one. He renewed the intifada in hopes of wearing down the Israelis' resolve and extracting concessions when the Israeli prime minister eventually returned to the negotiating table. But unknown to Arafat, Sharon had no intention of resuming negotiations. His short-term strategy was to provoke new violence in order to relabel Arafat as a terrorist rather than a negotiator; ultimately, Sharon intended to terminate the peace process entirely and bring about a shift in the regional balance of power that would guarantee Israel's security once and for all. Despite these different perceptions of what was at stake, the hostility and violence triggered by Sharon and Arafat in September 2000 had an irrepressible logic of its own. Within the year, the entire world, and not just the Middle East, would be overwhelmed by a wave of terrorism unprecedented in modern times.

On the Palestinian side, criticism of the Oslo Peace Accords was repeated in a litany of grievances: construction of Israeli settlements was continuing apace; Israeli sanctions and legal tricks were strangling the embryonic economy of the autonomous territories; the moment was never "right" for the creation of a Palestinian state. This sense of injustice was felt most strongly among the shabab—the young men of Gaza and the West Bank. The growth rate of the Palestinian population ranked among the world's highest, and these young people constituted a giant reservoir of frustration and resentment—nowhere more so than in the refugee camps within the boundaries of autonomous Palestine, which shelter impoverished families who were driven from their homes inside Israel's 1948 borders. Far from satisfying these youths, the Oslo Peace Accords radicalized them, because the PLO's recognition of Israel had deprived them of their last hope of returning home. Arafat, seen as a traitor to this cause, was the immediate target of their anger.

Lacking economic resources to distribute to his population, apart from a trickle of donations from the Arabian peninsula and subsidies provided by the European Union (which his entourage was turning to private purposes, according to persistent rumors), Arafat knew that he must provide an outlet for the frustration of the shabab. Otherwise, his Islamist opponents in Hamas and Islamic Jihad would act as platforms for the resistance. These organizations threatened to unite beneath the banner of Islam not just the marginalized youth of the camps but also the urban middle classes, who had been deprived of access to political networks—the only real sources of wealth.

In May 2000, Prime Minister Ehud Barak had ordered the Israeli army to withdraw from southern Lebanon, a territory it had occupied since June 1978. The move was justified domestically by Israel's sophisticated military technology, which made physical occupation unnecessary. Nevertheless, the army's withdrawal was celebrated with much fanfare in the Arab world as a real retreat—the first battlefield victory against an enemy on the verge of defeat. According to this view, Hezbollah's war of attrition in Lebanon, spearheaded by frequent suicide bombings against which no military defense was possible, was both the reason for Israel's withdrawal and the proof that violence through terror—which the Arab press called "martyrdom operations"—could force the Jewish state to buckle. Hezbollah had found Israel's Achilles' heel. With its small population, its prosperous and developed economy, and its democratic ethos in which every citizen's life counted, Israel was not willing to make the sacrifices necessary to overpower a poor, densely populated Arab-Muslim territory—a place where obsolete political structures and bleak economic options made life so dismal that voluntary self-sacrifice was something of a rational choice.

By instigating the Al Aqsa intifada, Arafat took a calculated risk. The very term *intifada* invoked the spontaneous Palestinian uprising of December 1987 that had tarnished Israel's reputation on television screens worldwide. The image of a child with a stone in his hand facing down an Israeli army tank suddenly transformed the descendants of Nazi Holocaust victims into oppressors of a dispossessed Third World population. Audiences everywhere watched as the Palestinians acquired the symbols and language of victimhood and turned them against the Jews. With the second intifada, Arafat sought to restore the luster of this political rhetoric to the cause of a Palestinian state, and in the process to wipe away a decade of ineffectual byzantine negotiations and accusations of negligence and corruption.

But in the political climate of the new millennium, nationalism could take Arafat only so far. To be successful, he had to take over the discourse of Islamic politics, which presented Palestine as a stake in a religious conflict and its liberation as the goal of a universal jihad. Al Aqsa mosque was built at the southern end of the Haram Sharif, across from the Dome of the Rock. There, according to Muslim tradition, the Prophet Muhammad ascended to Paradise (the *miraj*), making this complex the third holiest site of Islam, after Mecca and Medina. By taking as his reference point Al Aqsa as well as the 1987 intifada, the president of the Palestinian Authority was positioning himself as the most ardent champion of a religious as well as a nationalist cause. His aim was to checkmate not just Israel but Hamas and Islamic Jihad as well.

Unlike the intifada of 1987, this second intifada was no spontaneous uprising. It was controlled from the top down by the Tanzim, "the organization," an arm of Arafat's political party, Fatah. Internally, Tanzim's tactic was to stir up the impoverished young insurgents in the camps and direct their rebellion exclusively against Israel. With this mobilization, Arafat hoped to deflect their animosity from the Palestinian Authority and to prevent his Islamist opponents from co-opting the uprising. Externally, the intifada was designed to pressure Israel to make concessions. Success on these two fronts would not only advance the cause of nationalism but also restore to the aging revolutionary the aura of leadership he had lost. As both the instigator and the embodiment of the resistance, Arafat was attempting to revive the charismatic role that he had played for most of his life, and to reverse the erosion of his power.

Tanzim circumscribed its displays of violence, targeting them at military installations or settlements in the territories. Gradually, it applied pressure on Israeli civilians in the expectation that they would sacrifice the settlements in return for peace and security within Israel's 1948 borders. The Tanzim cadres were careful to avoid actions that could be labeled as blind terrorism and incur international condemnation; they did not want to lose the support of "sincere democrats" throughout the world. Tanzim took as its model of operations Hezbollah's harassment of the Israeli army in Lebanon, which had "retreated" in May. Convinced by that episode that Israel's will was weakening, Arafat concluded that further displays of controlled violence would force Israel to return to negotiations eager to make a deal. This would turn out to be a grave political mistake.

During the previous July, a Camp David summit held under the auspices of President Clinton had ended without agreement. Instead of accepting Barak's offer of a second summit in the fall of 2000, the old Palestinian leader decided to raise the stakes by demanding the right of return for all Palestinians who had been driven out of Israel in 1948. This stipulation was designed to galvanize the loyalty of desperate youth living in refugee camps on the West Bank, in Jordan, and perhaps even in neighboring countries such as Lebanon and Syria—youth who were crucial to Arafat's constituency. But this move had unforeseen consequences. The majority of Israelis, including those in the peace camp, saw the Palestinian "right of return" as a challenge to Israel's very existence. Southern Lebanon, from the perspective of Tel Aviv or Jerusalem, had not been an integral part of Israeli territory but a mere buffer zone, occupied temporarily for security reasons. The 1948 borders of Israel were another matter entirely. The Palestinians' right of return touched upon a point that, for Israel, was nonnegotiable: the Jews' own traditional "right of return" to their ancient biblical homeland, a principle that had become the cornerstone of Zionist doctrine. In espousing the Palestinian right of return, therefore, Arafat stripped the Palestinian cause of most of its friends in Israel, and perhaps even of leftist Jews worldwide. Ariel Sharon was waiting in the wings to take advantage of liberal Judaism's disarray and sudden loss of faith in Arafat.

With the Al Aqsa intifada raging, Sharon became prime minister following early elections held in February 2001. He owed his success not just to the violence but to the confusion that Arafat's double-dealing, as both partner and adversary, had caused Barak. In much the same way, after the assassination of Yitzhak Rabin, Benjamin Netanyahu owed his 1996 electoral victory against Shimon Peres to Hamas's violent attacks on Israeli civilian targets. In both cases, a Palestinian group's decision to play worst-case-scenario politics had ensured the triumph of a Likud hawk over a Labor Party moderate. Elected on a platform of Israeli security, Sharon now had a popular mandate to extinguish Arafat once and for all. He escalated a campaign of repression calculated to crush the Palestinian Authority and force its president to retaliate. Along the way, he signaled to the world that the Israeli army's withdrawal from southern Lebanon in May 2000 did not represent any weakness whatsoever.

Faced with this rising tide of violence, the United States, as sponsor of the peace process, rediscovered the gesture of Pontius Pilate, himself once the guarantor of the Pax Romana in Palestine. By washing his hands of the Al Aqsa intifada and its consequences, the newly elected president, George W. Bush, claimed to have learned a lesson from his predecessor's mistakes. Clinton stood accused by the Republican camp of debasing the U.S. presidency by negotiating personally with the unsavory Arafat, whom the Bush administration refused to recognize as a head of state. After taking office just a month before Sharon's election, Bush let it be known that he did not want to get involved in the peace process.

In the close November presidential election, Arab Americans had voted massively for Bush, the scion of a Texas oil dynasty that had traditionally been sensitive to Arab interests. They rejected Al Gore, the Democratic candidate who enjoyed the backing of most American Jewish organizations and whose vice-presidential hopeful, Joe Lieberman, was a devout and conservative Jew. The Arab

world considered it an excellent sign when a younger member of
the Bush family was elected. In 1991, his father had pressured Israel's Yitzhak Shamir into meeting Palestinian leaders at the Madrid summit—an event that marked the United States' formal recognition of the Palestinian nationalist cause. When Bush Sr. was
then defeated by Bill Clinton in 1992, many Arabs saw it as a "sanction" by American Jewish voters who were supposedly keen to punish the elder Bush for forcing Israel's hand. In Arab capitals, it
seemed logical that the son should be eager to avenge the family's
honor against the Jewish/Israeli faction that had defeated his father, and to renew his family's pro-Arab policies.

But the Arab world had no inkling of the influence that neoconservatives had come to wield backstage at the White House.
Convinced that the Oslo peace process was a trap for Israel, this
group of intellectuals, politicians, and lobbyists sympathized with
the Likud Party, which in turn took strength from U.S. backing for
its hard, intransigent line. As early as 1996, in a memorandum intended for Netanyahu, a group of neocon academics expressed
the conviction that the logic of Oslo was out of date. According to
their view, a lasting settlement in the Middle East was contingent
on dealing with the Iraqi question—that is, eliminating Saddam
Hussein and replacing him with a pro-Western parliamentary democracy. This, they believed, was the only way to break Arab resistance to the state of Israel. The wider public paid no attention to
the document, but in retrospect it helps explain why Sharon undertook to repress the Al Aqsa intifada in a manner that would destroy the peace process, and with full knowledge that his action
would get a sympathetic reception within influential circles of the
new Bush administration.

In April 2001, when I visited Yasir Arafat and his entourage in
Ramallah, they still seemed unaware of this neoconservative influence. They expressed confidence in Sharon's "de Gaulle-like des-

tiny" and his reluctance to go down in history as the butcher of Sabra and Shatila rather than as the signatory of a durable peace with the Palestinian state—a goal toward which they believed the U.S. administration, as the sponsor of a peace process vital to American interests in the Middle East, would push him inexorably. Perhaps with an eye toward his own place in history, Arafat believed that Tanzim's controlled operations would cause his Israeli adversary to take stock of the Palestinians' resolve and return to the negotiating table, where he would make the necessary sacrifices to salvage a durable peace—particularly giving up the settlements that pockmarked the autonomous Palestinian territories.

But Sharon, secure in his American support, had no incentive to negotiate. The spiral of violence whipped up by the intifada and Israel's repression of the insurgents was good for him domestically. It damaged the credibility of his Labor opponents and guaranteed—whatever the brutal vagaries of terrorism—the support of most Israeli voters for his strong-arm tactics and hard-line rhetoric. Most important, the violence destroyed Arafat's reputation throughout Israel and the West. The "man of peace" whom Clinton had welcomed to the White House more often than any other foreign leader was now perceived as the person responsible for renewing the violence—an untrustworthy agitator who would soon lose most of his supporters in Washington and New York. As the doors of President Bush's White House closed in Arafat's face, his former allies in the American Jewish community—liberal supporters whom the Palestinians had cultivated patiently for decades—felt betrayed, bewildered, and embittered.

On the ground in the Palestinian territories, Arafat was unable to keep the uprising under Tanzim's control for long. In reaction to the growing unrest, the Israeli army moved swiftly to break the back of the intifada's leadership. The Palestinian people could do nothing to close this Pandora's box of violence—especially since no sign of the promised political benefits was forthcoming and repression had exacerbated the hostilities. As radicalism broke through Fatah's constraints, Islamist groups rushed back onto the scene. By the spring of 2001, Hamas and Islamic Jihad alike were carrying out spectacular, brutal suicide attacks that targeted buses and markets and aimed to kill as many Israeli civilians, including women and children, as possible. The policy of gradually escalating violence that Arafat envisaged had failed disastrously.

Suicide attacks soon won the support of preachers throughout the Muslim world, even among "moderate" Islamists like Sheikh Qaradawi, the star of a religious program on Al Jazeera's satellite television channel. He justified the killing of Israeli civilians by explaining that all Israelis, men and women alike, perform military service and, as reservists, constitute legitimate military targets for a jihad that seeks to recapture Muslim territory from impious occupiers. The mosques and the international Arab media revived the legitimacy of Hamas and Islamic Jihad, strengthening their hands against Arafat. Rejecting Arafat's controlled-conflict strategy as ineffective against Sharon's obstinacy and choosing instead to imitate the political strategy that had worked so well for Hezbollah in Lebanon, Hamas and Islamic Jihad hoped to transcend their narrowly Islamist support base and draw into their wake Palestine's nationalist movement.

The Islamists' first goal was to tip the balance of power within Palestine in their favor by mobilizing poor youths from the camps and radicalized students. To these frustrated young Arabs, a strategy of terror seemed a better answer than any Arafat had given to Likud extremism. It was no longer a time for negotiations. By summer 2001, the rise of terrorist activities had sidelined Tanzim's armed operations and pushed it out of the media spotlight. Arafat's claim to represent all Palestinians was damaged beyond repair. Yet publicly the Israeli government still held him responsible for all acts of violence, including suicide attacks, in his capacity as president of the Palestinian Authority and instigator of the Al Aqsa intifada.

In the weeks before September 11, 2001, the Arab world—and more generally the Muslim world, including Asia, Africa, and even the outskirts of European cities—was swept up in feelings of solidarity with the Palestinian cause and hatred of Israel's policies. While the U.S. government looked the other way, violence in Israel and Palestine became the focus of Middle Eastern conflict. During the preceding decade, the White House had used the peace process in a bid to defuse tensions in the region. Now, with years of delicate agreements a shambles and the Bush administration already preoccupied with plans to bring Saddam Hussein to his knees, the growing crisis in the Middle East had no outlet except eruption.

Al Jazeera relayed the daily news of a war in which "martyrdom operations" were acts of heroism. Funerals of fallen heroes were broadcast on Arab satellite television, and viewers mourned for victims of the Israeli army's attacks. In many cases, Arab and Muslim sentiment spilled over unreservedly into anti-Jewish hatred. Muslims perceived themselves as the collective target of a humiliation campaign inflicted by Israel, in collusion with the United States and its Western allies. The belief gained ground that George W. Bush, unlike Clinton, was no longer an "honest broker" but had gone over to Sharon's side.

The depth of bitterness among Muslims was matched only by their sense of powerlessness. The fatal weakness of Arab armies had never been revealed so harshly. Israel's crushing military superiority was so obvious that protests in Cairo and Damascus, or communiqués issued by the Arab League, were immediately dismissed as *kalam fadi*—hot air—by Arab public opinion. States had lost their credibility as political actors; activists had outstripped them. Israel's technological prowess, through its access to sophisticated American weaponry, was reasserted time and again in "targeted assassinations" of Palestinian political or military figures, most of them Islamist activists accused of perpetrating bloody attacks by suicide bombers. Invisible helicopters firing laser-guided missiles liquidated them one after another, in their cars or offices. Meanwhile, pro-Palestinian protests were quickly contained or squelched by neighboring Arab regimes as soon as these rallies showed any sign of challenging the state's passivity.

In the past, the military regimes that ruled most of the Arab world had justified their authoritarian character and their rejection of democracy and political pluralism by reference to the "Zionist peril." The armies that defended borders, guaranteed territorial integrity, and hunted down all manner of conspiracies attributed to Israel considered themselves entitled to absolute power. But the Soviet arms dealers who supplied these regimes had disappeared in 1992, and by 2001 everyone knew that no Arab army was capable of military parity with Israel, or even of responding to an attack or a threat in the form of a missile strike. The political regimes that had emerged from the barracks were damaged by this imbalance of power between Arab conventional forces and the Israeli army. Frustrated citizens, and especially young people, began to look for other means of resisting Israel; their unrest expressed their suspicion, if not outright condemnation, of the failures of Arab states and their associated institutions.

In the summer of 2001, a growing number of groups in the Arab and Muslim world, outside the narrow confines of radical Islamist militancy, began to see terrorism, in the form of suicide attacks, as an appropriate response—indeed, the only valid reply—to Israel's overwhelming technological superiority and to Sharon's determination to use terror to crush the Al Aqsa intifada. These "martyrdom operations" created a balance of terror of sorts against invincible smart weapons. But the world's moral condemnation of terrorism was unequivocal. Political forces that sought to use it were barred from the realm of civilized nations and relegated to the purgatory of rogue states. No nation or official institution could afford to take explicit responsibility for a terrorist act. More anonymous actors, who took Bin Laden and Al Qaeda as their icons, provided the ideal conduits for suicide attacks and gave them global resonance.

Despite the short-term political gains that bloodshed seemed to bring, it proved far more devastating for Muslim societies, which had no means to defend against it, than for Israel and the Western societies that were its primary targets. To understand how the terrorist option—and especially suicide attacks—came to express political power relations in the Middle East during the summer of 2001, we need to recontextualize the deterioration of the peace process and the ambiguities that presided over its implementation. Its architects hoped that these uncertainties would be swept away by a constructive impetus, but their hopes were not fulfilled.

IN THE EARLY 1990s, the collapse of the Soviet bloc altered the balance of power in the Middle East by depriving the USSR's clients of diplomatic support and military supplies. Israel had perceived these clients—primarily the PLO and Syria—as enemies that posed a direct threat on the battlefield, and now that threat had suddenly slackened. On the other hand, the first intifada, begun in 1987, had inflicted undreamed-of political damage by tarnishing Israel's moral legitimacy in the eyes of a young generation of TV watchers worldwide for whom the horrors of the Nazi Holocaust belonged to history rather than to memory, to black-and-white documentaries rather than full-color breaking news. The violence and repression of the uprising had also weighed on Israel's economy and society, by forcing citizens into policing duties that most of them despised.

The first intifada had taken its toll on the other side as well. Years of strikes and walkouts by Palestinian employees of Israeli firms, along with economic sanctions imposed by Israel, had bankrupted the Palestinians. Politics that had formerly been under the exclusive control of Arafat's PLO fell into the hands of the Islamists, led by Hamas, which was created at the beginning of the uprising. Islamist leaders became very visible in organizing the daily rock throwing and other acts of protest, and their activism swept them into power throughout the society, from universities to chambers of commerce. To compensate for the loss of essential supplies from the USSR, Palestinians became dependent on financial support from the Arab petro-monarchies, which were dominated by a conservative sect of Islam. These new patrons increasingly favored Hamas over the doctrinally less familiar PLO nationalists.

On August 2, 1990, more than two years into the intifada, Saddam Hussein invaded Kuwait. Arafat and the PLO applauded this audacious move, which they, like many Arabs, saw as a harbinger of Arab unity. If Iraq could maintain control of Kuwait's oil fields and refineries, the Palestinian cause would receive crucial financial and political support. Indeed, the "new Saladin" in Baghdad called repeatedly for the liberation of Jerusalem in order to buff up the legitimacy of his attack on Kuwait, a former "brother."

Kuwait's large and prosperous Palestinian community, besides contributing generously to the PLO, enthusiastically collaborated with the Iraqi soldiers. Saddam's army launched a few Scud missiles in the general direction of Tel Aviv, and when the Israelis did not retaliate, impressionable souls in the Palestinian territories believed victory was nigh.

The abrupt intrusion of the Iraq factor did not, however, alter the equation of conflict in the Holy Land in the way that Arafat predicted. In the immediate aftermath of Saddam Hussein's defeat at the hands of a U.S.-led international coalition, Palestinians were expelled from Kuwait, and the oil monarchies that had supported the coalition turned a cold shoulder to the PLO. The PLO's operating budget reached a historical low, while Hamas and Islamic Jihad, which had been more circumspect in expressing their sympathies during Operation Desert Storm, suffered no financial consequences.

But rather than punishing the PLO for its support of Iraq, President George H. W. Bush extracted a major political concession from Israel's leaders, by insisting that they negotiate with Palestinian representatives. To achieve this goal, Bush Sr. took advantage of the military paralysis Washington had imposed on Israel during the war and which continued in force. Israel had agreed not to respond to Iraq's Scud attacks, for fear that an assault on Iraq by the "Zionist entity" would inflame anti-Jewish passions on the Arab street, which would in turn pressure the United States' Arab allies to leave the coalition. The White House also capitalized on the fact that Israeli society, traumatized by the difficult security measures required by the intifada, was worn out and ready for a negotiated resolution to violence. Meanwhile, the PLO had torments and incentives of its own. Its ill-advised support for Saddam left it too cash-strapped to continue subsidizing the uprising and too demoralized to authorize strikes which, time after time, plunged the territories' inhabitants into misery. Meanwhile, Hamas's charity associations were bulging with petro-dollars to spread throughout Gaza and the West Bank. For his own political survival, Arafat had run out of alternatives to an American-brokered peace.

Thus, the United States forced both Israel and Palestine to send representatives to the Madrid peace talks in December 1991. This first encounter between negotiators from the two camps set in motion a process that appeared irreversible throughout the last decade of the twentieth century. At Rabin and Arafat's initiative and later under President Clinton's auspices, peace between Israel and Palestine was secretly negotiated in the Oslo Accords and enshrined in a Declaration of Principles, signed in Washington on September 13, 1993.

What prompted the sole global superpower to throw itself wholeheartedly into solving the problems of the Middle East? U.S. policy toward the region first began to take shape in the immediate aftermath of World War II. During the first four decades of the twentieth century, the Americans had been bit players in a zone dominated by the colonial powers. But with France and Great Britain weakened after six years of brutal war, and with the Soviets threatening to expand into the warm seas, the United States emerged from the Yalta Conference as the new protagonist on the Middle Eastern scene.

On February 14, 1945, after leaving the Crimean spa town where he had met Churchill and Stalin to establish spheres of influence in postwar Europe, President Franklin D. Roosevelt visited the Suez Canal and received the king of Saudi Arabia, Abd Aziz Ibn Saud, aboard the USS *Quincy*. In return for Saudi oil deliveries to Aramco, a U.S. consortium, Roosevelt agreed to protect the kingdom over the long term. Almost half a century later, when Saddam invaded Kuwait, Operation Desert Shield placed U.S. troops on the Saudi border with Kuwait, demonstrating the hardiness of that postwar arrangement.

After Yalta, an American presence gradually replaced that of Great Britain in the quasi protectorate of Saudi Arabia, once described by pundits as "made in England." The new mode of U.S. influence was intended to be indirect, focused on exploiting the outstanding oil fields in the kingdom's eastern region, where an "American colony" was established. The Middle East contained, in unparalleled quantities and at rock-bottom prices, the fuel reserves essential for any major power. To Washington and Moscow alike, it was clear that control of global petroleum resources would be the key to developing a military-industrial complex; and that, in turn, would ensure victory for one bloc or the other in the Cold War. The oil companies of the European colonial states were sidelined as second stringers to these two major players.

Thus, through FDR's negotiations aboard the *Quincy*, the United States gained a foothold in a region which, by the beginning of the new millennium, would dominate America's foreign policy priorities. During the intervening Cold War years, however, Washington was mainly concerned with preventing and containing—or repressing, if necessary—pro-Soviet initiatives by various communist, socialist, or "progressive" parties and movements in the region. If they managed to seize power and to sign alliances or friendship treaties with Moscow, these regimes would threaten the West's oil supplies. Israel was not yet a prism through which American eyes would focus on the Middle East. In 1956, in fact, after Nasser nationalized the Suez Canal, Washington wasted no time in pressuring Israel, along with France and Britain, to withdraw its troops from Egyptian soil. Paris and London were obvious targets, since the United States had a strong interest in relaxing their grip on the region; but Tel Aviv was also compelled to retreat.

The United States' vision of Israel's role in the Middle East changed dramatically in June 1967, after the embattled nation stunned its Arab neighbors by invading and occupying the Palestinian territories, Sinai, and parts of the Golan Heights in the Six Day War. France had been Israel's principal ally up to that point, and Paris had provided the Israelis with the Mirage supersonic bombers which ensured their mastery of the skies during the war. But the Israeli occupation of Palestine caused General Charles de Gaulle to make an about-face. In his renowned press conference of November 27, 1967, the general declared: "Israel attacked, and in six days of combat reached the objectives it sought. Now, it is organizing an occupation that cannot fail to be accompanied by oppression, repression, and expulsion on the territories it seized; there, a resistance has arisen that, in turn, Israel describes as terrorism. It is quite clear that the conflict is merely suspended. It can only be resolved by international means." The French government acted on these premonitory words by declaring an embargo on arms shipments to the warring countries.

The United States promptly took over the job of exclusive ally to Israel, but France's defection was just one factor in the decision to make the Jewish state a pillar of a new U.S. Middle Eastern policy. For the Americans, the Six Day War was interpreted primarily in terms of global antagonism between the West and the Soviets. In this bloc-centered reading, the Arab–Israeli dimension of the conflict was marginalized; the important point was that Israel had triumphed over two clients of the Soviet Union: Egypt and Syria. (Jordan, though a client of Great Britain, also lost territory—the West Bank of the Jordan River—and subsequently parted ways with its two former allies.)

While President de Gaulle foresaw the long-term risks of occupation and the threat of terrorism in the region—recurring themes up to and including the attacks of September 11—President Lyndon Johnson saw support for Israel as a short-term opportunity to score a welcome victory against Moscow. This power play in the Middle East served as a handy counterweight to the deteriorating situation Johnson faced in Vietnam, where the war was going badly for the Americans. The attraction of a global reckoning caused the United States to override its balanced policy in the Middle East, where previously the major political consideration was maintaining the flow of oil. As for Washington's Arab allies, such as Saudi Arabia, they had become too dependent on American support to offer any opposition to Johnson's political alliance with Israel—or so people reckoned in the White House.

Domestic politics also factored into Johnson's pro-Israel policy. The civil rights movement of the 1960s brought significant advances not only for African Americans but also for American Jews, who in previous decades had been victims of various discriminatory policies—especially quotas in university admissions and hiring—which limited their access to the political establishment. As these children of Ashkenazi immigrants came of age, they enjoyed considerable social and intellectual mobility compared with their parents, and as young adults they went on to take influential positions as government employees, teachers, social workers, and left-wing activists. For many of these newly affluent Jewish Americans, solidarity with Israel bridged the gap between the socialist ideals of their parents and their own issues of Jewish identity.

Jewish American organizations, still anchored to the left of the political spectrum in those years, were active in mobilizing against the Vietnam War. For President Johnson, rapprochement with Israel provided an opportunity to reestablish ties with these organizations and attempt to regain their political support, which he had lost in Vietnam. But Jews were not the only Americans to welcome a foreign policy favorable toward Israel. To people of diverse origins and backgrounds, the Israeli cause seemed just: they believed it was morally necessary to defend a small, democratic Western country, founded by Holocaust survivors, against the threats of a hostile Arab environment which some saw as reactionary, others as pro-communist.

While the Democrats, for reasons that were both ideological and religious, were eager to embrace the Israeli cause, the Republican Party demonstrated greater sensitivity toward the oil conglomerates and their Arab partners on whose territory the oil fields were located. After 1968, when the White House passed from Democratic to Republican hands, American policymakers tried to walk a tightrope between these competing interests. The Nixon administration wished to ensure an abundant, dependable, and cheap supply of oil while simultaneously asserting the nonnegotiability of security guarantees for Israel. These Cold War gymnastics were especially risky because since the 1950s, beginning with Premier Nikita Khrushchev, the Soviet Union had jumped at every opportunity to exploit Arab resentments.

The "division of the world" that resulted from Yalta had not established clear borders between the two blocs in the Middle East, as it had in Europe. Nasser, who had been fascinated by the American model when he seized power in 1952, turned to Moscow in frustration when the West refused to finance the construction of the Aswan High Dam. By confiscating the property of the bourgeoisie, nationalizing the banking sector, and imposing agrarian reform in the countryside, he established Egypt as a socialist nation—and in the process undermined the possibility of a civil society that could restrain his praetorian power. In Syria and Iraq, the Baathist regimes that took control in the 1960s established a firm political-military alliance with the Kremlin and imitated the Russian model by nationalizing factories, collectivizing agriculture, and destroying the entrepreneurial middle classes. Faced with these Soviet inroads and encouraged by domestic opinion, the Nixon administration increased its support for Israel. Along with the shah's Iran, Israel seemed to be the military outpost most likely to limit pro-Soviet contagion in the eastern Mediterranean, where a vaguely defined "Arab Cold War" was raging.

Nixon's support for Israel, however, cast a shadow over relations Washington was cultivating with the Gulf oil monarchies. It forced Saudi Arabia to intensify its anti-Israeli declarations of faith in order to conceal from its own population the nation's very real political dependence on the United States. At the same time, Saudi Arabia had to deflect the condemnation of more "progressive" Arab capitals in Egypt, Syria, and Iraq that had achieved ideological hegemony over the region at the time. As early as the 1960s, the pro-American oil oligarchies had recognized their need for an alternative legitimizing discourse to counter the Arab socialism of Nasser and the Baathists. This requirement was eventually met by modern Islamist doctrine. By advocating a political system based on the injunctions of the Quran and the sacred texts of Muslim tradition, this ideology offered an alternative utopia that could mobilize the Arab masses.

Islamist political doctrine originated with the Society of the Muslim Brothers, founded in Egypt at the end of the 1920s with the political goal of establishing an Islamic state. Taking as its slogan "The Quran is our constitution," the Brothers sought to bury both nationalism and socialism alike, in theory and in practice. But the secular ideologies they opposed were unknown or of no interest in the deserts of Arabia and neighboring states where the Muslim Brothers had taken refuge. There, rigid religious belief, shaped by local tradition, was hardly capable of replying to global challenges or to fickle political alliances with the United States.

The combination of the Brothers' political agenda with this rigid version of Islam (generally termed salafism, in reference to the pious ancestors—al-salaf al-salih—who were deemed to embody the purity of Islam's fundamental doctrines) would prove to be an explosive blend that would detonate throughout the region and then the whole world.

After Israel's 1967 victory over Nasser and the pro-Soviet regimes in the Six Day War, the United States' Middle East policy found itself gradually torn between its firm support of Israel and its obligations to oil monarchies whose legitimating ideology was drifting slowly away from the West. Inexorably, Arab states in the Persian Gulf moved from a conservative but pro-American form of Islam to explicit estrangement to marked hostility, expressed first toward Israel and then toward its U.S. sponsor.

A clear expression of this hostility occurred during the October 1973 War. Known in the region as the Yom Kippur or Ramadan War, it was launched by Egyptian and Syrian armies to prove they were capable of military initiative against the Israeli army. This surprise attack hit Israel on the most important feast day of the Hebrew calendar, but whatever initial advantage the Arab armies enjoyed was quickly overwhelmed by the Israeli counterattack. Massive airlift deliveries of American military equipment figured prominently in the Israeli counteroffensive. But when the petroleum-exporting countries decided to implement a progressive embargo on oil shipments to Israel's Western allies, Israel was forced to halt its advance on the road leading from Suez to Cairo.

The embargo caused a series of spikes in the price of crude that were felt throughout the following decade, making the oil monarchies fabulously rich and the U.S. position increasingly uncomfortable. The war had forced Washington to come down firmly on Israel's side, in order to guarantee the victory of its ally in the face of a surprise attack. But for the first time since the 1945 agreement aboard the *Quincy,* the Arab oil-producing countries had used petroleum to achieve a degree of political autonomy from the United States. During almost three decades of Cold War, in return for Washington's protection from the Soviet Union, the oligarchies had kept their promise to limit their financial ambitions and had refrained from using their resources to apply political pressure on Israel. All of this changed with the October War. Yet, ironically, the rising price of oil set in motion an Arab–Israeli peace process under the United States' exclusive auspices that would work to the detriment of the Soviet Union and its Middle Eastern clients.

Anwar Sadat had led Egypt's assault on Israel as a show of Arab military strength, but also as a strategic prelude to negotiating a peace with Israel on the best terms possible. A reversal of alliances in 1974 had brought Egypt out of the Soviet camp and placed it under U.S. protection, where Israel was already firmly ensconced. The Egyptian president understood that making peace with his enemy—who was also his new friend's friend—was the price he must pay for the return of the Sinai, lost to Israel in 1967. Making peace would also reap large sums in economic aid that Sadat desperately needed to redress Egypt's deteriorating social situation, which the excesses of the Nasser years and a subsequent population explosion had destabilized.

Egypt's separate peace isolated it from other Arab countries, but it also precluded any conventional Arab military offensive against Israel in the foreseeable future. Without Egypt's army, war was impossible, and in that sense the Camp David Accords, signed in March 1979, seemed an unequivocal diplomatic triumph for the United States. The Carter administration guaranteed Israel's security by bribing its principal enemy, after tearing it from the Soviet embrace. Washington hoped that the accords, by soothing tensions between Israel and its Arab neighbors, would smooth relations between the United States and the privileged Arab oil producers.

This diplomatic architecture rested on fragile foundations, however. First, by eliminating the conventional military threat to Israel, the fragile peace would allow another type of threat to surface: violent revolts in the territories occupied or controlled by Israel, such as Palestine and southern Lebanon. Reeling from one dead-end strategy to the next, opposition movements in these areas evolved toward the "terrorism" that de Gaulle had predicted following the Six Day War. Two additional sources of instability originated farther to the east but sent aftershocks throughout the region. In February 1979, the Islamic Revolution brought Ayatollah Khomeini to power in Iran as cries of "Death to America" rang out. And in December the Red Army invaded Afghanistan, setting off an anti-Soviet jihad covertly financed by U.S. secret services and the Arabian peninsula's oil monarchies.

Though Iran voluntarily left the American sphere of influence, it did not seek refuge in the Soviet camp. Despising the USSR as much as the United States, the Shiite Islamist militants who seized power in Tehran grounded their republic elsewhere, in the slogan "Neither East nor West—Islamic Revolution." After launching an assault on the U.S. embassy in Tehran in November 1979, the revolutionaries disregarded conventions that had been respected throughout the Cold War by taking American diplomats hostage. One year later, with the Iranian hostage crisis unresolved, President Jimmy Carter, the architect of the Camp David peace, was voted out of the White House.

Iran's expansionist ambitions were quickly countered by Saddam Hussein, who, with the blessing of the Reagan administration and America's European allies, began a long and bloody war against his eastern neighbor in September 1980. Iran relied on unconventional arms, including the mass suicide of young sans-culotte Shia, the bassidji, who marched off to blow themselves up in Iraqi minefields, their heads swathed in martyrs' bands proclaiming "Allahu akbar." The Islamic Republic opened a second front in the region by taking Western hostages in Lebanon through the manipulation of local Shiite radical organizations. These actions went hand in hand with suicide bombings: booby-trapped trucks driven into an American and French multinational buffer force in Beirut in October 1983, and the following month, in Tyre, against the headquarters of the Israeli forces that had been occupying the south since 1982.

Such "martyrdom operations" had been exceptional, if not entirely unknown, in the political culture of even the most extremist Sunni movements, where the deliberate cultivation of death was commendable only as a last resort. Sunnis considered suicide an abomination against the Creator, who alone gives life and alone may decide when to take it from his creatures. But revolutionary Shiites—who considered the martyrdom of Imam Hussein, "the prince of martyrs," as exemplary—had fewer scruples in this regard. The tactics inaugurated by revolutionary Iran were exported to the Arab world via extremist Lebanese Shiite organizations, inspired by the imam Khomeini. These human "weapons" conveniently made up the deficit in conventional arms in the Arab camp.

Having concluded its separate peace with Egypt in 1979, Israel gave itself permission to invade Lebanon in 1982, in order to shut down the Lebanese bases from which the PLO had been lobbing rockets toward villages in northern Israel. This police operation, dubbed Peace in Galilee, aimed to remove the final threat to Israel's borders. Whatever its justification, the Israeli campaign became etched in the collective Arab memory by massacres at the

Palestinian refugee camps of Sabra and Shatila in Beirut's suburbs. There, brutal murders were carried out by Lebanese Christian militias, as the Israeli occupation forces, under the orders of General Ariel Sharon, then Israeli minister of defense, looked complacently on.

Operation Peace in Galilee achieved its mission of liquidating PLO strongholds in Lebanon. But a more formidable enemy rose up to take the PLO's place: the Shia resistance, spearheaded by Hezbollah. Arabs across the ideological spectrum came to see Hezbollah's trademark tactic—suicide attacks—as legitimate simply because the explosives experts of "Allah's party" had managed to find the only weak spot in Israel's armor.

The harbingers of suicide operations thus appeared first in the east, then in the center, of the region at the very moment when the peace agreement signed by Begin and Sadat was spreading a false sense that the United States had scored a palpable diplomatic victory. The United States drew Cairo—then the region's foremost Arab capital, due to its demographic weight and cultural influence—into its orbit before it was challenged by the Gulf cities of Dubai and Qatar, headquarters of the Al Arabiyya and Al Jazeera satellite television channels. But Egypt, the ace in Washington's hand in 1980, proved of little value against Israel's enemies by the end of the twentieth century. In this new regional game, the most important cards in play were terrorism, the transnational Arab media, expertise in global financial operations, and Internet communications between Tora Bora, Bali, and Tampa.

WASHINGTON PERCEIVED the 1979 Camp David treaty as having buttressed Israel's security, and Beltway pundits predicted that the

Islamist militants' virtuous jihad against the Red Army would complete this process. During the 1980s the Palestinian cause lost its centrality in the revolutionaries' imagination, as radicals flocked from the four corners of the *umma* (the Muslim world) to assist the jihadists. Afghanistan was an Islamist, not an Arab cause, and its first goal was to defeat the infidel Red Army, not to destroy Israel. The shift of tensions toward the east, far from Israel's territory, was a respite all the more welcome in the Jewish state because various Palestinian jihadists—such as Abdallah Azzam, a native of Jenin and a herald of the Arab brigades in Afghanistan—seemed to understand that it was impossible to defeat Israel by force of arms. Instead, they went off to fight—even to die, as Azzam would—in a great battle against the godless Soviet menace, partially subsidized and armed by Tel Aviv's strategic ally in Washington. The United States saw the jihad in Afghanistan as an opportunity to deal Moscow a death blow while weakening Iran, the enemy of its oil allies in the Gulf region.

Tehran reiterated its hostile declarations against "America's lackeys," as it described the petro-monarchies, and especially against Saudi Arabia. The Shiite mullahs despised the intransigent Sunnism of the kingdom of Saud, which portrayed the Shia as barely Muslim deviants *(rafidun)*. As long as Iran was at war with Iraq, tension in the region focused on the fate of the Gulf oil fields, not on Israel's problems with Palestinians. Saddam Hussein's armies faced Khomeini's in a horrifying trench war that lasted eight years and bled their countries dry, killing hundreds of thousands and devastating productive capacities on a massive scale. Iraq's battlefield successes owed much to American arms, and as the confidence of the Gulf oil suppliers in U.S. foreign policy rose, oil prices began to fall. Meanwhile, the victory of the Sunni mujahedeen in Afghanistan, bankrolled by Saudi Arabia and trained by Pakistan under CIA supervision, put paid to Iranian hopes of galvanizing the rest of the community of believers in its Shiite revolution.

Unable to triumph over Saddam Hussein on the battlefield, Ayatollah Khomeini had to accept a cease-fire in the summer of 1988. But in an attempt to make a last stand in the name of Islamist revolution, he issued a fatwa against Salman Rushdie for his *Satanic Verses* on February 14, 1989, just as the Soviet army was preparing to withdraw from Kabul the very next day. This astonishing death sentence by religious decree effectively overshadowed the final military defeat of the Soviet Union. But beyond its media success, Iran's spectacular pronouncement failed to arrest the shift in power toward the United States' petro allies in the Gulf. When Khomeini died in June 1989, he took with him Iran's hopes of exporting an Islamic revolution to the rest of the world.

The Soviets' withdrawal from Afghanistan, followed by the fall of the Berlin Wall in November, paved the way for the USSR's dissolution. The United States had rid itself of its greatest enemy courtesy of a guerrilla proxy war waged by international jihadist brigades. In the service of a larger project, the destruction of the Soviet Union, it had promoted radical Sunni Islamism in Afghanistan and throughout the Middle East. But at that heady moment in history, American policymakers persuaded themselves that the radical Sunni movements they had supported for the occasion were ephemeral, fragmented, under control, and destined to disappear once the United States and its allies ceased arming and financing them.

The liabilities accrued from the decision to entrust to Saddam Hussein the United States' containment strategy for Khomeini's Iran became obvious in early 1990. Bankrupted by war, faced with crude prices at rock-bottom levels, and harassed by Arab petro-monarchies that refused to grant it a debt moratorium, Iraq attacked and conquered Kuwait on August 2. The Iraqi army was routed from Kuwait the following spring by a U.S.-led international coalition, but Saddam Hussein's precarious regime was left standing at home. When Iraq's Shia, who had been the victims of savage political and cultural repression by the Sunni Baathists in the 1980s, rose up in rebellion in the middle of the Gulf War, the Bush Sr. administration encouraged them but then failed to offer concrete assistance. The retreating Sunni Republican Guards found themselves in an excellent strategic position to turn on the Shia rebels in the south and drown them in their own blood.

The United States' behavior toward the Shia during the Gulf War mystified many observers, and when the second Bush administration invaded Iraq in the spring of 2003, President Bush Sr. was asked why he had not eliminated Saddam's regime in 1991, when it would have been possible to do so more easily. He responded that he enjoyed no U.N. mandate to do so at the time—a sarcastic retort, some believed, since George W. Bush so clearly ignored U.N. opinion in the run-up to the 2003 invasion.

Leaving sarcasm aside, however, we can look for an explanation of President George H. W. Bush's hesitation in the prevailing political atmosphere of the Middle East. In 1991 an invasion of Iraq would have fragmented the exceptionally broad coalition behind Operation Desert Storm. Arab leaders in particular would not have accepted an invasion of Iraq by "imperialist" American arms—despite Iraq's own penchant for invading its neighbors. They would have had a difficult time justifying such interventionism to the Arab street, which was generally unwilling to accept Operation Desert Storm itself. Furthermore, a despot's removal by a foreign army, with backing from the local civil society, might plant ideas about radical reform in other Arab countries.

Cairo was no less reluctant than Damascus or Rabat to allow the coalition's U.N. mandate to be overstepped, and that mandate was limited to restoring Kuwaiti sovereignty. The "betrayal" of Iraq's Shia must be seen in the light of these constraints. The Sunni petro-monarchies of the Arabian peninsula—the United States' treasured clients—were more troubled by the prospect of Shiite domination in Iraq, and possibly the revival of Shiite revolutionism in Iran, than they were by the prospect of dealing with the Sunni leader Saddam Hussein, despite his having given them such a fright.

The punishment meted out to the Iraqi regime was a U.N.-controlled embargo and economic sanctions. These measures hit the Iraqi population hard, ravaging civil society by breaking its supply lifelines to the rest of the world. But this mattered little to the member-states of the victorious coalition: above all else, they sought to "freeze" Iraq and render it innocuous to its neighbors. This solution offered the additional advantage of reducing Iraq's petrol extraction and export capacities to their lowest possible levels. By squeezing the global supply of oil at a time when prices were low, Iraq's neighbors increased their own market share.

Beyond the internal equilibrium of Gulf geopolitics, however, the decision to put Saddam's regime on a short leash resulted from a crucial geostrategic choice at the heart of America's Middle East policy—a choice that seemed to promise, finally, the reconciliation of two contradictory goals: guaranteeing Israeli security and ensuring oil supplies. By forgoing the opportunity to overthrow the tyrant in Baghdad and choosing instead to preserve the coalition's integrity—and by making this choice following a lightning-quick war in which the devastating superiority of America's military technology was demonstrated beyond question—George Bush Sr. used the immense political capital at his disposal to apply leverage on the Israeli–Palestinian conflict. The United State's military victory in Kuwait allowed him to breach the political and military impasse created by the first intifada. Neither Arafat nor Shamir had any other option: Arafat was discredited by his support for Iraq and ruined by his Gulf sponsors' financial abandonment; Shamir was damaged by the media's coverage of the intifada and by the United States' refusal to let Israel respond to the Scud attacks on Tel Aviv. Both were forced to obey the Pax Americana President George H. W. Bush imposed. Fresh from his triumph in Operation Desert Storm, he used the December 1991 Madrid peace conference to design a coherent Middle East policy, one that would harmonize the region's specific constraints. That its architect was a Republican president who had built his private fortune on Texas oil was hardly irrelevant. It was precisely that sensitivity to Arab concerns which operated as a powerful constraint on Israel's demands.

Israel, in fact, had undergone a double setback in aligning its interests with the United States'. By preventing Shamir from responding to Iraqi Scud attacks, Washington treated Israel's security concern as a secondary consideration. And once again, when Bush forced Shamir to participate in the Madrid peace conference, paving the way for Israel's recognition of the PLO, he prevented Israeli leaders from putting forth their security interests as trumping all others. Washington's attitude was determined by its own calculations, and the Bush team made it utterly clear that Israel was to enjoy no privileges against the imperatives of U.S. energy security and oil economics. Israel would not set the agenda. This was the basis for resolution of the Arab–Israeli conflict according to the unambiguous interests of George H. W. Bush's administration.

This show of strength could have been imposed on the parties only in the exceptional circumstances of that time: the USSR's decline, the successful liberation of Kuwait, the demonstration of the

United States' military superiority, and a consensus on a "New World Order" reached among the states of the Middle East and within the international community as a whole. But despite this historic convergence, some sections of Arab society, as well as in important elements of the Israeli establishment, lacked conviction at best and only grudgingly marched to Washington's orders. Meanwhile, on the U.S. domestic front, the economy was faltering, and President Bush was unable to translate his military and diplomatic successes into an election victory in 1992. On the international scene, the United States' Middle East triumph could not be replicated on the African continent, where in 1993 Operation Restore Hope, whose mission was to reestablish order and security in Somalia, ended in disaster when eighteen American soldiers were killed by Islamist militants, fresh from the Afghan jihad battlefield, and their bodies dragged through the streets of Mogadishu for all the world to see. In response, President Clinton promptly withdrew American troops from the Horn of Africa.

Beneath the conventional geostrategic power relations that prevailed after Operation Desert Storm, other actors had begun to appear. The American setback in Somalia was just the first sign of the radical Islamist operations whose tortuous course throughout the 1990s would culminate in the September 11 attack on New York and Washington. During a decade of illusory Arab–Israeli peace, through aborted guerrilla campaigns in Algeria, Egypt, and Bosnia, global terrorism was on the rise. Not a single strategymaker paid enough attention: the defeat in Somalia was consigned to history as a mere bump on the road to a U.S.-imposed peace in the Middle East—though, as Bin Laden himself would later mention, this was the first battleground where Afghan-trained jihadists tested their fighting skills against U.S. soldiers, and found them less tough than the Red Army.

During both of his terms in office, President Clinton deepened the logic of a Palestinian–Israeli peace within the framework defined by his predecessor. However, by entrusting the portfolio to pro-Israel Democrats, he tipped the balance away from the pro-oil Republicans whose views had triumphed in Madrid. The new team was close to Israel's Labor Party, which had seized power, under Rabin and Peres, after trouncing Shamir in June 1992. These new arrangements were reassuring to most of Israel's supporters, who were confident that General Rabin would not take lightly such questions as the security of the Jewish state. On September 13, 1993, following discreet talks in Oslo between Arafat's and Rabin's envoys, the Palestinian and Israeli leaders signed a Declaration of Principles in the White House Rose Garden. This extraordinary gesture, broadcast across the world, symbolized the beginning of the path to peace.

Still, no one nurtured illusions about the parties' true feelings— as evidenced by Rabin's very visible revulsion at shaking Arafat's hand, despite Clinton's jovial encouragement. Arafat needed to offer his people an autonomous Palestinian territory, even a fragmented one, to counter the political advances of the Islamists. Rabin's government had expelled 415 Islamist activists to Lebanon in mid-December 1992, after the kidnapping and execution of a border guard on Israeli territory, and the Islamic resistance movement was basking in the glow of this success. In the face of critics (who would compare the territories over which the Palestinians exercised limited authority to apartheid South African's Bantustans), Arafat returned to Gaza and Jericho in 1994 as a liberator.

As for the Rabin government, it was keen to get rid of the difficult problem of policing Gaza, which was depleting the energy and morale of its citizen-soldiers. By the terms of the Oslo Accords, this function would be subcontracted to the Palestinian Authority. The Palestinian police force and security services, armed with light weaponry, were supposed to rein in Hamas and Islamic Jihad, but under no circumstances, at least in principle, were they to threaten the state of Israel.

The negotiations that began with the signing of the Declaration of Principles in Washington was dubbed the Oslo *process*, to emphasize the idea that these principles were merely a starting point for negotiations, not an agreement. The term "process" signified both that peace between Palestinians and Israelis was intended to spread to the rest of the Arab world (bringing the aborted peace initiative undertaken by Sadat and Begin in 1979 back to the table) and that economic renewal would complete the process by offering the governments involved—Israeli, Palestinian, and Arabs in general—tangible dividends they could redistribute to their peoples.

Still, the accords must be seen as the positive product of two negatives: neither Arafat nor Rabin had an alternative, but neither wanted to make the first move toward peace, so great was the suspicion they harbored toward their unwilling ally. The catalyst was, as usual, the man who occupied the White House—in this case Bill Clinton, whose personal engagement throughout his presidency mirrored the previous efforts of Presidents Jimmy Carter and George H. W. Bush. The end of the peace process, marked by the beginning of the second intifada in the fall of 2000, would coincide precisely with the end of Bill Clinton's second term and the election of a successor who believed that the "logic" of Oslo was out of date.

The Arab states had their own reasons for acquiescing to the peace process. During the 1990s, new constraints were bearing down on the political culture of Israel's neighbors. Since achieving independence from European colonization, ruling elites had invoked the mantra of the Zionist danger on their borders as a way to justify autocracy, whether it was exercised by kin dynasties, military groups, religious sects, tribes, or a mixture of these elements. This imperious Sacred Union served as a pretext to block any kind of innovation and to seek out sinecures, using force to repress opposition if necessary. As a result, economic development and its corollary, social progress, were stymied. The states confiscated by these political elites, who faced no competition within their borders, paid a price in the currency of decline: failure to compete on the international scene, demographic explosion, and massive underemployment. In a bid to perpetuate their power in this deteriorating context, Arab leaders, cognizant of the limited effectiveness of the spells they cast to ward off the "Zionist enemy," required new resources. The United States' triumph in Operation Desert Storm had created a context in which economic, rather than political, dividends were on offer. At once coerced and convinced, they agreed to support the Oslo process, but only if such fruits were forthcoming.

That is why the United States' role as a broker of this multipurpose peace process was so critical. Only Washington could mobilize the resources that would transform a peaceful Middle East into an integrated, prosperous economic region. According to Shimon Peres's vision, Israeli know-how, Gulf oil capital, and Arab labor would eventually come together to enable the birth of a new regional civilization, a New Middle East. By anchoring Israel definitively within this virtuous economic circle as a vital partner, he would enrich the leaders of Egypt, Syria, and other countries through economic growth rates comparable to those of the Asian "dragons." By redistributing part of this wealth to the middle and working classes, these leaders would be able to buy the population's acquiescence in their continued rule at a time when neither ideology nor repression was as effective as it had once been.

For this utopian scenario to play out, the suspicion the peace partners harbored toward each other must be overcome, and an influx of international investments capable of financing the operation must be created as quickly as possible. Funding, however, was limited largely to political gestures. The European Union's commitments, for instance, enabled the functioning of the Palestinian Authority and the creation of extensive infrastructure projects in the Palestinian territories—most of which were devastated by punitive Israeli operations during the second intifada. Despite numerous international conferences, particularly those organized by the World Economic Forum in Davos, the private sector could not anticipate positive returns on its investments in the Israeli–Palestinian zone and failed to commit itself. At various round-table sessions at the Davos forum destined to encourage this process, where I was asked to sit as facilitator, I could not help but notice that the CEOs of large multinational corporations who were slated to attend did not show up, leaving the representatives of Palestinian water, Israeli gas, and Jordanian electricity companies to chat endlessly among themselves about their needs. No doubt these captains of industry had concluded that the payoff would not be worth a few hours of their time. When I asked specifically why they had been absent, some of them pointed out that the petro-monarchies were investing most of their enormous liquidity reserves in Western markets, thereby demonstrating their profound misgivings toward a region which they knew better than anyone. Why should foreigners take a risk that local investors shunned? This lack of faith in the economic domain had repercussions, barely three or four years after the Oslo Accords, in the political realm. Stalled investments and growth prospects that seemed increasingly illusory eroded confidence in the peace process among a growing fraction of ruling elites, both Arab and Israeli.

Meanwhile, Islamist movements continued to engage in sporadic violence, triggering Israeli reprisals and undermining Arafat's credibility. Clearly, the man responsible for order in Gaza and the West Bank was unable to prevent attacks on Israel. Yitzhak Rabin's assassination in Israel on November 5, 1995, by an ultra-religious Jewish extremist strengthened a feeling in some quarters that the peace process posed a potentially fatal risk to the Jewish state. When, in reaction to violent attacks by Palestinian Islamists, Benjamin Netanyahu was elected prime minister, it became clear that Jewish voters, reeling from shock, would not put their faith in the Oslo process, perhaps because they had lost faith in its American sponsor. Despite the return to power of a Labor-led coalition under Ehud Barak in July 1999, a large portion of the Israeli establishment was now skeptical.

These elites, many of them Jewish intellectuals originally from the left and even far left of the political spectrum, saw their interests reflected more accurately in the American neoconservatives' strategic vision, as represented by the newly elected administration of George W. Bush. The neocons wanted an alternative to the Oslo process, one that entailed reshuffling the entire Middle East deck, starting with replacing the regime in Iraq with a pro-American democratic political force willing to recognize Israel. This step required that Oslo be abandoned. Sharon's provocative stroll along the esplanade of Haram Sharif in September 2000 and Arafat's instigation of the Al Aqsa intifada implicated both men in this geostrategic vision—one a willing accomplice, the other unaware.

2

The Neoconservative Revolution

During the 2000 presidential campaign, Republican candidate George W. Bush repeatedly signaled his deep-seated hostility to nation-building. In contrast to President Bill Clinton, who had intervened successfully in the civil wars ignited by Yugoslavia's disintegration, candidate Bush expressed skepticism about using American troops and financing to rescue failed states, or to create new states out of ethnic or religious chaos. And for the nine months of his presidency prior to the surprise attack of September 11, 2001, Bush further distanced his position from that of his predecessor by refusing to become personally involved in the Arab–Israeli peace process. He chose instead to toe the line drawn by his secretary of state, Colin Powell: "The United States stands ready to assist, not insist."

The international press had a field day with America's "new isolationism." But in reality, two factions within the president's foreign policy team deeply disagreed about how the world's sole superpower should conduct itself in the face of erupting ethnic and religious strife. One group aligned itself with Powell, who reflected the State Department's tradition of international diplomacy, and with the CIA, whose culture of cautious realism stressed international order, not upheaval. This group relied on traditional multilateral instruments, such as the United Nations, while bringing the United States' uncontested political weight to bear in settling local disputes.

The opposite position, represented by the Pentagon's civilian directors, favored taking advantage of the nation's unprecedented status as sole superpower to radically transform the world order. This neoconservative group, which included Assistant Secretary of Defense Paul Wolfowitz, Vice President Richard Cheney, and Chairman of the Defense Policy Board Advisory Committee Richard Perle, called for dissemination of the American model of democracy around the globe, by whatever means appropriate—means that did not necessarily include multinational organizations such as the United Nations (which Wolfowitz and his colleagues considered outdated) and which did not preclude military force.

The September 11 attacks impelled George W. Bush toward the worldview of this second group. Having displayed unease and inexperience with regard to foreign policy during his campaign, Bush as president decisively committed the United States to a bold course of military interventionism—a policy unmatched since Franklin Delano Roosevelt's response to the Japanese attack on Pearl Harbor sixty years earlier. The United Nations endorsed the U.S. "war on terror" by giving the administration unqualified support for Operation Enduring Freedom in Afghanistan, which sought to destroy the Taliban regime that was hosting the terrorist mastermind Osama bin Laden.

The neoconservative "project" to restructure international order along ideological lines did not originate on September 11, although it received a great boost from that tragic event. And the decisions President Bush made in the weeks and months after the attack cannot be reduced to this one element. Nevertheless, in the months following September 11 the neocons enjoyed an extraordinary degree of influence at the highest decision-making levels of the Bush administration. Despite their relatively small number—a few dozen intellectuals and academics at most—these ideologues were able to sell their vision to the president and persuade him to forsake the more pragmatic diplomacy that had shaped American foreign policy, for the most part, since the Vietnam War.

The roots of neoconservatism can be traced back to the 1960s, to a group of disaffected activists, many of whom were liberals or radicals before turning their backs on their comrades in arms. Denounced as traitors by their former friends, they were mocked in the pages of the left-leaning publication *Dissent* as "neoconservatives." The slur became their slogan. As one of the movement's founders, the essayist Irving Kristol, put it vividly: "A neoconservative is a Liberal who has been mugged by reality."

The versatile Kristol spent most of his career at New York University, but he was also at home in the para-academic world of think tanks and independent foundations. Kristol was the quintessential neoconservative. The son of a poor Jewish immigrant family from Brooklyn, he attended New York's City College during the interwar years and joined the youth association of the Trotskyite Fourth International's American section. The militants of the Young People's Socialist League met every day in the same corner of the school cafeteria, where they shared their humble egg or peanut butter sandwiches, remaking the world while keeping a cautious eye on the Stalinist contingent of communist students at the next table.

From this formative experience, which he often evoked with a hint of nostalgia, Kristol retained several distinguishing traits, even after he went over to the right. The anti-Stalinism of those years fed a lifelong suspicion of the USSR, strongly manifested during détente, which he saw as a Stalinist trap. His student participation in minority politics nurtured a proclivity for creating iconoclastic publications, such as *The Public Interest*, which he founded in 1965 and which became the mouthpiece of the new movement. He also discovered a penchant for infiltrating larger groups to spread his ideas. The high point of this strategy was the neoconservatives' takeover of the American Enterprise Institute, created in 1943. Once a radical advocate of class struggle, Kristol continued to confront the rigid, complacent convictions of the American political establishment after he became the voice of the neoconservative movement.

The person whose work helped Kristol articulate this worldview was Leo Strauss. A German Jewish immigrant of the previous generation, Strauss began his career as a philosopher during the Weimar Republic. Its collapse under the hammerblows of communism and Nazism forced him into exile in 1937. As a professor at the University of Chicago after 1949, Strauss examined the causes underlying the twentieth-century rise of totalitarian "tyrannies," as well as their acceptance by the people and the failure of intellectuals to challenge them. He attributed this process to a rejection of universal verities in favor of relativism, historicism, and what Max Weber called "axiological neutrality."

Applied to the world situation in the 1960s and early 1970s, Strauss's political philosophy translated into a warning against any attempt at "convergence," in the name of realpolitik, between the United States and the USSR. For him, there could be no moral equivalency between democracy and totalitarianism, good and evil. When necessary, democratic societies must be willing to use force against evil in order to survive. Yet during the last years of his life, Strauss looked on in despair as American university campuses boiled over in protest against the Vietnam War, questioning the use of force to defend democracy against the expansion of communism in Southeast Asia.

A profound pessimism regarding the common people—so easily seduced by the century's demagogues—marked Strauss's work. In the popular rhetoric of Nazism or communism he heard echoes of the Sophists whom Socrates fought with the weapons of philosophy. In the interests of a people who were by nature flighty, Plato deduced that the best political order proceeded from a philosopher-king, educated in civic virtue, who could recognize truth and good. As an interpreter of Machiavelli, Strauss took this thinking a step further, by rationalizing the prince's lying to the people or hiding information, if necessary, when it was in their own best interests. According to Strauss, secrecy and deception, along with force, were valid instruments of leadership when wielded for the greater good of democracy.

By 1980 the "revolution" initiated by Kristol and inspired by Strauss had become an integral part of establishment politics. Some of the neoconservatives who would eventually rise to power under George W. Bush were already beginning to make their mark on American foreign policy, especially in the Middle East and Central Asia. In 1981 Reagan inherited the United States' financial commitment to a jihad launched by the mujahedeen against the invading Red Army in Afghanistan. The Afghan cause had been taken up first by President Jimmy Carter at the end of his term (on the initiative of his National Security adviser, Zbigniew Brzezinski) in reaction to his administration's failure to free American hostages in Iran. The young neoconservatives who came to Washington during the Reagan years seized upon the Afghan conflict as a proxy war against the Soviet Union, part of a broad global strategy to combat communism around the globe.

It was in pursuit of this single-minded Cold War strategy that the so-called Iran-Contra affair emerged. In a complex covert operation carried out by high-ranking members of the Reagan White House, a pro-American, anti-Sandinista (that is, anti-Marxist) guerrilla movement in Nicaragua was financed through the illegal sale of spare parts to the Iranian air force under Khomeini. The ayatollah, who had released the American hostages on the first day of Reagan's term after holding them for 444 days, was now at war with his neighbor, Saddam Hussein, and he needed American military back-up. Members of the Reagan administration hoped that by secretly supplying arms to Iran, they could eventually influence moderates to move the country in a pro-Western direction. But in the meantime, Saddam Hussein was also receiving military assistance from the United States, which maintained official neutrality in the conflict. Among the Reagan operatives who arranged the Iran-Contra deal while also aiding Iraq, the mantra was to defeat communism and promote the spread of democracy, freedom, and capitalism around the globe, using all means at their disposal. In pursuit of that mission, almost any political bedfellow would do.

The mujahedeen's jihad to turn back the Soviet invaders in Afghanistan benefited from the operational and financial backing of the CIA, as well as subsidies from the Gulf petro-monarchies. "Holy warriors" from different parts of the world—Arabs, Pakistanis, Indonesians, sometimes second-generation European Arabs—were supplied with surface-to-air Stingers, which they used to keep Soviet air power pinned to the ground. These state-of-the-art missiles, as convenient as a crossbow or even a simple slingshot, brought together Stone Age and digital technologies. A Stinger could be operated by an unskilled fighter on foot; and for a very reasonable ratio of price to damage inflicted, it could paralyze a conventional occupying army. After years of stalemate, the mujahedeen's counterattack forced Soviet President Mikhail Gorbachev to pull his troops out of Afghanistan on February 15, 1989. The Stinger's poisonous "insect bites" had caused the collapse of the Soviet mammoth, and its fall would bring down the global balance of power that had dominated world politics for forty-five years.

The Stinger was just one of a huge arsenal of "smart weapons" developed by the United States after World War II. Their origins trace back to Project Solarium, initiated by President Dwight Eisenhower in 1953 when the Cold War was at its coldest and the communist model was attracting growing numbers of adherents among Western workers and intellectuals alike. Summoning the best military and scientific minds of the time, Eisenhower commissioned three teams to work in parallel to develop a long-term military strategy most likely to ensure victory over the Soviet bloc. Smart weapons were developed within this framework, which favored quality over quantity, fighters' sophistication and creativity over simple obedience to orders, and precision strikes over blind bombardment—innovations that required considerable financial investment in research and development, information technology, higher education, and high-tech industry across several generations and presidencies.

The father of the new strategy was Albert Wohlstetter (1913–1997), a New Yorker who, like Irving Kristol, graduated from City College and earned a degree in mathematical logic from Columbia University. In 1951 he took a position at the RAND Corporation, a defense and information think tank in the Los Angeles area, where he threw himself wholeheartedly into strategic questions concerning the logical use of military force. While in California, he met and inspired a high school student by the name of Richard Perle, who would become one of the most influential neoconservative policy-wonks in George W. Bush's administration. After leaving RAND, Wohlstetter went to the University of Chicago in 1964, and there he joined a circle of like-minded academics which included the economist Milton Friedman, Leo Strauss, and a bright young disciple, Paul Wolfowitz, whose dissertation focused on nuclear proliferation in the Middle East.

Throughout the Cold War, presidents from both parties—from

Eisenhower and Kennedy to Reagan and George H. W. Bush— drew on Wohlstetter's expertise and confidential advice. In the 1950s his painstaking risk analysis had led the Eisenhower administration to withdraw Strategic Air Command bombers from overseas bases and to install strategic missiles in protected underground silos in the United States. These moves were part of his groundbreaking concept of "second-strike deterrence." At a time when the two superpowers were engaged in a ferocious competition to increase the number and size of their nuclear weapons, Wohlstetter pointed out that what a nation could do *after* it had been attacked would be the deciding factor in a nuclear war. His second-strike logic led the United States to develop the capacity for a massive retaliatory response to preemptive nuclear attack— a scenario that is credited with achieving deterrence during the Cold War.

But Wohlstetter did not limit his strategic thinking to nuclear weaponry. He understood that there must be more to the logic of military force than Mutually Assured Destruction (MAD)—a theory that he considered unsound and needlessly risky. If the principal weapons in a nation's arsenal were nuclear bombs, how, he asked, could it respond to a conventional attack against one of its allies, or to a war begun accidentally? Wohlstetter believed that the ability to use precise and decisive force in a restricted theater of conflict was crucial to U.S. military preparedness. Decisionmakers needed nonsuicidal options for responding militarily to regional flare-ups—options designed to destroy the enemy's weapons rather than its civilians and infrastructure.

Measured against the standard of "precise and decisive," the military action in Vietnam was an unmitigated disaster, in Wohlstetter's view. The United States lost that war because planners at the time—most notably Secretary of Defense Robert

McNamara and Special Assistant for National Security Affairs Walt Rostow—wavered between two missions: to promote a democratic state in South Vietnam that would champion American ideals, or to crush the North Vietnamese army by using American weapons to their full capacity on the battlefield. By accomplishing a little of both but not enough of either, and by favoring short-term tactical compromises over long-term strategic vision, Washington met with both military and moral failure. For Wohlstetter, military supremacy had meaning only if it was placed in the service of clearly asserted democratic values—a worldview at odds with political realists like Henry Kissinger.

Against the caution of the Kissinger school of diplomacy—which had gambled on the USSR's slow internal decay, the prohibitive cost of an arms race it could not avoid, and the fatal attraction of an inaccessible consumer society—Wohlstetter and his disciples advocated an aggressive, right-here, right-now strategy toward Moscow. They pushed the Reagan administration toward a "hard line," to cite the title of a book by Richard Perle, who was known in the Department of Defense as the "Prince of Darkness." The Red Army's eventual retreat from Afghanistan in February 1989, followed by the fall of the Berlin Wall in November of that year, and finally Gorbachev's resignation in December of 1991, marked an apotheosis for the neoconservative cause. These prodigal sons of the Reagan administration had triumphed not only over the Evil Empire but also over the Washington establishment, particularly the CIA, which had earlier greeted their fervor with annoyance. It was a heady success.

Two years after the Stinger-wielding Afghan guerrillas routed the Soviet Union, the new administration of George H. W. Bush, supported by an international coalition, turned back the Iraqi army's invasion of Kuwait in Operation Desert Storm—an exemplary practical application of Wohlstetter's theories regarding preemptive air strikes. In forty days of intense bombing in Baghdad and throughout Iraq, the U.S. Air Force destroyed the nation's communication system and annihilated most of its fighting power before American ground troops began their offensive. In both theaters—Afghanistan and Iraq—the loss of American soldiers had been minimized. In Afghanistan, the actual fighting had been subcontracted to bearded "freedom fighters" whose death on the battlefield cost American politicians nothing at home. And in Iraq, precision bombing destroyed the will to resist on the part of the Iraqi army, a fearsome giant with feet of clay. These successful implementations of the Wohlstetter doctrine were limited only by imperfections in the new technology—a problem that would be remedied during follow-up engagements in Afghanistan and Iraq after September 11, 2001.

Wohlstetter had been an early proponent of the Strategic Defense Initiative (Star Wars), a massive military research program launched during Reagan's second term with the goal of developing a defensive shield to protect the United States from missile attack. The demise of the Soviet Union made the missile shield unnecessary, but the research that began during this program paid off in new information and communication technologies that could be applied to smart weapons on the battlefield. This work came to fruition in fall 2001, as scattered groups of special operations forces on the ground in Afghanistan, equipped with laser markers and GPS devices, called in devastating air strikes. Fighter aircraft high overhead dropped precision munitions on the ill-trained and undisciplined Taliban—munitions that could wipe out enemy fighters while sparing friendly troops nearby. The Taliban were convinced that only Satanic intervention could explain the decimation of their ranks without a single shot being fired by Americans on the ground. Less than two years later, during the offensive phase of Operation Iraqi Freedom, smart weapons struck presidential palaces, ministries, and barracks with the same incredible precision, while traffic made its way tranquilly through Baghdad's avenues and across its bridges.

WOHLSTETTER'S VISION provided the means for converting precision weapons into decisive instruments of foreign policy. A military offensive no longer needed to annihilate the enemy indiscriminately, as did the Allied bombardment of Dresden. The new goal was to target the ruling regime while sparing civilians (whom the attackers wished to win over to their side) and the urban and industrial infrastructure (which could be used by the conquerors and by local leaders who supported them). This strategy combined military power with politics in a new way. In theory, it allowed the United States and its allies to target "rogue" regimes selectively and to punish the ruling elites of those countries while promoting and strengthening civil society.

Such an operational arrangement, which portrays military force as a carefully calibrated and highly effective instrument of foreign policy, presupposes a worldview in which realpolitik has given way to the pursuit of a morally determined foreign policy. In 1992, that worldview found its theorist in Paul Wolfowitz, Wohlstetter's disciple, whose star had risen over Washington during the presidential term of George H. W. Bush. As Richard Cheney's undersecretary of defense for policy, he had authored a "Defense Planning Guidance Paper" which set down the United States' strategic priorities in the wake of the Cold War. The document, leaked to *The New York Times*, described a project that would guarantee post–Cold War global supremacy for the United States through military confrontation with regional regimes that were likely to challenge its absolute hegemony. To that end, the paper called for a policy asserting Washington's power wherever America's vital interests exist—with oil supplies and Israeli security at the top of the list.

But President Bush, a former director of the CIA who was running for reelection, did not share Wolfowitz's worldview. He had built his personal fortune on petroleum, an industry that prefers political and financial realism nourished by long-term investment returns over ideological indulgence. If Bush had been reelected, the neoconservatives probably would not have played an important role in the administration's strategic vision. As it turned out, Bush was defeated by the Democratic candidate Bill Clinton, who stressed the domestic economy over international strategizing. The aging *enfants terribles* of the Reagan administration found themselves sidelined for another eight years.

Those Clinton years, in the eyes of the neoconservatives, were characterized by political and military spinelessness and moral wretchedness. But they provided Albert Wohlstetter with material for his last battle, fought in the former Yugoslavia. He argued that morality and strategy alike required wide-scale American action in support of the Bosnians against the Serbs. The Clinton administration hesitated at first, displaying what the neoconservatives interpreted as a moral failing and a strategic incompetence that its enemies would exploit. But eventually the Clinton White House adjusted its thinking about Bosnia in a way that was inspired by the 1992 Wolfowitz paper (to its author's explicit satisfaction) and acted to intervene against the Serbs and on behalf of the Bosnians, then the Kosovars. Andy Marshall, chief of the Pentagon's Office of Net Assessments, took up the global vision conceived by Wohlstetter and promoted by Wolfowitz and worked to apply it on the battlefield.

In March 1996, facing the prospect that Clinton would be reelected for a second term, Norman Podhoretz, founder of the right-leaning magazine *Commentary*, published an article entitled "Neoconservatism: A Eulogy." In this witty text, which had emerged from a conference at the American Enterprise Institute, he saw the movement's eclipse during the Clinton years as a sign that neoconservative thought was now part of a shared mindset that no longer needed to be put forward explicitly. "Having been a neoconservative for so long that I ought perhaps to be called a paleoneoconservative," Podhoretz noted, "I have good reason to mourn its passing. And yet I must confess that its death seems to me more an occasion for celebration than for sadness. For what killed neoconservatism was not defeat but victory; it died not of failure but of success." Neoconservatism, he argued, "came into the world to combat the dangerous lies that were spread by the radicalism of the 1960s and that were being accepted as truth by the established liberal institutions of the day." Its "two ruling passions," anti-communism and "its revulsion against the counterculture," no longer had an object by the mid-1990s. Communism had disappeared, and the only remaining traces of the counterculture were its commercial exploitation by the establishment.

But Podhoretz's announcement of neoconservatism's demise was premature. In the middle of the arid 1990s, *The Weekly Standard* appeared as a remake of what *The Public Interest* and *Commentary* had been in the 1960s. Edited by William Kristol, Irving's son, it featured short, provocative, and often funny articles rather than the deeper reflections to be found in the previous generation's publications. According to *The Weekly Standard*'s perspective, Bush Sr. and Clinton had both demonstrated their inability to learn the necessary lessons from the collapse of the Soviet bloc and to reevaluate the international system as well as the exceptional opportunity facing the United States as the only remaining superpower. The American government was lazily following the norms and institutions that emerged in the wake of World War II and that, according to *The Weekly Standard*, had became irrelevant with the fall of the USSR. It was time to realign and, if necessary, disrupt traditional diplomatic practices in order to promote the American model of democracy, capitalism, and vested interests around the globe.

Such ideas gained a foothold with the publication in *Foreign Affairs* of an article by Bill Kristol and Robert Kagan entitled "Toward a Neo-Reaganite Foreign Policy." Like Podhoretz's "eulogy," it was published in 1996 when all the signs seemed favorable for the reelection of the neocons' nemesis, Bill Clinton. But the outmoded foreign policy views of his pale Republican adversary, Senator Robert Dole, were no better. Against the lukewarm consensus that had resulted from a perceived anachronistic diplomacy, Kristol and Kagan called for a strategy of radical rupture. It was time for the United States to achieve the unparalleled military superiority envisaged during the Reagan years, by devoting at least a quarter of the federal budget to defense. Through a massive investment in advanced weaponry, the United States could guarantee world peace by dissuading potential enemies from attacking, and also promote democratic ideals by "putting pressure on right-wing and left-wing dictatorships alike."

The authors did not hide their contempt for James Baker, Bush's secretary of state, who had justified military engagement in Operation Desert Storm in 1991 by reference to the defense not of American values but of American jobs. Rather than offer such a tepid justification for military adventures, Washington should exercise a "benevolent" universal hegemony, which left no room for negotiation or compromise. "Civilized nations" would place themselves under its aegis, for their own good and that of humanity. Those who did not would be labeled rogue states and could expect to be brought to their knees sooner or later, if they refused to mend their ways.

This worldview found a home in June 1997, with the creation of a specially designed think tank headquartered in the same Washington building that sheltered the American Enterprise Institute and *The Weekly Standard.* Baptized by Kristol and Kagan as the Project for the New American Century (PNAC), this think tank admonished and excoriated politicians throughout the government in order to influence the foreign policy choices of the Clinton administration. Regular signers of the project's petitions would later become passionate advocates of unilateralism in George W. Bush's entourage: future vice-president Dick Cheney; future secretary of defense Donald Rumsfeld; future assistant secretary of defense Paul Wolfowitz; future undersecretary of defense for policy Douglas Feith; future Department of Defense Policy Board chairman Richard Perle; future ambassador to Afghanistan Zalmay Khalilzad; and future member of the National Security Council (with special responsibility for the Middle East) Elliott Abrams, who had been found guilty of lying under oath about his role in the Iran-Contra affair and was later pardoned by George H. W. Bush.

It was around the Middle East question that the think tank's deliberations began to crystallize, and it was there that the line separating "civilized nations" from "rogue states" was drawn. Part of the theoretical underpinning for this distinction was found in a 1993 article on the "clash of civilizations" published in *Foreign Affairs* by Harvard professor Samuel Huntington. This piece triggered impassioned debates which inspired Huntington to expand his thesis into an instant worldwide best-seller in 1996. In that book, Huntington presented Islam (and, secondarily, Confucianism) as the West's adversarial Other, a hostile entity framed by the author's famous statement that "the crescent-shaped Islamic world has bloody borders." His intention was to displace the Cold War confrontation between the West and the Soviet bloc farther east, toward yesteryear's Orient, where the belligerent overtones of the Saracen enemy were recast as today's radical Islamism, with its mingling of leftover communist propaganda and religious fanaticism.

But the comparison was misleading, since it suggested that the world of Islam is as centralized as the Soviet bloc once was (Chinese dissidence notwithstanding) and that Mecca really constitutes the Moscow of Islam. But the Muslim world is neither monolithic nor homogenous. It has many centers, all of which compete for hegemony over political and religious values. Islam's relation to the West, and to the modernity the West invents and disseminates, is more complex, historically fraught, and intimate than the clear-cut ideological and military antagonism that prevailed between the United States and the USSR. There is no Islamist Comintern with radical offshoots across the planet, blindly following the Stalinist line.

Huntington's clash of civilizations theory facilitated the transfer to the Muslim world of a strategic hostility the West had inherited from decades of Cold War. The parallel drawn between the dangers of communism and those of Islam gave Washington's strategic planners the illusion that they could dispense with analyzing the nature of the Islamist "menace" and could simply transpose the conceptual tools designed to apprehend one threat to the very different realities of the other.

The neoconservative movement played a crucial role in bringing about this rhetorical and theoretical permutation. It placed a facile way of thinking in the service of a precise political agenda, aimed at expanding the American democratic model into the Middle East—the only part of the world that it had not penetrated at the end of the twentieth century—and at modifying U.S. policy in the region to give Israel's security precedence over an alliance with the Saudi petro-monarchy.

Although the Soviet Union had disappeared, the twin problems of procuring access to the Middle East's superabundance of oil and ensuring Israel's security had not. Despite their repeated efforts to jump-start the Oslo peace process, neither George H. W. Bush nor Bill Clinton sought the evolution of political systems in the Arab world toward a pluralism that would enable educated, modern elites from the rising middle classes to share political power—the only possible basis for early democratization. The United States—and Europe, for that matter—failed to provide the conditions for any modification to the status quo because it was to their economic advantage.

Thus, the democratic aspirations expressed in the Arabian peninsula after Kuwait was liberated in the spring of 1991 found no sympathetic ears at the White House. Instead, the main concern during a decade of U.S. foreign policy was to maintain stability in the Gulf—the necessary condition for dependable world oil supplies to fuel the booming global economy. To the vast numbers of malcontents in the Middle East, the West's continued support for authoritarian regimes in the region appeared clearly as bad faith. As an alternative, Islamist ideology, presented as an indigenous political solution, became increasingly appealing. Whatever its expression, whether moderate or radical, conservative or revolutionary, peaceful or violent—even terrorist—Islamism asserted its authenticity and altruism, its lack of concern with anything but the interests of the people from whom it had emerged, rather than those of foreign powers or global oil producers.

As early as the mid-1990s, the neoconservatives had astutely identified this Western complacency and its corollary problem, the Middle Eastern resentment that feeds Islamist ideology. They formulated a battery of arguments in favor of a radical intervention into the region, one that would eliminate most of the authoritarian regimes currently in power and set in motion the wheels of democracy. The grievances against these regimes were of two types. First, they had failed to ensure the minimum social progress that would have allowed their populations to acquire the commodities and profits of globalization, as had happened among the middle classes in Asia and Latin America. There, multinational corporations manufacturing electronic components, textiles, machinery, or automobile parts had decentralized production.

Second, the frantic quest for oil revenues had led to widespread corruption among political elites and to a tradition of authoritarianism that had precluded the emergence of an entrepreneurial class capable of generating jobs and wealth and participating in a democratic process. The neoconservatives' writing about power structures in the petro-monarchies took on an almost left-wing tone, which won their analysis approval beyond the circle of the American right, including some Arab intellectuals. Their analysis was not radically different from that made in 2002 by the *Report on Human Development in the Arab World*, written by Arab intellectuals under the aegis of the United Nations Development Program, even if the remedy prescribed was different.

Beyond these general principles of political and economic democratization, another pressing consideration led the neocons to challenge the regimes in power in the Middle East: the imperatives of Israel's security and permanence. As early as the mid-1990s, the neoconservatives denounced as illusory the logic of the Oslo process, which exchanged the occupied territories for recognition of the Jewish state. In 1996, in a document communicated to Benjamin Netanyahu, who was running for election as Israeli prime minister, they expressed their complete lack of confidence in Israel's Arab peace partners and sketched out an alternative strategy. Entitled "A Clean Break: A New Strategy for Securing the Realm," the text, developed by a Jerusalem think tank, bore the signatures of Richard Perle, Douglas Feith, and others who would exert a powerful influence on George W. Bush after September 11, 2001.

This document asserted that Israel was paralyzed at home by the remains of labor Zionism, which had led to economic recession, and abroad by a peace process founded on the exchange of "land for peace" with the Arabs. Replete with danger, and a sign of weakness, this exchange had to be replaced by the logic of "peace for peace." The "clean break" of the title was intended to rebuild Zionism on a "new intellectual foundation," making it possible to "secure the nation's streets and borders" by restoring Israel's strategic initiative and by emancipating it from the constraints created by Oslo. Three main strategies were set out: a strategic alliance with Turkey and Jordan; a review of relations with the Palestinians (allowing the "right of hot pursuit" into territories under Palestinian authority of those who commit acts of aggression and enabling the emergence of alternatives to Arafat's power); and less dependence on the United States.

Israel, according to the report, could "shape its strategic environment, in cooperation with Turkey and Jordan, by weakening, containing, and even rolling back Syria." This effort could "focus on removing Saddam Hussein from power in Iraq—an important Israeli strategic objective in its own right—as a means of foiling Syria's regional ambitions." In the short term, the restoration of the Hashemite monarchy in Baghdad, with a monarch from Amman's ruling family, was advised; by influencing the Shiite religious centers in Najaf that would fall under their control, the Hashemites could help Israel separate Lebanon's Shia from Hezbollah, Iran, and Syria. "Israel's new agenda," the authors concluded, could "signal a clean break by abandoning a policy which assumed exhaustion and allowed strategic retreat by reestablishing the principle of preemption, rather than retaliation alone and by ceasing to absorb blows to the nation without response."

The "preventive" approach—analogous to the doctrine of preemption elaborated by Wohlstetter and Wolfowitz with regard to America's global strategy—took as its starting point the principle that Israel's security and permanence could be guaranteed only if the ruling oligarchies in neighboring Arab countries and in Iran were overthrown. These governments had compensated for their lack of political legitimacy and their own economic and social failures by fleeing into populist anti-Israeli rhetoric and guilty complacency toward Islamist militancy in its most virulent anti-Jewish form. To break this vicious circle, the Israelis had just one option, according to the neoconservatives, and that was to deliver a shock to the system which would bring down these governments and, ideally, promote a democratic alternative. New rulers elected by the people would no longer feel the need to mobilize the Arab "street" against Israel, especially if a new class of entrepreneurs who were creating wealth and jobs perceived that partnership with Israel was the best way of increasing prosperity.

The trigger of this process, whose goal was to foment a true revolution in American foreign policy in the Middle East, was the elimination of Saddam Hussein's regime in Iraq. Considered the tyrant of the region's main rogue state, he, above all, embodied the principal threat to Israel, and his elimination would deprive Israel's Arab enemies of one of their main sources of support. Most importantly, removing a despot who had caused his people to suffer terribly would provoke a democratic transition and the growth of a civil society. Iraq's reconstruction, financed by its abundant oil production, would usher in an era of prosperity throughout the Middle East. The Iraqi example would galvanize the populations of neighboring states to overthrow their own rulers—thus allowing the Middle East to become a "normalized" region, basking in the glow of the United States' benevolent hegemony, like Europe, Pacific Asia, or Latin America.

On January 26, 1998, on the day before the annual State of the Union Address, the Project for the New American Century addressed an open letter to Bill Clinton, signed by eighteen influentials from a broader political spectrum than the neoconservative movement—Donald Rumsfeld, Paul Wolfowitz, Richard Perle, Zalmay Khalilzad, Elliot Abrams, and Richard Armitage, among others. Expressing their conviction that the embargo and sanctions against Iraq had become ineffective after the U.N. weapons inspectors' withdrawal, the letter argued that it was no longer possible to be sure that Saddam Hussein was not producing weapons of mass destruction. "Such uncertainty will, by itself, have a seriously destabilizing effect on the entire Middle East. It hardly needs to be added that if Saddam does acquire the capability to deliver weapons of mass destruction, as he is almost certain to do if we continue along the present course, the safety of American troops in the region, of our friends and allies like Israel and the moderate Arab states, and a significant portion of the world's supply of oil will all be put at hazard." The only acceptable long-term strategy to counter that danger consisted in "removing Saddam Hussein and his regime from power."

The next day, President Clinton asserted in his State of the

Union Address that Saddam Hussein "could not defy the will of the world . . . I say to him, 'You have used weapons of mass destruction before; we are determined to deny you the capacity to use them again.'" Three days later, on January 30, Bill Kristol and Robert Kagan published an op-ed piece in *The New York Times* under the title "Bombing Iraq Isn't Enough." Opening with the words "Saddam Hussein must go," it closed with a visionary piece of advice: "If Mr. Clinton is serious about protecting us and our allies from Iraqi biological and chemical weapons, he will order ground forces to the gulf. Four heavy divisions and two airborne divisions are available for deployment. The President should act, and Congress should support him in the only policy that can succeed."

As a first step in this vast plan to reshape the Middle East, the liquidation of Saddam Hussein's regime was contemplated in the same terms as the elimination of communism. The eradication of the power apparatus—represented by the Baath Party and the military hierarchy—would enable Iraqi civil society to take its destiny in its hands. In Prague, Warsaw, and indeed throughout the former socialist bloc after the fall of the Berlin Wall, civil society had rebuilt itself on a democratic basis once the communist system had vanished. In the same way, the neoconservatives (who agreed on this point with many liberals and human rights activists) saw Iraqi society as the bearer of an equally democratic future.

According to this perspective, there could be no "cultural exception," whether Arab, Muslim, tribal, or other. Most neoconservatives were willing to gamble that Huntington's dire "clash of civilizations" would dissolve in democratization and the market economy—in keeping with the views of Francis Fukuyama, author of a 1992 book entitled *The End of History*. Himself a signer of the PNAC's open letter to Bill Clinton, Fukuyama had argued in his book that "a remarkable consensus concerning the legitimacy of liberal democracy as a system of government had emerged throughout the world over the past few years [and] that liberal democracy may constitute the end point of mankind's ideological evolution and the final form of human government, and as such constituted the end of history." Iraq and other countries of the Middle East should be allowed to adopt liberal democracy and participate in "the end of history," just like the rest of the world's nations.

But regime change in Iraq could come about only through external intervention. The solution the neoconservatives prescribed was a military initiative to use "smart weapons" to overthrow Saddam's regime. This plan would reverse the embargo's effects: instead of punishing Iraqi society without harming the regime, it would destroy the superstructure of the Baath Party and the military hierarchy while limiting "collateral damage" as much as possible. This Iraqi strategy redirected a number of guiding principles of the Cold War: it extended to Saddam's Iraq the modus operandi that had led to the USSR's collapse (that is, war); it made Israel's security a priority; it aimed to promote the dissemination of the democratic American model in the Middle East; and it purported to open the way to prosperity for the region and for the American firms that wished to do business there. Meanwhile, control over the world's main oil zone would be guaranteed and the oil supply would be balanced out to benefit the new Iraqi producer.

This military initiative in Iraq, which would require the United States to deploy its forces unilaterally if it could not obtain support for invasion from the U.N. Security Council, might never have seen the light of day had it not been for an exceptional set of circumstances: the unprecedented terrorist attacks on New York and Washington of September 11, 2001, which opened a new chapter of American history.

3

Striking at the Faraway Enemy

The surprise attacks on New York and Washington in 2001 came out of a clear blue September sky, shocking the West and shaking it to its foundations. The unimaginable collapse of the World Trade Center's twin towers—viewed in real time or within hours by people around the globe—left an indelible mark on the world's collective memory. Once standing tall as the proud symbols of America's financial power and global reach, these crumbling edifices now represented desolation and terror. Not since Pearl Harbor had the United States been the victim of a surprise attack on its own soil; but unlike the sailors and airmen who died at the hands of Japanese pilots, the three thousand civilians buried in the wreckage of September 11 were hostages in a war about which they knew nothing, against an enemy they could not name.

The bombings and suicide operations that preceded September 11—warning shots across the bow—did not prepare the United States and its Western allies for the impact of the 9/11 destruction. The attack seemed to be both a terminal and a founding explosion, a sort of Big Bang that ended a familiar chapter of history and inaugurated the return of barbarism—a senseless, incomprehensible apocalypse requiring an unprecedented response. President George W. Bush, with the strong endorsement of his neoconservative advisers, countered with a "war on terror," an initiative intended to bring forth a new world order from the overwhelming chaos and sense of dread. Transformations that had been on hold since the collapse of the Soviet Union suddenly took on renewed energy and urgency.

But the strikes of 9/11 were not unintelligible. They were in fact the most spectacular expressions to date of an ongoing and rational process designed by Islamic radicals to bring terrorism to the American homeland. Those who commissioned and executed the suicide hijackings saw them as neither beginning nor end but as simply the successful implementation of a predefined and long-range strategy. The insatiable death wish of the terrorists who carried out the attacks and the means they adopted were indeed fanatical, but from the perspective of the radical Islamist faction that masterminded the project, there was nothing irrational about the goal of this "martyrdom operation." The terrorists' plan resulted from deliberations informed by past tribulations and failures and from an analysis of the limits of American supremacy in the new international balance of power. Like their enemy the United States, they placed the Middle East crisis at the center of their strategy; but instead of flexing diplomatic or military muscle, they sought to gain political strength in the region by administering shrewd doses of terror around the globe.

In order to reconstruct the logic of those who planned the attacks on New York and Washington, we must retrace the converging paths of the two men who would become the chiefs of the Al Qaeda network: Ayman al-Zawahiri, an Egyptian citizen, and Osama bin Laden, a Saudi Arabian. During the 1980s "experiment" in Afghanistan, they began to formulate the notion of global jihad, and they put it to the test between 1992 and 1996, during their years of exile in Sudan. Learning from their successes and failures, Zawahiri and Bin Laden refined their militant theory and implemented it on a grand scale when they returned to Afghanistan under the Taliban's Islamic emirate between 1996 and 2001. During that period the area around Kandahar served as an incubator for combatants from all over the Muslim world who came there to train with Al Qaeda.

But behind this exceptional encounter between Zawahiri and Bin Laden is a larger story, involving the hybridization of two strains of radical Islamism—Egyptian and Saudi. Its unexpected progeny, global jihad, overturned the past logic of an imminent struggle against the "nearby enemy" (the regimes that held power throughout the region), in favor of an immediate, merciless war against the "faraway enemy" (the United States, Israel, and the West in general). Spectacular attacks on American, Israeli, or Western targets would resolve a major problem that had stymied Islamist radicals for over a decade: their inability to mobilize popular support to overthrow established regimes and replace them with an Islamic state.

In the Sunni countries, no political movement had come close to replicating the Shia unrest that caused bazaar merchants and the disinherited underclass to overthrow the shah of Iran in 1979. The insurrection against Hosni Mubarak in Egypt had failed, and the civil war in Algeria had fallen short of overthrowing the government. The Sunni ideologue Hassan al-Turabi managed to take power in Sudan in June 1989 through a coup d'état, and in 1996 the Taliban seized Kabul, thanks to Pakistani military support; but neither group was able to export their Islamist revolution, despite the plethora of Arab and Islamic conferences Turabi organized to that end. These disappointments, as well as futile attempts to turn Bosnia into an Islamist base within Europe, led Al Qaeda's ideologues, Zawahiri first among them, to switch gears and give priority to the international struggle and the media attention it would inevitably garner.

In an age of satellite television, Zawahiri reasoned, international media attention must replace the patient, close work of recruitment through Islamic charity associations that in the past had targeted potential sympathizers and militants. Television images of successful attacks, featuring hundreds of dead and wounded, would sow panic in enemy ranks while galvanizing the faithful and increasing their numbers. But above all, these events would encourage "martyrs" to come forth and take on future suicide missions in the name of the Islamist cause.

To understand how Zawahiri and his acolyte, Bin Laden, developed and implemented this new global strategy, we must appreciate how profoundly the defeat of the Soviet army in Afghanistan in 1989 modified the international context in which Sunni Islamists operated. The jihadists persuaded themselves that they had been the primary cause of this unprecedented victory against a superpower, rather than instruments manipulated by the world's other superpower, the United States. This conviction led them to deploy their forces in a new global project guided simultaneously by a mythical reading of Islamic history and a subtle appreciation of the fault lines in America's global hegemony.

This new project was based on an eschatological understanding of time, organized around the fulfillment of divine revelation. According to traditional Muslim belief, that revelation was realized under the Prophet Muhammad and his four first successors, between approximately 622 and 657 CE—the Golden Age of Islam. Since then, according to the worldview of Al Qaeda's ideologues, humanity has been caught between the positive, dynamic expansion of Islam around the globe and a negative movement toward corruption, under the influence of materialistic politicians. Instead of "commanding good and forbidding evil," as sharia (Islamic law) requires, these leaders govern according to their whim and self-interest.

The Islamist radicals gathered around Kandahar aspired to renew the original paradigm incarnated in the Prophet's life. They vowed to fight both an internal battle within the Muslim world aimed at replacing corrupt leaders with "rightly-guided" princes, and an external battle against "impious" foreign nations. These foreign infidels were seen, on the one hand, as Islam's enemies, whose endless conspiracies must be uprooted; but they were also perceived as its quarry, since they would necessarily come to embrace the one true faith in the end.

Zawahiri interpreted the jihad against the Soviet Union in Afghanistan as a repetition of a founding conflict during the early days of Islam in which "knights under the Prophet's banner" (the title of Zawahiri's most important work) destroyed the Persian Sasanid empire before turning against Byzantium. Like their glorious ancestors, the Afghan jihadists believed that they too had brought down one global superpower, and now these modern-day knights must recommit their efforts to wreaking havoc on the remaining one, the United States.

The mimetic simplicity of this worldview served Islamist ideologues well, for it unearthed and updated a long tradition of education dispensed to small children in Quranic primary schools and madrassas. It was also reminiscent of the Assassins, the medieval Islamic organization whose members, high on hashish (hence their name, *hashishin*, which translates as "assassins" in English), were trained by their chief, the so-called Sheikh of the Mountain, to become hired killers. The Assassins sacrificed their lives to stab and kill Frankish Crusaders in Syria and Palestine, as well as Muslim emirs whose jihad against infidel invaders was deemed tepid.

A more modern reference was to a *putsch*, in which a small vanguard carries out a coup and then reconstructs the social order from above—the opposite of a bottom-up strategy that mobilizes the masses to overthrow a despised regime. The political logic of the 9/11 masterminds carried on a tradition of military coups through which many Arab elites—first among them Gamal Abdel Nasser and his comrades in Egypt in 1952—seized power. The Islamists simply substituted their religion-based ideology for the socialism-tinged nationalism that was in vogue in the 1950s and 1960s.

Zawahiri's eschatological interpretation of global politics, with its medieval overtones, did not pose an obstacle to the mastery of modern, sophisticated communication and transportation technologies, monetary instruments, and weapons systems. Living fully in the electronic information age, the planners of 9/11 were aware of the influence of neoconservative thought in the United States during the 1980s and the anti-globalization critique in Europe during the 1990s, even if these American and European opinion-makers were oblivious to them.

Most Westerners got their first glimpse of Zawahiri—an Egyptian surgeon who became Al Qaeda's foremost political theorist—on Al Jazeera television on October 7, 2001, as he squatted beside Osama bin Laden at the mouth of an Afghan cave. Bearded, with a heavy, bespectacled face, he wore a turban and, like his companions, a hybrid outfit which suggested both the uniforms of the mujahedeen (Afghani holy warriors) and the costumes that regularly appear on Egyptian soap operas about the Prophet's life. In this video, the first from Al Qaeda to appear after the September 11 attacks—and timed to coincide with the first day of the United States' "war on terror" in Afghanistan—Zawahiri spoke out to rally supporters, representing the current struggle as a continuation of the Prophet's life and of the epic battles fought against the Crusaders in the name of Allah:

> For you, Muslims, this is the day of truth and sincerity, the day you face a test. This is your day. The new Quraish [the impious tribe of Mecca, which fought the Prophet Muhammad and which he ultimately vanquished] has ganged up on the long-suffering Muslims, much as the old Quraish and its brutes ganged up on the Muslims in Medina; so do as the Prophet's companions did. Young mujahedeen, faithful ulema who love Allah, this is a new Islamic epic, a new battle for the faith, like the great battles of Hittine [in which the Muslim armies triumphed over the Crusaders], Ain Jalut [where they defeated the Mongols] and the conquest of Jerusalem. The epic is starting again, so come defend the honor of jihad.

Of the three men who spoke in the video (the other two being Bin Laden and Abu Ghaith, a Kuwaiti citizen), Zawahiri was the one whose discourse was most politically grounded. Bin Laden attempted to appeal to a universal morality and to turn the accusation of terrorism against America by incriminating it for "over eighty years of humiliation" that the Muslims had borne, as well as the present suffering of Iraqi children and the Palestinians. Zawahiri, on the other hand, addressed himself first to the self-interests of the American people, calling on them to dissociate themselves from their government, which was leading them "into a new war it is certain to lose, and in which you will lose your children and your property." Then taking up the cause of the Palestinians, he said, "You, American people, and the whole world: know that we will not tolerate a repetition of the Andalusia tragedy [the end of Moorish rule in Spain] in Palestine. We would rather see this whole [Islamic] nation perish than see Al Aqsa mosque destroyed, Palestine Judaized, and its people expelled."

In this appeal—a harbinger of the carnage in Madrid on March 11, 2004, when Al Qaeda bombed four commuter rail trains and killed 191 people—Zawahiri was drawing upon a tradition of perpetual jihad against foreign enemies, Jewish and Christian, and against idol worshipers who threaten the Prophet. All were vanquished by the faithful in past battles, just as their descendants will be vanquished by today's Muslims. The great deeds of September 11 were the work of the movement's vanguard, but they were not the final consummation of its vision.

The entire scenario—the cave, the outfits, the exhortations—suggested that Zawahiri and Bin Laden were playing out, in full costume, the epic story of the Hegira, or Flight from Mecca, which marked the beginning of the Islamic era in 622 CE. Islamist history must always return to its beginning, they seemed to be saying, to the foundational rupture of the Flight: it both grounds and justifies, through the exemplary nature of its origins, today's jihad against faraway enemies. Having shattered New York and Washington, this battle would go on to sow death in Tel Aviv, Djerba, Bali, Mombassa, Casablanca, Istanbul, Riyadh, and Madrid.

THE MAN PRIMARILY responsible for formulating this political strategy was the scion of a family from the Egyptian intellectual aristocracy that had seen better days. On his father's side, Ayman al-Zawahiri descended from men of science, both sacred and profane: prominent doctors of medicine and pharmacology as well as eminent imams from Cairo's Islamic university, Al Azhar. His family name originated in the town of Zawahir, in Saudi Arabia, between Mecca and Medina. But in the 1860s Zawahiri's great-grandfather moved to Tanta, in the Nile Delta, leaving behind poverty-stricken, pre-petrol Arabia for the prosperity and promise of Egypt, where the population explosion had not yet taken its toll.

On his mother's side, Zawahiri traced his lineage back to the powerful Azzam clan, also originally from the Arabian peninsula. The Egyptian branch—claiming descent from the Prophet—was known principally through the life of Zawahiri's grandfather, Azzam Bey, who was educated at Al Azhar University and then in London and who served as dean of Cairo University's Faculty of Literature as well as Egypt's ambassador to Saudi Arabia (twice, under King Faruq and the Nasser regime) before founding Riyadh University. Azzam Bey's brother, Azzam Pasha (Zawahiri's great-uncle), a physician educated in England, served as a deputy during the Egyptian monarchy. An ambassador and the author of, among other works, *The Eternal Message of the Prophet Muhammad*, Azzam Pasha was the Arab League's first secretary-general, from 1945 to 1952. In addition to this very illustrious career, he gained the family's blessing by marrying off his daughter (Zawahiri's mother's cousin) to the eldest son of Saudi Arabia's King Faisal, Prince Muhammad, who founded the Faisal Islamic Bank.

Ayman was born in Cairo in 1951—a year marred by corruption, violence, and political assassinations. King Faruq's dynasty was unable to withstand the collapse of the European colonial order and the nationalist aspirations of the urban middle classes, the effendis. When the Free Officers took power in a coup d'état on July 23, 1952, President Nasser brought Arab nationalism to life in Egypt, and in the process implemented socialist policies that destroyed the careers of the educated, salaried class to which the Zawahiris belonged. Ayman's father, a university professor of pharmacology, resettled the family in Maadi, a residential suburb south of Cairo, but in a dusty lower-middle-class neighborhood rather than in the opulent villas near the Sporting Club, where French and English were spoken over afternoon cocktails. Zawahiri's parents were pious but without affectation. At a time when Egypt's relations with Saudi Arabia were at a nadir and sympathizers with the Muslim Brothers were rotting in prison (if they had not managed to flee across the Red Sea and into exile in Saudi Arabia), Arab Islamist militants were wise to keep a low profile.

In 1966, following its campaign against a "new Brotherhood conspiracy," the Nasser regime condemned and executed Sayyid Qutb, the Islamists' foremost thinker, after subjecting him to lengthy torture. His lawyer was Mahfuz Azzam, another of Zawahiri's great-uncles. Qutb's agony served as a trigger for the future theoretician of global jihad. While students across Europe and America were joining left-wing Marxist or Maoist movements, Zawahiri, a student at a public secondary school in Maadi, and a few friends who were also shocked by Qutb's execution set up a clandestine Islamist group. It lasted fifteen years, until Sadat's assassination in 1981, though it underwent many changes, and at its apogee in 1974 had only forty-odd members.

Qutb's thought played a foundational role for Zawahiri: "Qutb's call for faith in Allah's Oneness, for submission to His sole authority and sovereignty [hakimiyya], was the spark that enflamed the Islamic revolution against Islam's enemies throughout the world," he wrote in *Knights under the Prophet's Banner*. Zawahiri's secret organization aimed at overthrowing the Egyptian regime that persecuted Muslims and establishing in its stead an Islamic state based on sharia. The means was jihad, which he defined as "an armed putsch . . . requiring cooperation between civilians and the military to achieve its goal."

Zawahiri did not modify this strategy after Anwar Sadat came to power in 1970 following Nasser's sudden death. Even though Islamist militants were no longer the targets of merciless government repression, Egyptian university campuses filled up with bearded young men who were encouraged by Sadat's now pro-American regime to help root out any remaining left-wing militants. Recognizing the danger, Zawahiri remained in the political underground throughout his years in medical school, where he performed brilliantly and did nothing to betray the intensity of his radical commitments. A Jewish American journalist who had converted to Islam remarked when he met him midway through that decade that Zawahiri, with his huge glasses, resembled nothing so much as the left-wing City College intellectuals of thirty years earlier in New York.

In 1974 an Islamist group led by a Palestinian exiled in Cairo, Salih Sirriyya, attempted a coup against Sadat. It failed, and its leaders were arrested, sentenced to death, and executed. Nevertheless, this first attempt to use violence in overthrowing an infidel regime pleased Zawahiri, who disapproved only of its lack of preparation, its amateurish approach, and its hastiness. He interpreted the attack, however, as a sign that the radical Islamist movement had overcome the taboos preventing it from using force to attack the nearby enemy.

In 1980 Zawahiri, now a physician, joined an Islamist medical NGO whose assignment was to bring aid to the Afghan mujahedeen, then in the first year of their jihad against the Red Army. His four-month stay in Peshawar and Afghanistan, followed by a briefer sojourn the following year, confirmed Zawahiri's belief that only armed struggle would lead to Islam's triumph and that Afghanistan offered the best battleground for victory. In the month following his second return to Egypt, in May 1981, however, Zawahiri was drawn into the whirlwind that led up to Sadat's assassination on October 6.

An Islamist electrical engineer by the name of Farag sketched out the leader's assassination in a pamphlet entitled *The Hidden Imperative*. The Islamist movement must seize power immediately, he said, by eliminating the corrupt "devious prince" who governed Muslim lands. If the militants began with the "faraway enemy"— Israel—the despot would turn the struggle to his advantage. Farag's ideas emerged from a critical analysis of the use Arab nationalists had made of the conflict with Israel in order to impose the sacrosanct Arab Union and legitimize the repression of any form of opposition.

The ranks of Islamist radicals like Farag who dreamed of overthrowing the Egyptian regime had grown while Zawahiri was in Afghanistan, and some army officers had been recruited for a violent coup. Zawahiri did not participate in their preparations, but he got word of the assassination plot a few hours before it was carried out. He tried to dissuade the killers, since he considered their operation premature and destined to fail. The murder of Sadat went according to plan, but, as Zawahiri had predicted, Sadat's death bore no lasting fruit: it did not bring an Islamic state into being, despite a brief uprising in Asyut, in Upper Egypt, the Islamist stronghold.

Sadat's vice president, Hosni Mubarak, came to power and undertook a vast repression campaign against all activists. The principal conspirators were rounded up and executed, but those who belonged to the second tier served only a few years in jail. Zawahiri was among them. In early 1982, when the trial opened, his co-detainees designated him as their spokesman, for his English was better than the others'; shouting to the international press from the courtroom cage in which they were kept, he denounced the Egyptian government's use of torture. This was the first time that Zawahiri's round, bespectacled face had appeared on news agency pictures and television screens. Otherwise, he remained anonymous except among the handful of specialists who were investigating the phenomenon of Islamism.

In prison, Zawahiri associated with the major players of radical Islamism, among them the blind sheikh Omar Abdel-Rahman, who would later play a role in the first attack on the World Trade Center in 1993. After prison, the sheikh would also become the leader of Gamaa Islamiya, a rival of Zawahiri's group, Egyptian Jihad Organization. The Gamaa's strategy in Egypt during the 1990s was guerrilla warfare at close quarters: stalking and assassinating representatives of authority, Egyptian Christians, tourists—preferably, but not exclusively, Israeli—as well as other nearby targets. Gamaa Islamiya caused about a thousand deaths before the group's leading emirs called for the cessation of armed struggle, following the November 1997 massacre of fifty-eight tourists in Luxor. That senseless act had cut Gamaa Islamiya off from the last remnants of its popular support. Zawahiri advocated the opposite strategy: a jihad in 1989 focusing on state representatives and army and police officers. This closely targeted strategy, born out of necessity since his group was far less numerous than Gamaa Islamiya, was in the end no more successful.

The interrogations, torture, and socialization of prison turned most of the men rounded up by Mubarak into hardened militants, thirsty for revenge: they would become the foot soldiers of terrorism. Zawahiri's feelings were more complex and ambivalent: under torture, he had assisted the police in trapping one of his comrades. Muntasir al-Zayyat, a repentant Islamist radical and the author of a critical biography of Zawahiri, speculates that the shame of this all-too-human weakness was one cause of Zawahiri's final departure from Egypt in 1985, after he had served his time in prison.

Zawahiri relocated in Jeddah in Saudi Arabia, where he worked in a medical dispensary. Just an hour's drive from Mecca and the seat of the principal youth organization linked to the Muslim Brothers, the World Assembly for Muslim Youth, Jeddah was also the bastion of the Bin Laden family and the hub of enlistment in the Afghan jihad, via Peshawar in Pakistan. In 1986 Zawahiri arrived for the third time in what was then the global capital of radical Islamism. During that stay, he met the man who would give him the financial means to fulfill his ambitions: Osama bin Laden.

Six years younger than Zawahiri and seventeenth among the fifty-two children sired by Saudi Arabia's public buildings and public works magnate, Osama bin Laden was hardly an austere Islamist intellectual. Unlike Zawahiri, he had not experienced clandestine activism in his youth; instead, he exhibited the psychological and cultural dissociation typical of wealthy Saudis, who tend to be more pious at home than abroad. Osama's religious devotion had undergone eclipses. But like many children from influential Saudi families, he signed up to support the Afghan jihad in the early 1980s. That was when he discovered religious devotion and a militant commitment that gave his life meaning.

At the time, the Saudi monarchy did not consider such military proclivities suspicious—quite the contrary. The dynasty saw only advantages in a guerrilla war against the Red Army—a war which, with America's protection and acquiescence, it encouraged and financed. On the regional front, a struggle in the name of Islam against the Soviet Union's communist atheism provided a counterweight to Khomeini's impassioned calls to arms against America, the "Great Satan." Perhaps a glorious Islamic military victory, studded with "miraculous" victories in the Afghan mountains, would restore some credibility to the peninsula's conservative Arab regimes in the eyes of young people who were susceptible to the revolutionary rhetoric of the ayatollah in Tehran.

In autumn 1979 the Saudi monarchy had been shaken when a group of young local activists, along with foreign students educated by the kingdom's major religious figures, occupied the Great Mosque in Mecca. Their intention was to carry out a jihad against the House of Saud, which the rebels accused of being corrupt and hypocritical and of displaying its adoration for Allah only to disguise its idolatry of the dollar. By exporting the most enthusiastic of these activists to the Afghan military theater, the Saudi royal family hoped to distract them from domestic concerns.

When the jihad's young fighters arrived in Afghanistan, a Muslim Brother of Palestinian origin, Abdallah Azzam (no relation to Zawahiri's maternal relatives), welcomed them and took them in hand. Azzam was well known in political circles as the jihad's herald, celebrating it in countless articles and conferences around the world, from American university campuses to Pakistani training camps. He was careful to direct his rhetoric against the Soviet Union and the Muslim world's pro-socialist regimes, not against the United States and its regional clients. He stirred up the sentiments of young people by reminding them that one day Islam would reconquer Andalusia in Spain, but he was careful not to sully the reputation of the Gulf's conservative petro-monarchies or that of the United States, which was providing weapons, advisers, and subsidies for the bearded fighters pouring into Peshawar.

As coordinator of aid and services for the mujahedeen, Azzam was also in a good position to separate the wheat from the chaff—the offspring of pious, wealthy families on the Arabian peninsula from impoverished North African or Egyptian activists, just out of prison and brimming with extremist ideas. While exiled to Jeddah, Azzam had been Osama bin Laden's teacher and mentor, and the young Saudi's fabulous wealth made him a target of Azzam's attention when Osama arrived in Afghanistan. Bin Laden quickly fell under the spell of this Muslim Brother. Like a number of young men in his social group, Osama had been educated in the very conservative milieu of Wahhabism—an extremely dogmatic conception of Islam that still holds sway in the kingdom today. In Afghanistan, Azzam introduced the language and thought of the Muslim Brothers to the young Bin Laden, introducing him to a worldview that transcended the Arabian desert and channeled his ardor toward devotion to the cause of Islamist reform.

Between 1986 and 1989, as victory over the Red Army became more likely, violent conflicts began to divide the different factions of jihad fighters. They bickered over the movement's future global strategy and wrangled over financial matters, such as how to maintain the activists after the war, many of whom, including Zawahiri, had settled in Peshawar with their wives and children. In the course of these conflicts, Zawahiri gradually managed to replace Azzam as Bin Laden's spiritual mentor. His harsh accusations against the Muslim Brothers provided the content for a sectarian tract, *Sixty Years of the Muslim Brothers' Bitter Harvest*, that circulated among Islamists in the late 1980s.

Back in the 1950s and 60s, when members of the Muslim Brothers had fled repression under Nasser in Egypt and under the Baathists in Syria and Iraq, King Faisal had welcomed them to Saudia Arabia with open arms. At a time when a wave of nationalist fervor was sweeping the Arab world under the charismatic influence of Nasser, a Soviet client, the Saudi kingdom had come to depend on the support of reactionary and unsophisticated *ulema* (doctors of Islamic law), who were very knowledgeable about the balance of tribal power in the Arabian peninsula but ignorant of changes in the rest of the world (which they believed was flat) and therefore poorly armed to do battle against the socialist propaganda machines of Cairo, Damascus, or Baghdad. Saudi Arabia welcomed the Muslim Brothers because they bridged the gap between the kingdom's intellectually weak religious fundamentalists and the pragmatic agenda of the Saudi dynasty. The government rewarded the Brothers handsomely for their service, and the Brothers jockeyed for better position by making sure never to quarrel with their Saudi partners.

But according to Zawahiri's tract, the Brothers had sacrificed the ideals of jihad for their personal comfort and the material benefits that meddling in the Gulf's financial circles had brought. They had even accepted the "impious" notion of democracy, holding that the people could be a source of sovereignty, when all sovereignty is Allah's alone.

As these squabbles among jihadist factions were bouncing off the minarets around Peshawar, the Soviet army withdrew from Kabul on February 15, 1989, overcome by American weapons, particularly surface-to-air Stinger missiles. Having achieved its goal, Washington also rapidly withdrew its resources from Afghanistan, and the struggle for increasingly scarce financing grew more bitter, as did controversies over the future of jihad after the Afghan victory. Zawahiri's anti-American line, which represented a minority position as long as the CIA was providing support for the jihad, gained adherents at the first sign that Washington was backing away from the Islamists. Violent clashes ensued, and on November 24, 1989, Abdallah Azzam was assassinated. The perpetrators were never discovered.

The path was now open for Zawahiri to exert unchallenged influence over Osama bin Laden, whose rapid ideological evolution and suspicious acquaintances were beginning to worry the Saudi secret services. On a trip home in 1989, Bin Laden's Saudi passport was confiscated, and he could not leave the kingdom until his escape in 1991. During that time, he observed the arrival of hundreds of thousands of soldiers from the coalition that President George H. W. Bush had organized to expel the Iraqi army from Kuwait. For Bin Laden, the "cause" was now becoming clear: secular America, with its soldiers, tanks, and military bases, was befouling the land of the Muslim holy sites and was therefore the ultimate enemy that Islam must destroy. With that realization, the political destiny of the public works multimillionaire from Jeddah was permanently joined to that of the surgeon from Cairo.

Before a direct confrontation could take place between militant Islamists and the United States, however, it was necessary to launch a preliminary offensive against America's regional allies, foremost among them the states where Bin Laden and Zawahiri were citizens. In December 1988, violent incidents had pitted radical Islamists against the police in a Cairo neighborhood. Militants from Egyptian Jihad Organization—which followed Zawahiri—launched assassination attempts, some successful, against government figures and dignitaries. From Peshawar, Zawahiri had coordinated much of the violence, expecting that it would hasten Mubarak's fall.

But the radicals' capacity to take action abroad was inhibited by Bin Laden's unplanned stay in Saudi Arabia and by fierce disagreements within the Islamist movement over Saddam Hussein's invasion of Kuwait. It was only after the United States and its allies restored Kuwaiti independence in the spring of 1991, through Operation Desert Storm, that the Bin Laden–Zawahiri coalition

became an axis of resistance against the new regional order imposed by the United States. The centerpiece of that order was the
Madrid conference in the summer of 1991 which initiated the
peace process between Israel and its Arab neighbors.

Events did not go well at first for the Bin Laden–Zawahiri alliance. Among jihad fighters on the Afghan-Pakistani border—a
zone populated by horse-riding Pashtun and characterized by en-
demic tribal violence—the situation began deteriorating rapidly
after the conquest of Kabul. The motley coalition of mujahedeen
that had settled in the Afghan capital was torn by ferocious in-
fighting, and the strongmen of Kabul—sensitive to American and
Saudi encouragement as well as the concerns of Benazir Bhutto,
then prime minister of Pakistan—began to pressure the brigades of
foreign jihadists to disperse.

In 1992 Bin Laden and Zawahiri, accompanied by their families
and closest followers, set off for Sudan, where Hassan al-Turabi was
offering a safe haven for Islamist activism, on the condition that
Bin Laden would invest several hundred million dollars in Sudan,
which most Western countries were boycotting. In return, Sudan
would become a sanctuary for the jihad fighters, a place where
they could set up a truly international operation.

In that same year, new fronts in the armed jihad opened up
in Egypt, Algeria, and Bosnia, all inspired by the Afghan model.
Natives and foreigners alike—all former Afghan combatants—entered these theaters through channels organized in Khartoum by
Osama bin Laden's network. Other important dispatch points were
Yemen, the Bin Laden family's country of origin before it settled in
Saudi Arabia; London (dubbed Londonistan), where spokesmen
set up websites, contacted the pan-Arab press, conducted public
relations work, and proselytized; and cities on the Persian Gulf,
where financial operations and monetary transfers were carried out

through Islamic and some conventional banks but also through the *hawala* system, which was based on an exchange of IOUs that leave no written trace. This complex and growing web of connections, which Bin Laden and Zawahiri had started to spin in the late 1980s in Afghanistan, would be dubbed Al Qaeda, an Arabic word meaning "the base."

THAT RADICAL ISLAMISM was breeding international terrorism was obvious to the U.S. intelligence services by the first half of the 1990s, but they did little to act on that knowledge. Whether through negligence, ignorance, the work of obscure forces, or an excessively complex game of manipulation that turned against its authors, the United States managed to let two leaders of the most extreme form of Egyptian Islamism obtain visas to enter the United States without encountering a single obstacle. One of these men, Sheikh Omar Abdel-Rahman, known to U.S. intelligence as the founder of Gamaa Islamiya in Egypt, operated freely as a cleric in Jersey City until he ended up in an American prison for his involvement in the first attack on the World Trade Center in February 1993. The other man was none other than Ayman al-Zawahiri, who met with Muslim scientists in Silicon Valley later that year to raise funds for the jihad against America. He was accompanied by a double agent who reported his actions to the FBI, but he was not arrested, detained, or deported.

In late 1992, in the last months of his presidency, President George H. W. Bush deployed 25,000 American troops to Somalia to help end the state of anarchy prevailing in the Horn of Africa. The Islamist literature roundly condemned Operation Restore Hope as a bridgehead designed to destabilize Sudan and overthrow Turabi's regime, and some Afghan jihad veterans went to fight the American invaders. Somalia provided the terrain on which these jihad guerrillas carried out life-size tests of their tactics, exploring the weaknesses of the American expeditionary corps and the political vulnerability that would result from military setbacks. When President Bill Clinton withdrew American forces from Somalia in early 1993 after a Black Hawk helicopter was shot down and the bodies of American soldiers were dragged through the streets of Mogadishu, the United States' enemies learned a valuable lesson they would apply a decade later in war-torn Iraq.

The jihad network's publishing center in Londonistan linked up the various battles being waged in different spots on the globe, and for the first time a coordinated global jihad took shape. Now an attack in Egypt was echoed by an event in Algeria; the conditions for liberation of French hostages in Algeria required the release of two radical Islamists from Saudi prisons; the Algerian GIA's publication put together in London carried up-to-the-minute editorials on the jihad in Bosnia, Egypt, and Chechnya.

Taking advantage of that network, in 1995 Zawahiri, now back in Sudan, planned two violent attacks on Egyptian interests abroad. The first was an attempt to assassinate Mubarak during his visit to Ethiopia on June 26. This was foiled, but just barely. The Egyptian government responded with a harsh crackdown on militants and activists, and in reply Zawahiri had his henchmen blow up Egypt's embassy in Islamabad, Pakistan, in November. That operation was also a life-size test: as Zawahiri later reported in *Knights under the Prophet's Banner*, at that time Western embassies were too closely guarded for the offensive means available to his organization to be effective. But by August 7, 1998, a revised plan for a closely coordinated double attack on U.S. embassies in Kenya and Tanzania would be firmly on track.

The four years during which Bin Laden and Zawahiri were based in Khartoum (1992–1996) correspond to the most aggressive phase of local jihads. In comparison with national groups such as the very active GIA in Algeria, the name of Al Qaeda was virtually unknown at the time, and its contributions to international jihad had not pierced the consciousness of U.S. intelligence forces. Bin Laden himself was perceived merely as an enemy of the Saudi regime, not as a jihadist obsessed with anti-American terrorism. Zawahiri was still mainly concerned with Egypt, though he already preferred spectacular action targeted at the regime's high-ranking figures over minor disruptions.

But by 1996, local jihads everywhere—from Bosnia to Algeria and Egypt—were beginning to lose ground. After the failed attack on Mubarak, which had been planned from Khartoum, some people in ruling circles in Sudan considered the possibility of "selling" Bin Laden and his followers to the Saudis or the Americans, just as they had delivered the Marxist-turned-Islamist international terrorist Carlos to the French authorities the previous year. But neither Saudi Arabia nor the United States expressed any interest in buying Bin Laden and his network. So, for complex political reasons, on May 18, 1996, he was smuggled aboard a private jet and deposited in Kandahar, the capital of the Afghan Islamic emirate. There, fanatical young Taliban reformers, educated in devoutly religious schools in Pakistan and operating with Pakistani military support and America's tacit approval, were leading a triumphant offensive that, in September, would wrest control of Kabul away from the mujahedeen commanders who had become corrupt strongmen.

For the Al Qaeda leadership, 1996 was the hinge year, the moment during which strategic decisions were made that would ultimately lead to September 11. Local jihad was now recognized as a failed strategy. Zawahiri's fierce opposition to a truce in Egypt and Algeria did not disguise his lack of human resources to enforce the continuation of hostilities there. He had put together a journey to Chechnya, where he thought conditions for international jihad were excellent, since the Caucasus terrain most closely resembled Afghanistan in the 1980s and the Russian army presented the same fundamental characteristics, and therefore the same weaknesses, as the Red Army. The Russians imprisoned Zawahiri at the end of 1996 and then, through inefficiency or some miscalculation on the part of the secret services, let him go.

Meanwhile, on August 23, 1996, from his new hiding place in the mountains of Afghanistan, Bin Laden circulated a "declaration of jihad against the Americans occupying the land of the two holy sites." The text, about ten pages long, redefined the principal goal of jihad as Saudi Arabia's liberation from its American protectors. Earlier in July, a booby-trapped truck had blown up in the U.S. army barracks at Khobar, in the heart of the Saudi oil zone, giving substance to Bin Laden's intention, although sources at the time did not unanimously agree that Bin Laden was responsible for the damaging attack.

A year and a half later, in February 1998, a second declaration, signed this time by Bin Laden, Zawahiri, and the leaders of various radical Islamist groups around the world, announced the creation of the World Islamic Front against Jews and Crusaders. The document, which made no mention of Al Qaeda, called for "the killing of Americans and Jews wherever they may be." The strategy's implementation began with twin attacks that ravaged the U.S. embassies in Tanzania and Kenya on August 7, 1998, the anniversary of the day on which, eight years earlier, King Fahd had invited American troops onto Saudi territory to defend it against Saddam Hussein's army, which had just invaded and plundered Kuwait. In October 2000, a dinghy packed with explosives pulled alongside the battleship USS *Cole* as it was entering the port of Aden and exploded, killing seventeen sailors. The timing required for the success of these attacks once again served as a practice run for the exquisite coordination that the airplane hijackings on September 11 and the Madrid bombings in March 2004 would require.

As deadly as the attacks in 1998 and 2000 were, they targeted military men or diplomats (as well as a great number of Kenyans and Tanzanians) and took place in lands that the average American television viewer would consider exotic. They somehow became part of the daily tally of losses and gains reported in the news, where all sorts of atrocities and distractions numb the senses. Failing to perceive any political consequences favorable to the radical Islamist cause, even knowledgeable observers did not interpret these opening shots as warnings of a larger fusillade, seeing in them only proof of the ineptitude of Bin Laden's network. These acts of terror were read as expressions of frustration from a movement seemingly incapable of truly mobilizing the supporters required to overthrow governments.

Although they seemed to carry the earmarks of desperation, these attacks were in fact part of a gradually escalating strategy intended to resonate less among the masses than among potential candidates for martyrdom—the men who were being recruited for the camps of Afghanistan to begin preparing for the apocalypse of September 11. These militants, educated in the West for the most part, must have the discipline, intelligence, and training to carry out complex operations; but more important, they must be able to shift back and forth between the rational mindset they had cultivated during their studies of engineering, urban planning, medicine, or administration and an alternate mindset that infused suicide attacks with metaphysical meaning and value.

From documents published in the months following September

11, as well as testimony and interrogation transcripts that are still incomplete, we can reconstruct the thinking that informed the planning of the attacks and the methods of recruitment. Zawahiri's *Knights under the Prophet's Banner,* which became widely known through long extracts published in the London-based Saudi newspaper *Al-Sharq al-Awsat (The Middle East)* in December 2001, provides many clues.

First, Zawahiri presents a worldview comparable—but in reverse—to Samuel Huntington's famous clash of civilizations. According to this perspective, "the battle is universal" and "the Western forces hostile to Islam have clearly identified their enemy—which they call 'Islamic fundamentalism.' Their former enemy, Russia, has joined them." They have at their disposal six main instruments to combat Islam: the United Nations; humanitarian nongovernmental organizations (NGOs); the corrupt leaders of Muslim peoples; transnational corporations; data exchange and communication systems; and finally press agencies and satellite television channels. Of the items on Zawahiri's list, the jihadists efficiently turned at least three against their enemies: the Islamic humanitarian NGOs, the Internet, and to a certain extent Arab television networks that broadcast from the Gulf.

"Against this alliance," Zawahiri continued, "a coalition is taking shape, made up of jihadist movements in the various Islamic lands and the two countries that jihad has liberated in Allah's name: Afghanistan and Chechnya." Written at an unknown date but almost certainly after the Al Aqsa intifada broke out in September 2000, this text referred to Chechnya as "liberated." Russian troops were indeed suffering heavy losses in 2000, and specialized websites were presenting the jihad fighters who followed "Commander Khattab" (a Saudi citizen and the figurehead of the Afghan veterans in Chechnya) as knights straight out of an epic adventure, complete with heroic deeds, miraculous interventions, the muti-lated corpses of Russian soldiers, and (the coup de grâce) blond Slavic prisoners smiling after their conversion to Islam. By December 2001, when the text was published in London, however, neither of the two countries was any longer under the control of radical Islamism, and during the summer of 2002 Commander Khattab himself would die in combat.

At the time when Zawahiri was writing, the jihad coalition was taking its first steps; but soon, he said, it would witness a spectacu-lar increase in its ranks. "Free from servitude to the dominant Western empire, it bears a promise of destruction and ruin for the new Crusaders [fighting] against Islamic land. It seeks revenge against the gang-leaders of global unbelief, the United States, Rus-sia, and Israel. It demands the blood price for the martyrs, the mothers' grief, the deprived orphans, the suffering prisoners, and the torments of those who are tortured everywhere in the Islamic lands—from Turkistan in the east to Andalusia." This last refer-ence, in the imagination of the target audience, was to the con-quest of the Iberian peninsula by Tariq bin Ziyad in the seventh century and the Reconquista in 1492 by the Catholic kings. To the jihadists, this fifteenth-century defeat and humiliation must be erased by conquering Spain anew and reintegrating it within Islam. The commuter rail bombings in Madrid in March 2004 would be part of this strategy.

Finally, Zawahiri explained, "Our age has witnessed a new phe-nomenon that is gaining ground continuously: the young combat-ants who abandon their families, countries, property, studies, and jobs to seek a place in which to carry out jihad for the love of Allah." In these first paragraphs of his book's conclusion, Zawahiri set out his vision of the world and contemporary international rela-tions: the enemy, made up of "the Western forces hostile to Islam" and led by the unholy trinity of the United States, Israel, and Russia, would find itself confronted with "young jihad combatants" who were willing to relinquish everything in order to accomplish their goal.

The text then described the clarity of the battle at the turn of the twenty-first century, after a phase of discouragement caused by failures during the early 1990s. Zawahiri observed that "every movement passes through a cycle of erosion and renewal." The new factor bringing hope was "the emergence of the new contingent of Islamists that the *umma* [Muslim world] has awaited for so long. Only one solution: jihad! The children of Islam are now aware of that imperative, and eager to put it into practice."

If it is to win, Islamism must rethink relations between its "elite" and those whom Zawahiri—in an almost Marxist vein—described as "the masses." In the past, that elite had strayed from the absolute imperative of jihad or, at the opposite extreme, had proclaimed its own sanctity and infallibility, thus sinning by "methodological blindness." Jihad, according to the doctor, required a "scientific, confrontational, rational" leadership. Perhaps the targets of this accusation were those in Egypt who had called for an end to armed struggle in 1997 after the murder of tourists at Luxor, or the GIA extremists in Algeria who had lost their cause in sterile violence. Zawahiri separated himself from both groups.

In its relations with the masses, the Islamist elite must make sure to mobilize the widest support base possible, and not to confront government authority alone. "The jihadist movement must move toward the masses, defend their honor, prevent injustice, and guide them along the path leading to victory." He followed with the admonition that "we must not blame the *umma* for not reacting or not being up to the task. We are to blame for not having been able to get our message across, not having been able to convey our compassion and the sacrifices we have made."

Still, Zawahiri, who after all was a son of the Egyptian aristocracy and the very embodiment of an Islamist elite, did not seem to believe that he had anything to learn from the masses. As his subtext made clear, he alone held the truth that would inspire the people with an energy that they seemed to lack. Throughout his book, ordinary Muslims were depicted as passive, sickly, and devoid of conscience. The elite must find the right slogans, the appropriate rhetoric, to rouse them from their indolence, endow them with a conscience, and convince them to join the jihad.

This vision, steeped in *realpolitik*, appeared to follow Machiavelli more closely than religious principles. Similar considerations regarding the Palestinian cause completed it. According to Zawahiri, secular Arab nationalists have milked every drop of political advantage from that conflict, while the Islamists, "who are the best qualified to lead the *umma* in its jihad against Israel, are the least active in championing the Palestinian cause and in spreading its watchword among the masses." Today, according to the author, Palestine offers the ideal opportunity for mobilizing people around jihad against the West, regardless of their religious commitments: "It is a rallying point for all the Arabs, whether or not they are believers!"

After establishing the cause that the jihadists must take up if they are to maximize their popularity, Zawahiri explained the military strategy to be followed. Given the enemy's extraordinary material superiority, it was necessary to choose actions that small groups could carry out to terrorize Americans and Jews. "It is entirely possible to kill Americans and Jews with a single bullet, a knife, an ordinary explosive device, an iron bar. It is not at all difficult to set fire to their property with a Molotov cocktail. With the available means, small groups can pose a threat to Americans and Jews." But this must take place in a context where the masses, inspired by the appropriate slogans, understand and support operations carried out by the "elite." Otherwise, "the Muslim vanguard runs the risk of general indifference at the killing of its members, and of fighting a battle in which it confronts government authority alone."

A deep fear of isolation runs through Zawahiri's text. The jihadist vanguard carries out military actions, but operations must take on exemplary value and be easily decipherable by targeted populations capable of identifying with them. Once those two pieces were in play—vanguard operations and support from the masses—some unspecified process would lead to the collapse of "apostate" regimes and the creation of Islamic states. These states would form the core of an Islamic caliphate that would eventually rule the planet. Anticipation of such a glorious future would bring on board not only believers but also other parties who were nostalgic for a dictatorship of the proletariat. (In a tragicomic illustration of this possibility, Carlos, the Marxist-Leninist terrorist, would convert to Islam and declare himself a disciple of "Sheikh Osama.")

That same anticipation allowed Zawahiri, who was constantly on the lookout for the most spectacular attacks possible using the greatest economy of human means, to take steps leading to the September 11 attacks. His goal was to take the battle to the enemy's own soil (mainly the United States but also Israel and Russia), "to burn the hands of those who are setting fire to our countries." In ironic homage to democracy, he declared that it was legitimate to strike Western civilian populations, and not just governments and institutions, because "Western voters vote freely. Therefore, these are the people who deliberately requested, supported, and encouraged not only the creation but also the perpetuation of the state of

Israel." These voters, however, "only know the language of self-interest, backed by brute military force. In consequence, if we want to hold a dialogue with them and cause them to become aware of our rights, we must speak to them in the language that they understand." This jihadist reading of the clash of civilizations would persuade activists to "prepare for a battle that is not confined to one region, but that targets both apostates at home and Judeo-Christian Crusaders abroad."

The struggle against the latter had priority, both because it served as a diversion from the assaults being launched on the Afghan and Chechen citadels and because "it is not realistic, at this stage, to concentrate on domestic enemies alone." Zawahiri set out the modus operandi clearly, down to the last details: "To inflict maximum damage . . . no matter how much time and effort such operations take"; "to concentrate on the method to follow in martyrdom operations, which constitute the most efficient means of inflicting losses on adversaries and the least costly, in human terms, for the mujahedeen"; "to choose the targets, the type of weaponry, and the method of deployment according to their impact on enemy structures"; and finally "to break the media blockade on the jihadist movement; this is a separate war, which we must launch in parallel with the military confrontation." Through the media, the masses must become convinced that this battle, while it is taking place, involves every Muslim.

Thus ends the long, detailed analysis that led a well-brought-up surgeon from Cairo, squatting in front of an Afghan cave, to speak out on a videotape which Al Jazeera television would broadcast around the globe on October 7, 2001. By hijacking commercial passenger jets and flying them into the World Trade Center, the Pentagon, and a Pennsylvania field, Zawahiri, Bin Laden, and their acolytes had not only delivered a "massive strike" against the faraway enemy but they had launched a media war that would prove even more deadly.

THE LAST PAGES of *Knights under the Prophet's Banner*, as they appear in the serialized version of December 2001, contain the most detailed, rational exposition I have seen of the reasoning that led to the September 11 attacks. The text allows us to understand how in 2001 two factors were brought together: one external and contingent (the second intifada and the crucial introduction of "martyrs" into the guerrilla tactics of the Palestinian struggle), and the other internal and necessary (the movement's longstanding determination to program its recruits to seek self-sacrifice with fanatical zeal and to follow orders without question).

As Zawahiri noted, the Palestinian–Israeli question continued to occupy a place of central importance in the Arab popular imagination throughout the Middle East, the Muslim world, and even parts of the Third World. Hezbollah was created in 1982 in Lebanon at the instigation of the Iranian Islamic Republic's secret services, which needed an armed proxy in Beirut that could do its dirty work, such as taking Western hostages. This terrorist organization introduced the concept of suicide bombings, which were very popular in Iranian revolutionary Shiism, into the vernacular of Arab political culture, where previously they had been little more than a oddity. By directing suicide attacks against Israeli targets—Tsahal patrols in the Lebanese security zone or Southern Lebanese Army militias, paid and armed by Israel—Hezbollah succeeded in transforming the way Lebanese citizens in general, including Christians, perceived this organization. Through its "martyrdom operations," a terrorist group sponsored by a foreign country managed to reinvent itself as the guardian of national sovereignty, then a political party with parliamentary representatives, and ultimately the repository of Lebanese patriotism. Seen as the "thrower" that had forced Israeli troops out of Lebanon in May 2000, Hezbollah became widely popular and immune to criticism.

Hezbollah also enjoyed enormous prestige in Palestine, and as a result, suicide attacks as a combat tactic were transposed to the Palestinian struggle. The Palestinian cause had long been inaccessible to the Islamists because it had been organized and controlled from the outset by Arab nationalists, which made it their touchstone. Thanks to Hamas's emergence and rapid ascent during the first intifada which began in December 1987, however, the Islamist movement to claim Palestine for its own gained ground, challenging the monopoly of Arafat's nationalist PLO.

For a brief time, the momentum of the Oslo peace process muddled the Islamists' efforts. In the eyes of many Palestinians, the brinkmanship of Hamas and Islamic Jihad appeared to be dividing and weakening Arab ranks instead of leading to a negotiated solution. But the peace process came to an abrupt end when Arafat and Sharon fell into a downward spiral of tension and violence beginning in the fall of 2000. Local Islamists were quick to understand and exploit the significance of these renewed hostilities. By spring 2001 they were already touting suicide attacks as the only efficient means of armed struggle against the hi-tech "smart" weapons supplied to Israel by the United States. In making this claim, they benefited from powerful relay points on Arab television and had considerable impact on public opinion. Just as Hezbollah had undergone a metamorphosis into the embodiment of Lebanese resistance, so Hamas and Islamic Jihad began to transform themselves into the spearhead of the Palestinian cause, with a thrust far beyond their immediate sympathizers in the Islamist movement.

From 1996 to 2000, while the Oslo process appeared to be on track, the Palestinian question was not a priority for the international jihadist movement. Zawahiri's territorial reference at that time was to the "citadels of jihad": the Taliban's struggle for control in Afghanistan and the fight against the Russians in Chechnya. Bin Laden's focus was the Saudi dynasty. But as it turned out, none of these spaces generated the kinds of slogans that could mobilize the masses to the cause of jihad. The Taliban suffered from a reputation as medieval, extremist fanatics. Chechnya, despite admiring websites devoted to this cause, weltered in obscurity, a concern only of specialists and the most active militants. And the monarchy in Riyadh, despite its numerous enemies, could claim a plethora of duty-bound clients across the world to protect its interests. As Zawahiri noted in *Knights under the Prophet's Banner*, "The Muslim *umma* will only participate [in jihad] if the masses understand the jihadists' slogans clearly," and the slogan with the greatest mobilizing power, according to him, was the call to jihad against Israel.

Ariel Sharon's deliberately provocative walk on the esplanade of the Haram Sharif in Jerusalem on September 28, 2000, and Yasser Arafat's subsequent decision to launch the Al Aqsa intifada provided Al Qaeda with a propitious occasion to "strike the grand master [of evil]," as Zawahiri called the United States, and to count on receiving optimal sympathy and approval from the "*umma*'s masses." The murderous struggle between the Israeli and Palestinian leaders, which claimed thousands of lives, set the political stage on which Bin Laden and Zawahiri would direct their "massive strike" against New York and Washington. In 2001, as Palestinians were being killed by Israeli soldiers, dirges for the victims mingled with hymns to the glory of martyrdom, and Arab television stations broadcast nonstop images of Israeli repression and funerals in Gaza, Jenin, and Bayt Jala. Al Qaeda's ideologues concluded that the political language of suicide attacks in Allah's name had acquired sufficient legitimacy on the Arab street. The fruit of martyrdom was ripe, and must be harvested without delay.

Seen in this context, the September 11 attacks completed, extended, and fulfilled the suicide bombings that the Palestinians had perpetrated against Israel for many months. By drawing connections between the two tactics—which Bin Laden did explicitly in his October 7 broadcast through Al Jazeera—the financier of the September 11 attacks tried to capture the political capital of sympathy and legitimacy that the Palestinian bombers enjoyed. But this transfer of legitimacy did not work fully in Bin Laden's favor. Luminaries of "moderate" Islamism, such as the TV preacher Yusuf al-Qaradawi (an Egyptian sheikh from Qatar who hosts the most popular religious talk show on Al Jazeera), condemned the hijackings. The anti-Israeli suicide attacks of the Palestinians could be justified as martyrdom, he said, since they were part of a defensive jihad aimed at reclaiming Palestinian Islamic land that had been usurped by the Jews. Furthermore, Israeli civilian victims in restaurants and on buses, women included, were soldiers temporarily out of uniform, since in Israel every Jewish citizen is either a conscript or a reservist. Thus, Palestinian bombers were "martyrs" in a just war, not "suicides." But the sheikh condemned the September 11 hijackers as suicides rather than martyrs because, contrary to Muslim teaching, they had unduly taken the lives Allah had given them. The difference, according to Sheikh Qaradawi, was that America is not a legitimate target of defensive jihad, and therefore martyrdom in a fight against the United States on its soil is not possible.

Bin Laden and Zawahiri nevertheless asserted their right to declare jihad—with holy martyrdom as its corollary—wherever and whenever they chose, and they discredited and ridiculed the traditional legal scholars who disagreed with them as "court ulemas," the turban-clad lackeys of apostate rulers.

But there were other differences between the suicide tactics employed by Palestinians and Al Qaeda, beyond the question of how martyrdom should be defined. Given that Israeli society had been militarized since its creation in 1948 and a state of war had existed since the second intifada, attacks that killed or wounded dozens of people by destroying a packed restaurant or a school bus could have devastating political consequences only through ceaseless repetition, which would destabilize the enemy. Small-scale suicide bombings have a short half-life in their effects on the enemy, even as they impose a significant toll on the society from which they emerge. Suicide bombings must attain their political goals quickly, before the terror they engender dissipates.

Yet in practice, it was difficult to sustain the repetition of suicide attacks in Israel at the level required to be effective. The Israeli intelligence services managed to prevent a considerable number of planned operations, and the use of laser-guided missiles to assassinate Palestinian organizers profoundly disrupted activist networks. The fight between "martyrs" and missiles was inherently unequal in the midterm and led to a rapid turnover of volunteers for martyrdom. Palestinian suicide bombers were sent to their deaths shortly after they signed up, as quickly as an Israeli target could be chosen by their contact organization. This hastiness increased the risk of failure, defection, and discouragement. By contrast, Al Qaeda's suicide squad followed a specific, precisely planned training program that spanned many months, during which they learned how to operate the planes they would fly to their deaths.

Unlike the enemy of the Palestinians, which was close by, easily identified, and the object of passionate daily resentment for a large part of the population, the enemy of Al Qaeda's 9/11 recruits was distant and imagined, a fantasy constructed by an elite group of Islamist intellectuals. Part of the genius of the Al Qaeda organization was its ability to choose its future martyrs carefully and prepare them through an indoctrination program adapted to long-term commitment while they waited for the right moment. At many points during their training and waiting in the United States, the resolve of these recruits could have weakened, but it did not—a testament to the effectiveness of Al Qaeda's brainwashing methods.

These methods seem to be similar to those of cults that deal with novice recruits. They relied on religious sources to emphasize the importance of "submission" (the literal meaning of the word "Islam"). Such submission must be absolute, and over the course of time must become synonymous with complete obedience and total subjection to the leaders' orders. Much of what we have learned about Al Qaeda's indoctrination comes from three copies of a document found among the belongings of the September 11 hijackers. It has been called "Mohammed Atta's Testament" in reference to the group's presumed leader, the Egyptian student of urban planning, based in Hamburg, though it was written by another hijacker, Saudi high school graduate Abdelaziz al-Omari, who was imbued with salafist conceptions. The FBI published a few fragments, and on its website posted four pages scanned from a schoolboy's notebook, in cramped Arabic script with words crossed out and revised.

The text itself abandons all deductive reasoning, indeed all intelligence, and adheres solely to a series of injunctions taken from the Quran and the Sunna (the Prophet's words and deeds), intended to guide the terrorists blindly at the moment when they took action. At that point, they had to leave aside the rational thought appropriate to the modern world and project themselves into a state of fanatical faith, one that would allow them to kill innocent passengers and experience their own imminent death as an accomplishment that would open the gates of Paradise:

> At the moment of hand-to-hand battle, strike like brave men who want none of this despicable world, and shout "Allahu Akbar"—this frightens the infidels . . . Know that the gardens of paradise are decked out for you with their most beautiful ornaments, and that the houris [the virgins with whom the martyrs will sleep] are calling you: "Come, O friend of Allah," and they are wearing their finest clothes. And if Allah grants one of you a victim's throat to slit, then carry out this sacrifice . . . Don't argue; just listen and obey. If you slit someone's throat, plunder his possessions, because that is the custom according to the Elected one [the Prophet]—Allah bless and save him—but on one condition: don't let yourselves be distracted by the spoils and forget what is more important. Watch out for the enemy, his betrayals, his attacks.

That memorandum, made up of orders to conform blindly ("Don't argue; just listen and obey"), precludes any notion of individual reasoning, since this could cause the martyrs to stray from the path of jihad and fail to finish the job. It is all the more surprising, given what we have learned about the 9/11 commando leader Mohammed Atta, whose thesis in urban planning received an excellent grade from his German professor. Its topic: how to preserve the pluralistic Islamic-Christian urban fabric in the traditional quarters of the Syrian city of Aleppo. In that work Atta praised the harmonious coexistence of Muslims and Christians—the very same Christians whose throats would be slit as the bookish

Hamburg University student turned the passenger jet he had hijacked into a weapon of mass destruction. The depth of the dissociation Al Qaeda managed to engender in its recruits was illustrated by the behavior of two of Atta's comrades, who watched a pay-per-view porn film in their motel room on the night of September 10—hardly an act of Muslim piety—and then the next morning performed their duty with unquestioning religious faith and total obedience to their masterminds' instructions.

The attacks on the twin towers and the Pentagon were not a thunderbolt out of the blue. They were part of a precise, carefully considered program that combined the logic of jihad, the operational tactics of guerrilla warfare, the opportunistic advantages offered by the Arab–Israeli conflict during the second intifada, and the political influence of neoconservative ideology on U.S. foreign policy—all of which worked to the advantage of radical Islamism.

4

Al Qaeda's Resilience

By striking forcefully at the Islamists' most distant and powerful enemy, Al Qaeda put its theories of global jihad to the ultimate test. The horrid spectacle of this deadly and delicately coordinated operation propelled the radical organization into worldwide prominence, and its subtle manipulation of the media during the following months demonstrated a sophisticated understanding of the global communication system. Al Qaeda began to speak with a voice out of all proportion to the small number of activists at its core.

Osama bin Laden's first declaration following the attacks was published without fanfare on September 28 in the Pakistani periodical *Umma*. There, he denied any responsibility for the hijackings, just as he had previously denied direct involvement in the bombing of U.S. embassies in Tanzania and Kenya on August 7, 1998, which left 258 people dead and over 5,000 wounded, and the USS *Cole* in November 2000. Instead, he placed the blame on America, "which has no friends," and on Israel's intelligence service, Mossad.

But on October 7—the day that the Pentagon launched its military operation in Afghanistan—Al Jazeera's broadcast of the videotape recorded in front of an Afghan cave introduced Bin Laden

and Zawahiri to a worldwide television audience. In this highly influential recording, Bin Laden praised the daring and courage of
"the blessed Muslim vanguard" who had given their lives for the
sublime cause of jihad. Though again he took no direct responsibility for the operation, he depicted the victims as sacrificial lambs
whose immolation would please Allah. Through the rhetoric of
holy war and religious sacrifice, Bin Laden hoped to dehumanize
them and forestall any compassion in the Muslim world for the
thousands of victims who had died in the multiple attacks of September 11.

Al Qaeda's activists and their sympathizers viewed the successes
of that day as an extraordinary symbolic victory for Islam. Evidence
of this conviction came in the form of another videotape recorded
privately by the movement and then discovered by U.S. soldiers in
November 2001. The tape, which aired on December 21, was made
near Kandahar, where Saudi Sheikh Khaled al-Harbi, a veteran
who had lost both legs in Afghanistan, was received by Bin Laden.
Asked about the reaction in Saudi Arabia to the September attacks,
the sheikh replied: "Suddenly, we received the news, and everyone
was overcome with joy . . . Each of us said 'Allah is Great,' 'Praise
Allah,' and 'Thank Allah.' All day, we called to congratulate each
other. My mother was receiving calls constantly . . . There is no
doubt: it is a brilliant victory. Allah has given us this honor; He will
bless us and grant us even greater victory during this holy month of
Ramadan." Bin Laden commented that "in Holland, the number
of people who converted to Islam during the days that followed the
operations was greater, in total, than during the past eleven years."

Surprise and symbolism, along with games of media manipulation, could take the movement only so far, however. What was
needed was a conventional military victory, of the sort that had
driven the Soviet army from Afghanistan. But the only arms at Bin

Laden's disposal after 9/11 were subterfuge, evasion, and deception—the weapons of the weak. As soon as U.S. intelligence fingered Al Qaeda for responsibility, the United States brought its sophisticated military arsenal to the task of locating and destroying the organization's base of operations in Afghanistan. By mid-December ground forces of the indigenous Northern Alliance, assisted by hundreds of airstrikes called in by U.S. special forces, had gained control of Bin Laden's manmade caves in the Tora Bora mountain range. Many jihad fighters were killed or taken prisoner, but the main quarry—Osama bin Laden and Zawahiri—eluded capture.

The initial target of the war on terror was neither Afghanistan nor its population—whose hearts and minds the Americans were set on winning—but the terrorists who had taken refuge there. When these men proved hard to pin down, however, the Americans modified their goal accordingly. Instead of obliterating Al Qaeda, the new goal became the obliteration of the terrorists' Taliban hosts. The operation had fallen short of arresting or incapacitating the main suspects, but it had flung its net wide enough to catch thousands of accomplices and other small fry.

During the next two years, U.S. special forces, with their unmanned surveillance aircraft and GPS technology, seemed always to be just days behind Bin Laden and his band of nomads, who nevertheless managed to smuggle out several tapes that were broadcast by Arab television, together with messages that appeared on the Internet. In a litany of threats against the West and calls for the murder of unbelievers—including a tape aired on April 17, 2002, which finally admitted Al Qaeda's responsibility for the destruction of the twin towers—Bin Laden asserted Al Qaeda's role in post-9/11 bombings the world over, from Bali to Istanbul to Madrid.

Al Qaeda's resilience in the face of the Bush administration's war on terror revealed a major intelligence deficiency in the U.S. government. The means adopted by the United States to annihilate terrorism appeared to be inappropriate, and indeed Washington's very interpretation of terrorism seemed to be erroneous. That interpretation was derived from Cold War thinking about strategic options, which the neoconservatives in the Bush administration— their hand strengthened by the distortion effect of the September 11 attacks—took to their logical extreme. Just as the left-wing terrorist groups of the 1970s and 1980s were presumed by previous administrations to have some sort of obscure link to the Soviet bloc's intelligence services, the Islamist terrorists of 9/11 were presumed by the Bush administration to have some connection to Iraq and Iran— rogue states on an "axis of evil" that no longer included Moscow. Bringing those states to heel became the Bush administration's new goal.

Neoconservatives in Washington would not be satisfied with tracking down a bunch of haggard bearded men, hiding out in caves or motel rooms, who conducted their business through satellite phone connections and bank accounts in offshore tax havens. The United States required a worthy adversary for its war on terror—a nation with real estate to be occupied, military hardware to be destroyed, and a regime to be overthrown—not a terrorist NGO without status or headquarters, however devastating that NGO might prove to be. Washington's strategic planners were culturally incapable of grasping an actor that was not, in the final analysis, a state.

Following this misguided reasoning, the Pentagon's special services had no sooner destroyed the embryonic government of the Taliban in Afghanistan than strategists began making plans for the invasion of Iraq. What they did not do was move rapidly to eliminate the international network controlled by Bin Laden and

Zawahiri, primarily because they did not understand its nature and functions adequately. They gave it a vivid, reductionist name—Al Qaeda—but this served only to reify the network's fluidity, thereby masking its true source of strength. Naming the adversary created the illusion of having identified it. But that verbal representation replaced further analysis and short-circuited the search for operational concepts that could assimilate a complex reality and, in the process, restructure existing cognitive categories.

True, Bin Laden and Zawahiri had been buyers at the bankrupt Soviet bazaar, where nuclear warheads and other dirty weapons were on offer at yard-sale prices; they also had suspicious friends in Baghdad and Tehran. But they were first and foremost the privileged children of an unlikely marriage between Wahhabism and Silicon Valley, which Zawahiri had visited in the early 1990s. They were heirs not only to jihad and the *umma* but also to the electronic revolution and American-style globalization. Despite their beards and the soap opera costumes they donned for Arab television audiences, they had ambitions and interests in common with hackers and cosmopolitan golden boys everywhere.

The confusion of U.S. intelligence was visible from the administration's first attempts to identify, circumscribe, and define the nature of the new threat. The use of the word "terrorism" to describe the operation on 9/11 was already vague enough, but the confusion only increased as President Bush started to speak of a "war on terror." The phrase was engineered to heighten fear while simultaneously tapping the righteous indignation of citizens in "civilized nations" against barbaric murderers who would perpetrate despicable atrocities on innocent victims. But stigmatizing the enemy by calling them "terrorists" was of little help in defining the nature of the new threat they presented and creating ways to eliminate it.

After September 11, various arms of the U.S. government successively published and updated separate lists which, using different criteria, endeavored to identify these "terrorists." President Bush was first, with a fresh classification, Specially Designated Global Terrorist (SDGT), which allowed the United States to freeze assets belonging to twenty-seven organizations or individuals rumored to have links to the Al Qaeda network—a network that had not yet been defined in any way other than by this list.

Eleven days later, on October 5, the State Department's preexisting roster of Foreign Terrorist Organizations (FTOs) was updated and its content changed. On October 10, the FBI published its own Most Wanted Terrorists (MWTs), which included the names of twenty-two activists, all accused of having assassinated American citizens and all originally from the Muslim Middle East. On October 12, the Treasury Department froze the assets of thirty-three new individuals (of whom eighteen were already on the MWT list) and six organizations, which were added to the SDGT list.

On October 31, Attorney General John Ashcroft demanded that forty-six groups be designated officially as terrorist organizations; of these, nine were already on the SDGT list. On November 7, the Treasury Department froze the assets of sixty-two groups and individuals associated with the Islamic financial networks of Al Taqwa and Al Baraka, suspected of having links to Al Qaeda; these were added to the SDGT list. On December 5, the State Department updated its Terrorist Exclusion List (TEL) to include the thirty-nine individuals and organizations whose assets had been frozen by the Treasury Department.

These diverse inventories—the result of hasty cut-and-paste jobs on various groups, individuals, and bank accounts—captured the understandable disarray of America's intelligence efforts in the days and weeks following the 9/11 attacks. But because of the government's inability to comprehend the nature of the network that took Bin Laden as its iconic figure, the war on terror struck both below and above the heart of its enemy. The strategy of destroying the Afghan base and then annihilating Saddam Hussein's "rogue state" presented the advantage of being operational: it allowed the Pentagon to use its panoply of high-tech weapons, forged in the confrontation with the USSR and then adapted to vague new threats. But it missed the intended target. The very intangibility of the Al Qaeda network precluded a traditional military conquest.

During the first phase of the war on terror, U.S. strategists seemed to take the English translation of the network's name—"the base"—literally, imagining that the elimination of Al Qaeda's territorial base in Afghanistan would put the organization out of operation. By striking at the head, according to this reasoning, the tentacles would cease to be effective. But an interview that the Al Jazeera journalist Tayseer Allouni conducted with Bin Laden in October 2001 suggests why this interpretation was inadequate:

> The name Al Qaeda is very old. It came about without anyone really choosing it. The late Abu al-Ubaida Banshiri [an Egyptian activist, drowned in Lake Victoria in the spring of 1996, while he was organizing cells for the network in East Africa] had created a military base to train young men in the fight against the . . . Soviet terrorism. This training camp was called "the base" [Al Qaeda]. And the name spread. We are the children of one nation [umma], which extends from the Middle East to the Philippines, Indonesia, Malaysia, India, Pakistan, and as far away as Mauritania.

Bin Laden's explanation suggests that as the network evolved over time, its name came to have a double meaning. Originally, it designated a group of radical Islamists who were training together at one specific military base. But as the organization changed and developed, by extension the name became a metaphor for the dispersal of those fighters around the globe and for the web of communication links that held them together—a "database" that served as a microcosm of the *umma*, whose "brothers in Islam" could be found from the Philippines to Mauritania.

By intensely focusing strikes and searches on the physical facilities in Afghanistan, the United States demonstrated a failure to grasp fully the entirely different, and much wider, reality expressed by the name's double meaning. Perhaps the psychological mechanism of denial was at work in Washington's metaphorical lapse— denial of the intimate relationship that the Pentagon and the American intelligence services had nourished with Islamist radicals during the United States' proxy war against the Red Army on the same soil. By reducing Al Qaeda to a military-style base that could be pinpointed through special operations conducted by Green Berets and Gurkas and then destroyed by laser-guided airstrikes, perhaps Washington—and the neocons most prominently—hoped to avoid the difficult analysis of their own role in creating a monster.

With the invasion of Iraq, the Bush administration moved from the still unfinished pursuit of Al Qaeda to the overthrow of Saddam Hussein. Part of the incentive was to strike and destroy a tangible enemy, and in the process send a message to rogue states everywhere that the United States was not in a tolerant mood. But the rich folds of the anti-terrorism banner could accommodate and conceal the Bush administration's much larger mission—one that predated the attacks of September 11. That mission was to rebalance the power structure in the Middle East.

This prospect brought together two primary interests that had determined U.S. foreign policy in the region since the Second World War. The first was to reconcile, once and for all, the United

States' need for dependable oil supplies with its commitment to Israel's security. A regime installed in Baghdad that was dependent on the United States and friendly toward Israel could accomplish this goal. The second interest sought to encourage democracy and peace in this region of the world. The elimination of a dictator who had massacred Kurds and Shia in his own country, initiated devastating wars with his neighbors, Iran and Kuwait, and imposed a reign of terror on his people in the name of Arab nationalism, while monopolizing oil wealth for his clan, would go a long way toward bringing peace to the Middle East. Success at these two complementary goals—or so the wishful thinking went in Washington—would eliminate terrorism's root causes in the region, which grew out of political oppression, poverty, ignorance, and instability.

Depending on whether one wholeheartedly accepts or rejects these two dimensions of U.S. foreign policy as legitimate, the notion of eradicating terror through the invasion of a sovereign country can be seen as either a noble cause or a sordid pretext for imperial ambitions. But those who wish to transcend such impassioned value judgments must adopt a more critical attitude at every step along the road that stretches from September 11, 2001, to June 28, 2004—the date of the transfer of sovereignty to the Iraqi people. These two dimensions of U.S. foreign policy are in fact intrinsically related, and indeed incomprehensible when viewed independently. The complex meanings and signs encoded in U.S. operations in the Middle East during this period are not decrypted as easily as the administration's supporters and detractors have claimed.

As SHOCK AND CHAOS prevailed in the days following the strikes on New York and Washington, the U.S. government was forced to propose emergency reprisals, even though no one had yet claimed responsibility for the attacks. In impromptu remarks, President Bush described America's counteroffensive as a "crusade." In the United States, this term did not designate anything more than intense mobilization, and it carried no explicit connotation of the medieval Christian context in which it arose. Nevertheless, the choice of this word was a serious gaffe, and the American president retracted it immediately. He promptly visited Washington's principal mosque, contrite and barefoot, in order to erase the impression that the mobilization in question was directed at Muslims or at Islam in general.

The Bush administration sang the refrain of harmony with Islam again and again as the war on terror took shape. With equal conviction, many imams and a plethora of Islamist websites claimed that the real target of the war on terror was Islam, just as Islam had been the target of the medieval Crusades. By forcing President Bush's about-face, his adversaries scored the first point in a tense game of political rhetoric. His awkward reference to a "crusade" was at best a confirmation of the president's inexperience in dealing with international crises, even if it was not a Freudian slip that betrayed his subconscious desires. In the Muslim world, the significance was not dismissed so easily. Through acts of exegesis performed on the word by television preachers throughout the *umma*, the United States—itself the victim of terrorism—was turned into a repeat offender against Islam. Bush's "crusade" echoed the "Crusaders" Bin Laden was denouncing in his declarations and confirmed the content of his propaganda. Al Qaeda's circle of sympathizers widened as a result of Bush's misstep.

From there, it was but another small step to the claim, made widely in the Muslim world, that September 11 had been set up by American and Israeli intelligence as a pretext for a "Crusader-

Zionist" offensive targeting the Middle East's oil wealth. In a further spin on the conspiracy theory, rumors spread from Cairo to Damascus and Karachi to Jakarta of an email message (never produced by anyone) that had supposedly advised Jewish employees at the World Trade Center to stay home from work on that fateful day.

Semantic problems aside, Washington's primary difficulty in the days after the attack was one of military strategy. Since the beginning of the Cold War, U.S. doctrine had been devoted principally to the concept of deterrence in various guises: the Soviets had to be dissuaded from ever launching a nuclear attack, the consequences of which would be devastating on their own territory. The result was a state of international tension that commentators termed a "balance of terror."

In his plans for 9/11, Bin Laden sought a balance of this type between America and Muslims (of whom he was the self-designated representative). "They understand only the language of attack and murder," he told the journalist Tayseer Allouni in October 2001. "Just as they kill us, we must kill them, to create a balance of terror. This is the first time in the modern era that terror has begun to reach a point of equilibrium between Americans and Muslims. Until now, American politicians did as they pleased with us. The victims could not even cry out . . . The battle is now inside America. We will work to carry it on, if Allah allows it, until victory or until we return to Allah, before the inevitable success."

The problem with September 11, from the standpoint of U.S. military strategy, was that the United States could not clearly define a stable territory against which its retaliatory missiles could be launched. Military modes of action and reaction, nuclear or conventional, were conceived to destroy territorial defenses, seize cities, control airspace, annihilate tanks, disrupt troop formations, shoot down planes, and overthrow regimes that physically occupied palaces, offices, and barracks. Bin Laden and his allies had no homeland or territory: they were at best refugees in Afghanistan, under Taliban control. That Mullah Omar, the emir who ruled over Kandahar, had fallen under the spell of his Saudi guest did not circumscribe the network any more clearly within that country's borders.

Yet in the early phase of the war on terror, most of the means and resources employed to track down the terrorists focused on annihilating Al Qaeda's Taliban hosts through the occupation of their national soil. U.S. strategists were apparently convinced that Bin Laden, Zawahiri, and the rest, even if forced into their Tora Bora lairs in the high Pashtun mountain ranges, could be captured or exterminated during the course of the campaign to wipe out the Taliban regime.

Bin Laden's counteroffensive recognized that, under the right circumstances, rhetoric and satellite propaganda can be on equal footing with unmanned bombers and cruise missiles. He responded to the Afghan invasion on October 7 with a call to Muslims worldwide to take up arms in a universal jihad against America. In Afghanistan itself, however, this jihad was ineffective, and the attack against the Taliban represented a stunning victory for state-of-the-art U.S. weaponry. In an exemplary application of the military doctrine of Albert Wohlstetter, the U.S. military minimized human losses among troops and "collateral damage" among civilian populations through the use of special forces and "smart bombs."

The attack also represented a success for U.S. intelligence services, which had unified disparate ethnic groups—mainly Tajiks and Uzbeks—into a fighting force called the Northern Alliance. These tribal warriors, equipped with American technology, carried out most of the ground offensives, including the final march on Kabul. The Muslim troops who fought and ultimately overthrew the Taliban silenced the preachers on Arab television channels who were inciting the world's Muslims to take up arms in defense of Islamic territory that was being invaded by unbelievers. Once Mazar, Herat, Kunduz, Kabul, Jalalabad, and finally Kandahar had fallen to forces composed of Afghan Muslim soldiers, the religious foundation for the call to jihad fell away. Confusion reigned when the first images were broadcast of Arab jihad fighters being bound with wire, taken prisoner, and even mistreated by members of the Northern Alliance—fellow Muslims whom the jihadists were supposedly delivering from the infidels.

From both a military and a psychological point of view, the Afghan operation appeared to be a triumph for the United States. American soldiers had gained a foothold in former Soviet republics in Central Asia—Muslim countries rich in oil and gas and anxious to shake off Moscow's postcolonial dominance. Furthermore, since NATO had played only a marginal role, this victory belonged to the superpower alone. And for the first time, perfect electronic integration of air, sea, and land forces had been tested on the battlefield, where they performed splendidly. The Pentagon's control of the commons—sea, sky, and space in the theater of conflict—was absolute, as it would be in the conventional phase of the Iraq War a year and a half later.

Given the stated goals of the war on terror, however, Operation Enduring Freedom was a Pyrrhic victory. Despite the severe blows the Al Qaeda network had suffered—its data seized, many of its activists captured or killed—the elimination of its physical base in Afghanistan did not eradicate Al Qaeda's effectiveness. Attacks started up once more, and as they increased, the double meaning of the metaphor became clearer: this organization did not consist of buildings and tanks and borders but of Internet websites, satellite television links, clandestine financial transfers, international air travel, and a proliferation of activists ranging from the suburbs of Jersey City to the rice paddies of Indonesia. The U.S. military force had taken Tora Bora with bombs and missiles, and British commando squads had explored the depths of the caves where Bin Laden had been filmed; but the prey would not be found there.

In deciding to eradicate the Taliban, Washington revised the logic that had dominated U.S. policy in Afghanistan since the Soviet withdrawal in 1989. In the manner of police strategies that encircle and contain certain forms of delinquency by coordinating surveillance with neighborhood gang leaders and pimps, the U.S. strategy toward Afghanistan had tacitly encouraged the Taliban to harbor the lost soldiers of jihad, who had nowhere else to go once the armed struggles in Algeria, Egypt, Bosnia, and Kashmir had failed. On the surface, the United States adopted a practice of benign neglect, but in reality Pakistan's support for the rising Taliban movement and its occupation of Kabul in 1996 would have been ineffective, indeed inconceivable, without Washington's consent. In 1996 Bin Laden himself, along with his entourage, was transported to Kandahar from Sudan with the United States' blessing, when his presence began to hinder a regime seeking to escape international condemnation. Neither Washington nor Riyadh wished to put the Saudi multimillionaire on trial, although Khartoum was willing to turn him in. Rid of Bin Laden, Sudan felt the pressure from Washington lift. Meanwhile, communication and transportation problems between Afghanistan and the rest of the world made it unlikely that jihad would be exported from this remote region—so common wisdom had it.

The inanity of this red-light-district strategy became apparent as early as August 23, 1996, when Bin Laden made his jihad declaration and began transforming Afghanistan into a base from which to launch the attacks of 1998, 2000, and 2001. Yet American policy toward the Taliban did not shift. On September 11, however, the sheer magnitude of the destruction required a thoroughgoing revision.

The war on terror directed at the Taliban was analogous to the behavior of police when delinquency transcends the terms of the gentleman's agreement between gang leaders and the forces of order. At that point the police often besiege a stronghold, seizing caches of arms, handcuffing unsavory criminals, and even demolishing buildings. But these dramatic crackdowns, which often make the evening news, serve only to encourage the proliferation of criminal behavior outside the besieged zone when no social measures are taken to counter the factors giving rise to the delinquency. In the same way, the crackdown on the Taliban's Islamist halfway house served to disperse many Al Qaeda jihadists around the world. Alerted in plenty of time, they fled with the innkeeper. As Bin Laden, Zawahiri, and Mullah Omar vanished into the Pashtun valleys, they left behind only their accounts and some addresses—small consolation indeed.

A communiqué from a group speaking in the network's name and signed Qaedat al-Jihad (Jihad Base), which appeared on the Internet on April 26, 2002, announced: "Allah has allowed us to protect most of the Arab forces and lead them to safety. There were about 1,600 mujahedeen, from all over the Muslim world, spread along four main fronts: north of Kabul, Kabul, Kandahar, and Jalalabad. About 325 became martyrs, 150 were taken prisoner, and over a thousand fled. Through Allah's grace, over 300 families were evacuated. The total number of martyrs is nine women and ten children." Even if these numbers were skewed for propaganda purposes, the fact remained that many jihad fighters had been able to get away.

The fall of Kabul and the arrest or death of many Islamist activists obliterated the network's physical infrastructure but did not affect the network's ability to reconstitute itself elsewhere, albeit on a smaller scale, and to launch a series of attacks during the following years. Al Qaeda needed only to demonstrate to potential "martyrs" that it had escaped destruction and was continuing to serve the cause of jihad until the inevitable defeat of the Western imperialists and their Muslim clients. To that end, it had only to show itself through attacks that were preceded or followed by communiqués attributed to Bin Laden or Zawahiri.

The targets were chosen carefully, according to two criteria. The first was the impact of terror on the enemy; images of dismembered, bleeding bodies broadcast to the farthest reaches of the earth were intended to panic and demoralize the West and foster dissent in its ranks. The second criterion was the impact of terror on potential "martyrs"; as the alleged moral dimension of the attacks increased from the perspective of Muslims, the popularity of the movement would grow and more recruits would volunteer for martyrdom. On this scale of values, Jews, then Americans, followed by Westerners in general, and finally their "apostate" Middle Eastern agents were targets ranked in descending order of legitimacy.

In the framework of jihad, none of Al Qaeda's intended victims were "innocent." Jews were the preferred targets, not just in reference to the state of Israel or Ariel Sharon's policy toward Palestine but in an essential, ontological sense. Thus, in October 2001 when Tayseer Allouni asked Bin Laden if he agreed with the concept of a clash of civilizations, he received this reply:

> Absolutely. The [holy] Book states it clearly. Jews and
> Americans invented the myth of peace on earth. That's a

fairy tale. All they do is chloroform Muslims while leading them to the slaughterhouse. And the massacre continues. If we defend ourselves, they call us terrorists. The
Prophet said: "The Hour will not come until the Muslims fight the Jews and kill them." When a Jew hides behind a rock or a tree, it will say: "O Muslim, O servant of
Allah! There is a Jew behind me, come and kill him!"
Those who claim that there will be lasting peace between us and the Jews are unbelievers because they
disagree with the [holy] Book and its contents.

Bin Laden was drawing on a literal interpretation of one of
the Prophet's sayings, the kind of interpretation preferred by
salafist preachers in order to convince their fellow Muslims—under threat of excommunication—that murdering Jews is their duty.
This interpretation differed from that of preachers who emerged
from the Muslim Brothers, such as Sheikh Qaradawi, who justified
the killing of Israelis, but not of Jews in general, as part of the jihad to reconquer Palestine, a usurped Muslim land. Americans
could not be presumed innocent either, according to Bin Laden;
but here his arguments were less assured and underwent several
changes over time.

In an interview with Hamid Mir, a Pakistani journalist, which
was published in the Lahore daily *Dawn* on November 7, 2001, the
leader of Al Qaeda, asked to justify the murder of innocents in
light of the teachings of Islam, snapped:

This is a major point in jurisprudence. In my view, if an
enemy occupies a Muslim territory and uses common
people as human shields, then it is permitted to attack
that enemy. For instance, if bandits barge into a home
and hold a child hostage, then the child's father can at-

tack the bandits and in that attack even the child may
get hurt. America and its allies are massacring us in Palestine, Chechnya, Kashmir and Iraq. The Muslims have
the right to attack America in reprisal . . . The September 11 attacks were not targeted at women and children.
The real targets were America's icons of military and
economic power.

As if the weaknesses of his argument were visible even to himself, Bin Laden followed a different line of thinking in his next explanation: "The American people should remember that they pay
taxes to their government, they elect their president, their government manufactures arms and gives them to Israel, and Israel
uses them to massacre Palestinians. The American Congress endorses all government measures and this proves that [all] America
is responsible for the atrocities perpetrated against Muslims. [All]
America, because they elect the Congress."

As for the many non-Americans who died when the twin towers
collapsed—and in particular Muslims in whose name the jihad
was carried out—Bin Laden settled the question by noting: "The
Islamic sharia says Muslims should not live in the land of
the infidel for long." This argument was also used by the GIA
in the 1990s to justify the massacre of Algerian civilians, through
communiqués transmitted by London's Islamist media. Like Bin
Laden, these activists had been indoctrinated in the Afghan jihad
training camps by the same salafist-jihadist ideologues.

According to Bin Laden's point of view, the slaughter of innocents is not terrorism. It is merely a minor reparation for the countless crimes and murders committed against Islam and Muslims
since the end of the 600-year-old Ottoman Empire in 1923. "What
the United States is tasting today is nothing compared to what we

have tasted for decades. Our *umma* has known this humiliation and contempt for over eighty years. Its sons are killed, its blood is spilled, its holy sites are attacked, and it is not governed according to Allah's command. Despite this, no one cares."

DESPITE AMERICA'S EFFORTS to run Al Qaeda to ground, in the period between September 11 and the transfer of sovereignty to Iraq, a series of attacks demonstrated Al Qaeda's global presence and its resilience. These attacks were designed to satisfy Bin Laden's two criteria: maximum damage to the enemy, and maximum popularity among the masses. Only the proportions varied, depending on local conditions.

On December 2, 2002, during Ramadan, and then again on December 6, on the occasion of the feast marking the end of the month of fasting, two statements were posted on websites that the movement used frequently. Signed respectively by the "political bureau of Qaedat al-Jihad organization" and Al Qaeda's usual spokesman, Sulayman Abu Ghaith, a Kuwaiti, they explained the significance of the two largely unsuccessful attacks in the Kenyan beach resort of Mombassa just a few days earlier, on November 28. This failed operation—in which two missiles launched against an Israeli charter plane were turned off course by its radar, and nine Kenyan employees, as well as the three suicide bombers, were among the fifteen people killed in an explosion at the Paradise Hotel—made it necessary to explain the goals of the network, which had been blurred by this fiasco.

Despite the absence of conclusive, absolute proof, most expert observers believed these statements were authentic. The fact that they were posted on the Internet instead of being broadcast on one of the Gulf's pan-Arab satellite channels (which fight for the privilege, hoping to increase their audience) suggests that the messages were intended primarily for potential sympathizers rather than for the masses, and that the goal of the postings was first and foremost to clarify and validate the political logic that underpinned the Mombassa attack.

The first statement was elaborate, exceptionally precise, and carefully argued. The second completed the first and claimed to authenticate it, thanks to Abu Ghaith's "signature" (although neither Bin Laden's nor Zawahiri's signature appeared). It is impossible, given the available evidence, to untangle the internal conflicts that may have motivated this curious double posting. But together, the statements offer a fairly accurate representation of Al Qaeda's strategy after its dismantled base spread across the real and the virtual world.

The statement issued by the "political bureau" ran as follows:

> In the name of Allah the Merciful, the Compassionate.
>
> Praise be to Allah, who has said:
>
> " . . . slay
>
> The Infidels wherever ye find them,
>
> And seize them, beleaguer them."
>
> Blessings and praise upon the most noble of prophets, Muhammad, and upon his people. In this holy month [Ramadan], and in these past ten blessed days, we would like to congratulate, first, our people in Palestine, and then all the Muslim *umma*. We delayed these congratulations deliberately, so that they would coincide with the two operations in Mombassa, Kenya, against Zionist interests, and so that our greeting would be more mean-

ingful in the circumstances under which the *umma* is suffering by the fault of its enemies, the Crusaders and the Jews.

Today, the mujahedeen have returned to this place, where the coalition of Jews and Crusaders was overcome four years ago, at the American embassies in Nairobi and Dar es Salaam, in order to strike this deceitful coalition once more; but this strike is against the Jews, and it bears the following message: whatever you inflict by way of war damages, occupation of our holy sites, criminal acts against our people in Palestine—by killing children, women, the elderly, by destroying houses, uprooting trees, and maintaining your siege—will not go unpunished. You will suffer the same, and more if Allah allows it. Your children for ours, your women for ours, your old people for ours, your buildings for our homes. In retaliation for the siege you have imposed on our lives and survival, we will besiege you with terror and fear, we will hunt you down, with Allah's permission, wherever you are, on land, at sea, or in the skies.

The mujahedeen have kept their promise to Allah to cause His religion to triumph. They have kept their promise to the *umma* to end its humiliation and degradation, by launching painful strikes and victorious operations, with Allah's assistance, against the treacherous coalition of Jews and Crusaders, wherever it is to be found. Praise be to Allah for what follows:

The destruction of the U.S. embassy in Nairobi;

The destruction of the U.S. embassy in Dar es Salaam;

The destruction of the World Trade Center in New York;

The destruction of the Pentagon;

The hijacking of the American airliner over Pennsylvania, intended to strike at the U.S. Congress.

America was maddened by all this. It was plunged into a state of shock and horror by all it saw and heard, without understanding the cause of its ill. It was shaken, its dignity was crushed into the ground, and it forced the entire world to rally behind its flag and fall into step with its iniquitous campaign—unprecedented in ancient or modern history—against this honest group of mujahedeen and against the Muslim *umma*. It thought it would be capable of winning the day and exterminating Allah's soldiers.

The entire world became a CIA office, following America around everywhere on earth and under the heavens, forgetting that Islam is devotion, that it grows stronger in hardship, suffering, and distress. This was demonstrated by the mujahedeen, who proved capable, with Allah's help, of targeting their strikes and launching attacks during a year when they were being hunted down. Since the Crusaders attacked Afghanistan in the middle of the month of Rajab 1422 [October 2001], they have accomplished the following:

The operation in Djerba, Tunisia, against the synagogue;

The shoe rigged with explosives on the American airliner;

The attack on French soldiers in Pakistan;

The attack on the [French] oil tanker in Yemen;

The assassination of marines in Falayka, Kuwait;

The destruction of the Bali discotheque, as well as other operations that took place on the same day in Indonesia;

The two operations in Mombassa against Jewish interests;

Dozens of operations in Afghanistan and elsewhere in various parts of the world;

Other operations, which we shall not mention for various reasons . . .

The statement that appeared four days later, signed by Sulayman Abu Ghaith, on jehad.net, in a bid to "confirm" the previous one, noted:

> While the nature of our activities in the previous phase prevented us from claiming responsibility for our jihad operations against this iniquitous alliance, today we find ourselves in a better situation and a more assured position, and can therefore do so. The mujahedeen are part of this blessed, victorious *umma*. They are the vanguard, which has devoted itself to fomenting confrontation with our enemies. This vanguard is not fighting in the *umma*'s place, but acts upon it like yeast, allowing it to rise and resist occupiers and invaders. It would be wrong to reduce jihad to one limited organization, because jihad is an essential part of faith, of the original doctrine that confronts Islam's enemies. It is part of the path shown by the Prophet Muhammad (peace and blessings upon him) and his companions.

These two statements, like many of the documents issued by the Islamist terrorist network, pose a problem of authenticity, since the Internet lends itself to infinite manipulation. Abu Ghaith's electronic signature proves nothing in itself. Only the fact that the statements were posted on a jihadist site well known at the time, and the fact that no one has disavowed them since, provides the documents with some external elements of credibility and veracity. Furthermore, they show a considerable degree of internal coherence; and the relation between the content and the actions to which the text refers, as well as the suggested interpretation, makes sense.

The interest of the two statements lies first in the list of acts to which they lay claim, an innovation justified by the "improved" circumstances in which the network found itself. This boasting affirmation should be read, however, as exactly the reverse: if the list was published as a show of strength, it was because the network was in fact going through a phase of weakness. In March 2002 Abu Zubayda, a 31-year-old Palestinian born in Saudi Arabia, had been arrested in Pakistan. An operations commander, he was close to Bin Laden, who had made him responsible for directing camps in Afghanistan and then for training terrorists even when he was very young. Some of these trainees—like the "shoe bomber" Richard Reid, a British convert who tried to blow up his shoe in December 2001 on a flight from Paris to the United States—had been arrested and had revealed vast amounts of information to their interrogators.

Above all, in September 2002 Khalid Shaikh Mohammed and his associate, Ramzi bin al-Shibh, the technical "brains" behind the September 11 operation, suffered the consequences of their carelessness after attempting to influence a documentary Al Jazeera was supposed to air in commemoration of the attacks on the United

States. While meeting an Egyptian journalist who worked for the station in Karachi, they allowed U.S. and Pakistani intelligence agencies that were trailing them to locate the group that had planned the attacks. In late September Bin al-Shibh, a Yemeni who had been slated to be a 9/11 hijacker but was unable to obtain a visa to enter the United States, was arrested. This opened the way to the capture of the planning and operations chief behind the attacks, Khalid Shaikh Mohammed. He was caught on March 1, 2003, hiding in a house in Rawalpindi that belonged to a deputy of Pakistan's main Islamist party. Born in 1965 to a Baluchi family that had settled in Kuwait, he was Ramzi Youssef's uncle, albeit only three years his nephew's senior. Youssef had planned the first attack on the World Trade Center in 1993 and was serving time in the United States.

The circumstances of these arrests, amid recurring doubts that Bin Laden was alive and still fit to command, hardly made the case for the group's efficiency and capacity to pose a global threat. Rather, they testified to the fissures in its security, protection and alliance networks, and communications policy. Furthermore, the network now had a new name, Qaedat al-Jihad, which combined "Al Qaeda" with the name of the Egyptian group led by Zawahiri, "Tanzim al-Jihad" (Jihad Organization) to create an expression signifying "Jihad Base." It also claimed to have acquired a "political bureau," an expression more reminiscent of extreme left-wing parties than of Islamist movements and one intended to suggest efficiency and political savvy at a time when these qualities seemed to be in question.

The first admission of responsibility for the September 11 attacks had taken the form of a the macabre video clip of the "testament" recorded by one of the hijackers, a Saudi citizen, Ahmad al-Haznawi al-Ghamdi. He made his statement before a picture of the twin towers, above which floated the slogan: "Expel the *mushrikin* [that is, the Jews and Christians, who worship other deities alongside the one true God] from the Arabian peninsula." This videotape, which was televised on April 17, 2002, by Al Jazeera, marked a break with the deliberate evasiveness that Bin Laden had adopted with his interviewers up to that point.

The date of this change in communication strategy is significant: it coincides with an Israeli army operation in the Jenin refugee camp aimed at dismantling explosives workshops and suicide-bomber training networks in the Palestinian territories. Israeli troops killed many Palestinian civilians and caused extensive property damage. Across the Arab world, outrage mingled with frustration and a sense of powerlessness. Thanks to a U.S. veto, the "Jenin massacre" was not discussed at the U.N. Security Council. With this first explicit, irrefutable admission of responsibility for the 9/11 attacks, the planners asserted to the *umma* that they were the only force able to strike a comparably powerful blow at the enemy.

This vendetta logic was visible in the two subsequent statements released in December 2002. At that time, Sharon's government had begun to build a "security fence" that would encircle Israeli space and isolate the eroding Palestinian territories, to the great distress not only of Arab public opinion but also of international institutions, which protested in vain. In retaliation for the "siege" Israel had imposed upon the Palestinians, the December 2 statement announced that it would besiege the Israelis on land, at sea, and in the skies—thus providing the Mombassa operation with a justification that was all the more necessary because the attack had fallen so far short of its goals. For Al Qaeda supporters, it was therefore crucial to reiterate that its militants were not acting in the *umma*'s stead but rather were the agents of its uprising against the "Jews and Crusaders"—that these militants would strike a blow for every blow received, while all the other representatives of the Muslim world faltered.

During the same month of December 2002, for three days running, the Arabic-language London daily *Al-Quds al-Arabi* published a pamphlet by Ayman al-Zawahiri entitled *Al-wala wal-bara
(Loyalty and Separation)*; it was also available on all the jihadist
movement's websites. A little over a year after the hunt for Al
Qaeda had begun, at a time when the invasion of Iraq seemed imminent, Zawahiri's statement did not discuss the operational or
technical aspects of the attacks that had taken place during the
previous months but echoed points made in his *Knights under
the Prophet's Banner*, which had appeared a year earlier. He reaffirmed the doctrinal foundations of global jihad and identified its
contemporary targets and goals.

To Arabic-speaking readers who were knowledgeable about
Islamic concepts, the reaffirmation was obvious even in the title.
Al-wala wal-bara is a canonical definition of Muslim identity, referring to a state of siege, especially during the Prophet's era, which
was rife with crucial conflicts, and to two subsequent historical
traumas: the loss of Andalusia to the Christian Reconquista between the twelfth and the fifteenth centuries and the fall of Baghdad to the Mongols, or "infidel" Tatars, in the thirteenth. The
phrase advocates enclosing Islamic identity within an internal citadel, in accordance with austere, intransigent criteria, to ward off
the threat of its imminent disintegration or corruption.

The term *wala* suggests friendship, loyalty, trust; *bara* evokes the
severing of ties, the absence of any relation. The correlation of the
two concepts enjoins Muslims to give their trust and friendship
only to Muslims, and to withhold them from unbelievers; infidels,
apostates, and hypocrites—non-Muslims—must be subjected to a
merciless jihad until they accept Islam or face extermination. The
Quranic verse most frequently cited in scholastic tradition stipulates:

O ye who believe!
Take not the Jews
And the Christians
For your friends and protectors:
They are but friends and protectors
To each other. And he
Amongst you that turns to them
(For friendship) is of them.

This last verse has been used repeatedly since the 1990s by ji-had fighters to justify the incidental killing of Muslims (often more numerous than the originally targeted enemy) during attacks against unbelievers, under the pretext that they should not have been nearby, since such proximity exposed them to suspicions that they were associating with the infidels. In the context of a war against unbelievers, the term *bara* or separation suggests that if Muslims do not break all ties of friendship or trust with unbeliev-ers—if they associate with some of them, for instance, to preserve their immediate interests—then Islam is in peril.

Some ulema used this reasoning to explain Baghdad's fall to the Tatars or the Reconquista of Andalusia. By contrast, during colo-nial times, which gave rise to critical introspection among Muslim elites who sought the causes of colonial domination in the Islamic world's backwardness, the notion of *al-wala wal-bara*, with its im-perative of separation from Europe, fell into disuse. It seemed more urgent at that time to learn the technologies and ways of thinking that had made European civilization dominant—even if that question was addressed, as it was by reformers like Jamal al-Din al-Afghani and his disciples, through the rereading of sacred texts. Once purged of accumulated tradition, the reformers imagined, these texts would allow them to bring the precepts of early Islam into line with European modernity. The result, however, was that men of religion lost their influence among Muslim intellectuals: the ulema had to give way, or at least accept the loss of their monopoly, to academics and thinkers who advocated nationalism, liberalism, secularism, or socialism.

The failure, a generation after the colonial era, of independent states that were founded on these principles reopened the way to those who rejected the ideals themselves. Believing that Western civilization had corrupted the Islamic world and was the root of all ills, they advocated its wholesale rejection. This philosophy, at its most extreme in Zawahiri's writings and Bin Laden's terrorist practices, unearthed the doctrine of *al-wala wal-bara* as a means to that end.

The premises of the doctrine can be found as early as the 1960s in the work of Sayyid Qutb, who advocated separation between the Muslim vanguard, which had to return to the Prophet's way of life in order to restore Islam's greatness, and what he termed *jahiliyya*, the modern world of ignorance and unbelief. Qutb, however, was not trained as a classical jurist, and he used a modern term more easily understood by readers who were superficially educated in Arabic: *mufasala*, which also means separation but is not a Quranic reference. On the other hand, *bara* emerged from a religious and scholarly tradition and, as used by Zawahiri, had a significance that only erudite Arabic speakers with a religious education could grasp instantly. Thus, Zawahiri's pamphlet constituted a sort of linguistic strong-arm tactic: it intimidated those who did not adhere to his views by attributing their disagreement to ignorance of the language used in the Quran.

The text was divided into two unequal parts. The first, twice as long as the second, set down the Islamic grounds for the doctrine of "loyalty and separation"—implying that newspaper readers or Internet surfers had forgotten them. The second specified the doctrine's modern application, thus mobilizing the resources of religious tradition in the service of jihad. In the first part, Zawahiri offered his own potpourri of Quranic verses, prophetic sayings, and analyses and glosses by legal scholars to demonstrate that Muslims are forbidden from associating with "infidels." In his argument, there was no trace of the tolerance for "people of the Book"—especially Christians and Jews—upon which Islam's apologists insist. Zawahiri lumped them all together indiscriminately: they were all infidels, who must submit or be killed. The same applied to "bad Muslims," the apostates and hypocrites who do not heed the call to jihad and who for their own sordid reasons prefer to associate with infidels, thus precipitating their fall in this life and the hereafter.

Zawahiri drew heavily on the fatwas (legal opinions) that Ibn Taymiyya pronounced in the thirteenth century, as the Tatar invasion was under way. That invasion would culminate in the conquest of Baghdad, the capital of the Abbasid caliphate. These references were hardly coincidental: the U.S.-led coalition was preparing to attack Baghdad and would launch its invasion three months after the publication of Zawahiri's tract. The point, therefore, was to read the forthcoming war not as a battle for democracy, as the neoconservatives in Washington saw it, but as a sort of remake of the devastation the warring Tatars had caused seven centuries earlier. This view would revive one of the two major disasters (Andalusia being the other) that have marked the history of Islam.

Thus, Zawahiri recycled the traditional ulema's most radical rulings, passed centuries earlier in a time of imminent peril, but imbued them with an unchanging and binding character that made them applicable to the circumstances of today. Zawahiri's first target was the Muslim leadership—the kings, emirs, and presidents of states close to Iraq, from Egypt to Pakistan via the monarchies of the Arabian peninsula—that was preparing to participate in the American invasion by providing troops or allowing the use of military bases or air space. In so doing, Zawahiri was taking no great risk, since he was echoing an opinion that transcended jihadist circles: in Qatar, which would become the headquarters of the U.S. attack on Saddam, Sheikh Qaradawi had spoken out along the same lines. Conveniently for U.S. military operations, he disappeared from the screen of Al Jazeera (which broadcasts from Qatar) to undergo a surgical procedure—one which he had put off repeatedly in the past and which required a period of convalescence that coincided with the period of the U.S.-led invasion.

Saddam Hussein was a secularist whose Baath Party the Islamists despised. But they felt that his crimes, no matter how grievous, could not justify a Muslim alliance with a non-Muslim coalition, especially since those non-Muslims were acting with the perverse intention of corrupting belief and obedience to Allah. Thus, according to Zawahiri, who took the argument further than Qaradawi, any Muslim ally of America against Saddam Hussein was by definition an apostate whose blood it was permissible to spill. The ultimate goal of the Judeo-Crusaders, to use the term popularized by the World Islamic Front against Jews and Crusaders in 1998, was to occupy and thereby annihilate—symbolically if not in reality—Islam's holy sites, and therefore to strike a fatal blow against Islam itself. Israel's occupation of Jerusalem was merely the prelude to a U.S. occupation of Mecca and Medina.

By putting forth a theological argument to buttress a feeling of anxiety and humiliation that was widespread in the Muslim world but was rarely made explicit, Zawahiri continued to compete for the hearts and minds of believers and to seek their acceptance of Al Qaeda as its belligerent vanguard. No alliance or friendship with the infidels was permitted, though dissimulation was an acceptable strategy when the enemy occupied a position of strength, as in India and China or on the outskirts of European and American cities. Through such dissimulation of allegiance, the community's ranks and strength could grow, until the time was right for jihad. Against the apostate regimes (lackeys of the Judeo-Crusaders), against the ulema, thinkers, journalists, and intellectuals who served those princes and spent their time inventing pretexts to delay the struggle, young people of the Muslim world were duty-bound to join the jihad caravan wherever it could be found: "Young Muslims must not await anyone's authorization. Jihad against Americans, Jews, and their allies among the hypocrites and apostates is mandatory on all Muslims." Thus did Zawahiri conclude his pamphlet. In 2003, a new group of activists heeded his call.

THE ATTACKS CARRIED OUT in 2003 opened a new phase of violence, bringing it back to the Middle East, where, in mid-March, the U.S. army had begun its invasion and occupation of Iraq. A stated goal of this operation was to eradicate terrorism by overthrowing a tyrant and establishing a democratic regime that would spread its influence throughout the region. For Al Qaeda and those who shared its hostility to the U.S. presence, attacks within the region would demonstrate to the world that Washington's hopes were absurd.

With the exception of strikes in Iraq, to which we will return later, the series began in Saudi Arabia. On May 12, thirty-five people were killed in a residential complex in Riyadh as Secretary of State Colin Powell was visiting the capital; nine of the victims were Americans. On May 16, in Casablanca, the targets were "Jewish and European," but all forty-five of the victims were Muslims. On November 8, in Riyadh again, seventeen people were killed, all Arabs (including some Lebanese Christians). On November 14 and 20, in Istanbul, a synagogue, a Jewish center, and a British bank were targets of explosions. A local Islamist newspaper ran the headline: "Sixty-nine dead, but only six Jews."

The high proportion of Muslim victims in the 2003 attacks suggested less "professionalism" than Al Qaeda had demonstrated in the previous year. If Zawahiri and others sought to mobilize the *umma*, this shotgun approach was counterproductive. In Saudi Arabia, Morocco, and Turkey, the population rejected terrorism virulently, cutting the radical Islamists off from many potential supporters—as had been the case in Egypt in 1997, when the Luxor massacre caused widespread revulsion. On the other hand, the suicide attacks demonstrated the growing localization and decentralization of the terrorist network, following the arrest in March of the network's chief operations planner, Khalid Shaikh Mohammed. This new crop of suicide bombers consisted of natives: Saudis, Moroccans, and Turks, trained only superficially by some compatriot who had been in an Afghan or Pakistani camp. The amateurishness of the attacks translated into relatively weak coverage by the world media, in contrast with operations in 2001 and 2002, which had been remarkably effective in popularizing the cause of jihad.

Balancing out such decreased effectiveness, however, was the fact that terrorism had proliferated beyond the practiced activists in Bin Laden's circle, most of whom were now serving prison sentences or were in U.S. custody. This troublesome evolution suggests that terrorism could become routine in these countries, in much the same way that it has become routine in Palestine, Israel, and, increasingly, in Iraq. Violence inspired directly or indirectly by the ideology of *al-wala wal-bara* and similar doctrines has spread to the slums, among networks of delinquents financed by dope-peddling and sundry petty trafficking. Their bombs are cheap and easy to make with ammonium nitrate and have devastating effects. Al Qaeda, in a sense, has become a franchise, with Bin Laden merely the logo for small-time operations managed by independent micro-entrepreneurs working under license to purvey terrorism.

Nowhere was the indigenous character of the new terrorism clearer than in the May 16 attacks on Casablanca and the March 2004 bombing of the Madrid trains. The suicide bombers in Morocco died as they detonated their charges in places with Jewish or European connotations: the alumni association of the Universal Israelite Alliance, a Jewish-owned restaurant, a hotel where Israeli tourists were staying, the Jewish cemetery, and the Casa de España club, where Spaniards socialized during colonial times but which is frequented only by Moroccans today. Just as the 9/11 hijackers had slit the throats of those who tried to resist, the attackers in Casablanca used long knives to slit the throats of porters, policemen, and guards on duty before blowing themselves up with a primitive fertilizer-based mixture.

All the victims were Moroccans, which confused the message received by a population that was supposed to rally to the jihad and its goals. The terrorists, too, were Moroccans: ten of the twelve were from one shantytown neighborhood on the outskirts of Casablanca. Most of the suicide bombers were barely educated, though a few had managed to escape for a time before falling back into poverty, and several had attempted to emigrate secretly to

Spain, in hope of finding work there. None had a direct link to Al Qaeda; none had trained in Pakistan or Afghanistan. Their indoctrination had been an entirely local affair, carried out through the sermons and speeches of imams from the salafist movement, some of whom had been educated in Saudi Arabia and sought to impose Islamic order in the slum, to "command good and forbid evil." They did this by sending out militias armed with sticks and whips to hunt down unmarried couples, petty dealers, people who drank alcohol, and "immoral women."

One of these imams was thought to be the Moroccan representative of the salafist-jihadist militant Abu Qatada, whom many considered to be the most radical figure of the London-based Islamist movement. Another had already ordered several executions by stoning or decapitation. Yet another, at the same time that Zawahiri was writing his pamphlet, had circulated a small treatise also titled *Al-Wala wal-Bara*, which incited readers to engage in immediate jihad against the Moroccan regime, which he saw as "falsely Muslim."

A few of the May 16 suicide bombers had discovered Islam recently; some had been petty criminals, drug addicts, or alcoholics; but all had been delighted by the September attacks. Won over by Osama bin Laden's charisma, they were desperate to imitate him. Encouraged by the imams to act but unable to cross the Straits of Gibraltar to enter Europe, they chose instead to leave the misery of the slums behind for good and head toward Paradise, where their status as jihad martyrs guaranteed them extraordinary rewards.

The Casablanca attacks resulted from a mix of Al Qaeda's ideology with the social frustrations of dispossessed young men who decided, under the influence of radical salafist imams, to translate their political impotence into terrorism. This primitive hybrid had a fatal flaw, however—the Islamists' failure to convince the *umma* that a struggle which killed so many innocent believers was just.

Their sympathizers may not have objected to the massacre of Jews, Americans, Europeans, and other infidels—indeed, may even have rejoiced—but they drew the line at killing fellow Muslims. In November 2003, when a bloodbath in Riyadh claimed only Arab victims, the same sentiment prevailed, and the jihadist imams had to issue an apology. The Madrid massacre, by contrast, killed mainly infidel Europeans. Though it was carried out by Moroccans linked to the Casablanca movement, this time a group of more experienced jihad fighters, trained directly by Bin Laden's network, was in charge.

Al Qaeda's "Moroccan émigré" connection had caught the attention of investigators following September 11. It had gained visibility mainly through the arraignment of Moroccans who had crossed the borders into France and Germany. Most famous among them was Zacarias Moussaoui, arrested in the United States, and Mohamed al-Mutasaddiq, arrested in Hamburg. Spain's role as a revolving door for terrorists had become clear: its large population of Moroccans included many illegal residents. In July 2001, the principal meeting to plan September 11 in Tarragon had been attended by Mohammed Atta, the chief of the U.S. commandoes, and Ramzi bin al-Shibh, the Yemeni who served as liaison officer with Khalid Shaikh Mohammed and Bin Laden. At the time, the Spanish police and judiciary had no experience in the surveillance and pursuit of radical Islamist groups, and control techniques at border checkpoints were inefficient. This lack of expertise allowed Bin Laden's followers to use Spain as a sanctuary and a base: activists and financial transfers alike passed through it. But a series of extremely thorough investigations and subsequent arrests after 9/11 disturbed this tranquil arrangement and provided data that linked the attacks in Madrid and Casablanca to Al Qaeda soon after they occurred.

The Madrid train bombs exploded early in the morning, as commuters on four trains were traveling toward Atocha station. Spain was nearing the end of its election campaign, and the Aznar government had sent troops to Iraq despite strong public disapproval. The prime minister therefore faced left-wing opposition that had made troop withdrawal part of its platform. If these early trains had been running on time on March 11, they would have converged at the station just as the bombs exploded. The railway station itself would have collapsed, killing thousands. Only delays in train departures limited what would have been the gravest massacre in European history. As things stood, 191 people were killed and thousands were crippled for life.

The parallel with September 11 was immediately striking: just as Atta and his accomplices had chosen to target air travel, which is emblematic of transport and communications in the United States, the Madrid terrorists targeted trains, since in Europe railway travel epitomizes efficient transportation. Other shared traits on 3/11 were the early hour and the choice of four trains, to echo the four planes of 9/11.

The Aznar government's immediate reaction was to blame the Basque terrorist group ETA. This tactic, adopted with a view toward the elections, backfired as soon as the first Islamists were arrested and the evidence of their involvement came to light. Voters punished the government severely, refusing to allow Aznar to derive political capital from the attacks, as George W. Bush had done successfully in 2001. Zapatero, the socialist leader who defeated Aznar, reiterated his promise to withdraw Spanish troops from Iraq, and a statement from Al Qaeda "saluting" this decision announced that a truce would be called in Spain. This precedent, coming on the heels of Zapatero's inopportune declaration, aimed to show that Bin Laden and his associates could use murder and blackmail to influence domestic policy in European states. But its true value—or the lack thereof—was revealed on April 3, when a bomb set to blow up under a high-speed train full of passengers traveling from Madrid to Seville was discovered and defused in time.

A statement in Arabic, communicated to the London daily *Al-Quds al-Arabi*, claimed responsibility for the Madrid attacks on the day they occurred. The text was signed by the Abu Hafs al-Misri Brigades (al-Qaeda), in reference to an Egyptian (*Misri* in Arabic), Mohamed Atef, a.k.a Abu Hafs, a former police officer who had become Bin Laden's military and security chief and who was probably killed in the American bombardment of Afghanistan on November 16, 2001. The text referred to an earlier communiqué, issued on March 2, which denied that Al Qaeda's Sunnis had been involved in any way in the bombing that had killed hundreds in Karbala, Iraq, that day. It thereby incriminated the United States in the attack on the world's greatest Shiite pilgrimage site, at a time when Shiites and Sunnis in Iraq were sealing an alliance that would result in an uprising against the U.S. occupation the following month.

After three Quranic citations intended to legitimate the operation from an Islamic point of view, the text began as follows:

> Operation trains of death.
>
> The Abu Hafs al-Misri Brigades affirmed in a previous statement [Al Qaeda's statement about the attacks on Karbala and Baghdad], dated Muharram 11, 1425, which corresponds to March 2, 2004, that operations would follow . . . and the brigades have kept their word . . . The death squadron has successfully made its way deep into Crusader Europe, and has dealt one of the pillars of the Crusader alliance [Spain] a painful blow . . . This is only part of the settlement of old scores with Crusader Spain,

America's ally in its war against Islam . . . We in the Abu
Hafs al-Misri Brigades do not worry about the deaths of
so-called civilians . . . Is it permissible for them to kill
our children, our wives, our old people, and our youth
in Afghanistan, Iraq, Pakistan, and Kashmir? Is it then il-
licit for us to kill them?

After recalling and justifying other attacks, giving coded instructions to other brigades that stood "ready to act," announcing America's imminent destruction by a "winds of black death" operation,
said to be ninety percent organized, the statement closed, before
the customary praise of Allah, with a "warning to the *umma:* do not
approach civilian and military installations belonging to Crusader
America and its allies."

It is significant that the statement made reference to "old scores"
to be settled with Spain. Whether by coincidence or intentionally,
the towns from which the booby-trapped trains departed bear Arab
names, as do many cities in the Iberian peninsula, recalling Muslim Andalusia: Alcala de Henares (from the *al-qala,* the fortress),
and Guadalajara (from *wadi al-hajara,* rocky river). The Islamic
reconquest of the peninsula was explicitly on the salafist-jihadist
agenda, starting in the 1980s with the pamphlets and sermons of
Abdallah Azzam, spokesman for the Afghan jihad, when he was
still the U.S. government's favorite anti-Soviet freedom fighter. Jihad in the Iberian peninsula is a binding duty for Muslims because Spain and Portugal constitute Islamic lands usurped by infidels (even if they were usurped six centuries ago), like Israel and
Bosnia, for example. It is therefore perfectly legitimate to conduct a "defensive jihad" there, one which targets the non-Muslim
population, including civilians, until that population submits anew
to an Islamic government. Today, most Muslims consider these

ideas bizarre, but the minority who believe them have the means and the will to transform this doctrine into a terror machine and to galvanize the fringe of sympathizers who were repelled by the massacre of Muslims in Casablanca or Riyadh but who do not object to the killing of infidels, which a jihadist interpretation of the sacred texts prescribes.

Beyond these doctrinal considerations, the Madrid attacks had significance in two other respects. First, they demonstrated that Al Qaeda "professionals" had taken operations in hand once more and were capable of issuing statements that would place their operations in a global context and provide the key to their interpretation. After the text just cited, a tape claiming responsibility for the attacks reminded listeners that they had taken place "exactly two and a half years after September 11." Bin Laden and his associates have demonstrated again and again an obsession with symbolic effects that multiply the material impact of terrorist attacks.

Second, once the amateurishness evident in the Casablanca massacre of Muslims had been corrected, the Madrid bombings confirmed that "natives" were being charged with carrying out large-scale actions on the ground. The links of the main suspects to the inner circles of Al Qaeda were strong, but most of the other Moroccans involved in the attacks were only remotely related to the network and had been recruited on the basis of neighborly relations, friendships struck up at the mosque, or family and tribal ties in northern Morocco or in underprivileged areas of Tangiers and the Rif. In other words, they bore no resemblance to the September 2001 cadres who had entered the United States to carry out professional attacks but had no links with either American society or local Muslim associations.

On the down side, from the perspective of the war on terror, the indigenous character of the new terrorists makes it difficult to distinguish the attackers from their environment. Local communities often tell the press that the suspects were nice, well-brought-up young men, hard workers, and good Muslims. On the up side, intelligence agents can usually infiltrate home-grown organizations with less difficulty. The arrests in Spain were made very quickly, thanks to the many clues these unprofessional terrorists left behind. Similarly, eight British citizens of Pakistani origin were arrested soon after the discovery of a large stock of ammonium nitrate near London on March 30, 2004. The primitive plot was foiled easily; but it would have been no less deadly had it been conducted as planned.

Adding up all of these attacks, one can conclude that, as of the summer of 2004, the U.S. government's war to eradicate terror has thus far been unsuccessful, despite the massive resources mobilized and the restrictions imposed on public freedom—most critically the imprisonment, without trial or sentence, of hundreds of people on the U.S. military base at Guantanamo. Guantanamo is to the state of law what offshore tax havens are to trade. This detention facility would find a moral (if not a legal) justification only if the interrogations carried out there shed light on the September 11 attacks, helped to capture those who were responsible, and prevented their recurrence, in the United States or elsewhere. Although official spokesmen (uncorroborated by any verifiable information) assure the world that arrests have been made thanks to information obtained in Guantanamo, the two individuals with whom Al Qaeda is identified—Bin Laden, the charismatic financier, and Zawahiri, the ideologue—are still alive and at large. Abu Zubayda, the Palestinian, Ramzi bin al-Shibh, the Yemeni, and Khalid Shaikh Mohammed, the Pakistani, may be under lock and key, but their arrests have not stemmed the attacks.

As for the eradication of the Taliban regime, it may well have deprived Islamist terrorists of their sanctuary, but it has not had the expected effect of destroying the movement or, for that matter, establishing a viable government in Afghanistan. Hamid Karzai enjoys Washington's backing as well as funding from the international community, but he has not managed to extend his authority beyond Kabul. The remainder of the territory is under the control of tribal warlords, as it was in the early 1990s before the Taliban imposed order.

Finally, the American offensive, which owed much to reasoning inherited from the Cold War, lost valuable time while it focused on the Afghan infrastructure, on overthrowing the Taliban, and especially on the war in Iraq. It set about cutting out the visible parts of the terrorist tumor, but it did not have a systemic cure for the cancerous cells that were metastasizing throughout the world. Terrorism, with a new face, has now spread around the globe, and Washington bureaucrats cannot easily recognize it.

Does this mean that Bin Laden and Zawahiri won the war on terror? On the contrary: the principal goal of terrorism—to seize power in Muslim countries through mobilization of populations galvanized by jihad's sheer audacity—has not been realized. Taliban-controlled Afghanistan, the only state governed according to sharia, has been liquidated, even if its successor state is hardly a political success story. In Sudan, General Bashir has placed Hassan al-Turabi under house arrest and is making friendly overtures to Washington in the hope of a lucrative petroleum-based collaboration. In Libya, Colonel Muammar Qaddafi, who made terrorism the modus operandi of international relations long before Al Qaeda came on the scene, has "recanted" and admitted his responsibility for the attacks that destroyed American and French airliners over Lockerbie and Africa. Qaddafi has paid considerable damages to the victims' families in order to return to the international fold and develop Libya's oil production, with help from Western technology.

But in Palestine—for many, the central focus of world unrest—the situation has continued to deteriorate. While Israeli civilians face increasingly murderous attacks every day, living conditions for Palestinian civilians are becoming more and more unbearable, and the spiral of violence and retaliation tightens. In March and April 2004, Israeli missiles killed first Sheikh Ahmed Yassin, the founder of Hamas, and then his successor, Dr. Abdel-Aziz al-Rantissi. If any further proof was required, these "targeted" assassinations showed that the one-upmanship initiated by Sharon and Arafat in the fall of 2000 will continue into the foreseeable future—a clear demonstration that the war on terror has not achieved its aims.

Finally, and ironically, the persistence of terrorism handed the United States a pretext or a justification—depending on one's point of view—for invading Iraq, overthrowing Saddam Hussein's oppressive regime, and placing American troops in the heart of the most oil-rich region in the world. The occupation—met by devastating resistance—quickly devolved into a quagmire.

Zawahiri conceptualized the use of terrorism in 2001 by positing that dramatic strikes against the "faraway enemy" would terrorize the "nearby enemy"—the heads of state in the Muslim world—and facilitate their overthrow. He was counting on jihad activists to mobilize the masses through grand actions broadcast by Arab satellite television channels like Al Jazeera. Only this magnitude of action would slow the decline of jihad, which by the end of the 1990s had failed in Egypt, Algeria, Bosnia, and elsewhere. Bin Laden has proved a seductive spokesman for Zawahiri's ideas: his slow, composed tones, his husky voice, and his salafist-Afghan outfits gained him supporters on the strength of imagery alone, as the

Casablanca attacks demonstrated. But apart from some narrow and unlikely alliances with intellectuals or black sheep, a few random Islamic bankers, and young, dispossessed bombers, Bin Laden has been unable to unify poor urban youth, the Muslim middle classes, and the Islamist intelligentsia into a coalition capable of repeating the only triumphant Islamic revolution the world has ever seen: the one that took place in Iran in 1979.

Terrorism has missed its political aim, but it continues to manifest its resilience in the face of repression and to cause havoc around the world. It acts as a parasite on international relations and has begun to weigh on social relations inside some Western countries. The war on terror, on the other hand, measured by the political strategy of the Bush White House, has been successful to some extent in mobilizing international support to track down potential threats and, following 9/11, in rallying American voters behind President Bush's initiatives in the Middle East.

Whatever its successes and failures, the war on terror was only one piece in the mosaic of a "new American century" that neoconservatives held dear. In their Middle East strategy, the war on terror meshed well with calls for reform, which required the overthrow of Saddam Hussein's regime and the creation of a democratic, pro-American Iraq. Once that solid foundation was in place, the Bush administration planned to erect the two pillars of a grand structure for the region: security for Israel and protection of the world's oil supply. The war against terror, from its inception, was in many ways a hostage to this larger aim.

5

Saudi Arabia in the Eye of the Storm

In the days following September 11, America and the world struggled to absorb the news that fifteen of the nineteen hijackers had been Saudi Arabian nationals. Meanwhile, an emergency evacuation was taking place: one hundred and forty of the kingdom's subjects residing in the United States, most of them members of Saudi Arabia's extended ruling family or the Bin Laden family, were flown home. Three years later, the U.S. news media were still wondering about the privileges granted these flights, some of which were authorized on September 13, when most commercial and private planes were banned from U.S. airspace. None of the departing passengers seem to have gone through careful security checks, although the country had just suffered the most devastating attack in its history.

The congressional report on the events of September 11, submitted in December 2002 and published the following July, included twenty-eight blank pages classified as secret intelligence. When rumors flew in Washington that this material incriminated Saudi Arabia, Prince Bandar bin Sultan—ambassador to Washington and a favorite of the press corps, as well as a hunting companion of President Bush Sr.—requested that the censored pages be made public so that he could mount a defense. President George W.

Bush refused the request. The most adamant anti-Saudi lobbies needed no further evidence that the Bushes were bailing out a long-term business partner: the ruling family of Saud.

Beyond such polemics, the September 11 attacks served to reveal the unusual nature of U.S.–Saudi relations, shedding light on the ambiguities while leaving the murkiest details unclear. The post-9/11 evacuation marked the end of an era that began with promises exchanged on Valentine's Day, 1945, between President Franklin D. Roosevelt and King Abd Aziz Ibn Saud aboard the USS *Quincy*, moored in the Suez Canal's bitter lakes. By giving his political seal of approval to the enterprising American firms that had obtained concessions from the royal family to develop its oil fields, FDR established U.S. hegemony over a tribal kingdom that had previously been a vassal of Great Britain. He pledged U.S. military support to counter any threat to the joint—indeed, inextricable—interests of Aramco, the "free world," and the Saudi dynasty. This promise amounted to a guarantee of survival for a fragile, heterogeneous kingdom whose very existence had been declared official only in 1932. The entanglements of oil, West, and local monarchy tightened the Saudi–U.S. imbroglio; September 11 sliced through that Gordian knot.

For over half a century, this marriage of convenience gave both partners considerable freedom to develop their individual interests. On the Saudi side, tolerance for a sect of Islam practiced by various desert tribes evolved into a mania for Wahhabism. On the American side, concern for the beleaguered new nation of Israel gradually made Israeli security a linchpin of American foreign policy. As long as the Soviet Union threatened, each side forgave the other these indulgences, despite periods of tension. One such period began with the October 1973 War. Following the initial success of the Arab military offensive against Israel, an airlift provided the United States' embattled ally with weapons. In response, Saudi Arabia and other petroleum-exporting countries embargoed shipments of oil to the West. From that moment, petroleum became a political weapon wielded by Gulf-state producers, who made billions of dollars in inflated revenues during the following decade.

As fabulous wealth accrued to the dynasties and military regimes of the region, resentment festered among social classes excluded from petroleum dividends. The Islamist expansion of the 1980s was one major consequence of this disparity in wealth. But instead of clamping down on expressions of dissatisfaction, the Saudi dynasty sought to channel the frustration of activists into the Afghan jihad against the Red Army. This strategy posed no immediate threat to those in power, and it offered a welcome opportunity to repair Saudi–U.S. relations after the quarrels over oil and Israel that had kept them at odds in the 1970s.

With the enthusiastic assent of neoconservatives in the Reagan White House, Wahhabism was elevated to the status of a liberation theology—one that would free the region of communism. Washington and Riyadh, reunited through their shared anathema for the Soviet Union, renewed the vows they had made on February 14, 1945. What did it matter if one of the parties called the warriors freedom fighters while the other called them mujahedeen? When the Soviet Union dissolved in 1991, conservatives on both sides, who had coexisted comfortably as long as they fought a mutual enemy, turned on their partner with surprising virulence. Still, the original contract did not dissolve. As long as Washington considered Riyadh to be a swing producer in the global oil market, capable of influencing barrel prices, and as long as Saudi Arabia saw the U.S. military as the best guarantor of its survival against such rogue states as Iraq and Iran, the alliance would hold.

Perhaps more crucial than these geopolitical considerations, however, were private interests that predated the meeting between Roosevelt and Ibn Saud. The primary beneficiaries of the deal struck on the *Quincy* were not the two states concerned but, on one side, the shareholders in the American companies that had discovered oil in 1932 under the desert and built Dhahran's American colony on the eastern coast of the peninsula, and, on the other side, the Saud family's private treasury, which previously had been dependent on meager, unpredictable revenues from the pilgrimage to Mecca and subsidies from Whitehall but now tapped oil revenues directly before they flowed into the national coffers. For obvious reasons, these transactions did not show up on any public ledger, but observers have estimated that approximately five percent of total revenues are diverted to the dynasty's many princes. In 2003, the kingdom produced 8.866 million barrels a day, at an average selling price of $27.39. To that must be added all the commissions paid upon the signing of a contract.

Such unprecedented public and private wealth flowing into the kingdom allowed massive purchases of U.S. weaponry that financed state-of-the-art military R&D, crucial to Albert Wohlstetter's and the neocons' vision. Highways, public buildings, and other infrastructure, sometimes in association with the American giant Bechtel, made the Bin Laden Group rich. Its founder, Muhammad (Osama's father), became the king of concrete in Saudi Arabia thanks to an exclusive license he procured from the king to expand and restore the Great Mosque in Mecca and its environs. Muhammad died in 1967 in a plane crash over the mountainous province of Asir, while he was overseeing the construction of spectacular works along Highway 15—a road that winds between villages perched high on the mountainside, where the principal Saudi participants in the September 11 attacks were born.

As the complex web of financial interests and ideological solidarity between the United States and Saudi Arabia thickened in the 1980s, recruitment centers for the Afghan jihad opened up on American university campuses. Islamist student associations welcomed salafist preachers and activists of the Muslim Brothers from the Middle East, and they set up the movement's first English-language websites. Immigration laws favoring applicants from Muslim countries turned the United States into an Islamist haven where authorities imposed few restrictions on radical political movements. By contrast, in other "lands of unbelief," mainly in Europe, some activists were resorting to violence to press their cause, and governments were reacting with crackdowns and repression. While new mosques, financed mainly with Saudi money, were being erected in many European cities, terrorism of Middle Eastern origin, under the banner of Shiite jihad, claimed its first victims in France.

If Allah's sun seemed to be rising over the West, the principal reason can be traced back to a group of religious teachers active in Saudi Arabia two decades earlier, whose brand of Islam would eventually spread among Sunni Muslims worldwide. In the melting pot of Arabia during the 1960s, local clerics trained in the Wahhabite tradition joined with activists and militants affiliated with the Muslim Brothers who had been exiled from the neighboring countries of Egypt, Syria, and Iraq—then allies of Moscow. This blend of traditionalists and modern Islamist militants served the kingdom's interests well at first, because it countered the threat of a "progressive," pro-Soviet Islam—the brand preached at Al Azhar University in Egypt during the Nasser regime. But eventually this volatile mixture would explode in the Saudis' hands.

The phenomenon of Osama bin Laden and his associates cannot be understood outside this hybrid tradition. It is the offspring—monstrous, natural, or legitimate, depending on one's point of view—of the marriage between local Wahhabism and international Islamist activism, facilitated at the highest echelons by the complicit mediation of the United States and Saudi Arabia.

WAHHABISM IS A CORPUS of doctrines, but also a set of attitudes and behavior, derived from the teachings of a particularly severe religious reformist who lived in central Arabia in the mid-eighteenth century. Muhammad bin Abdul Wahhab was a contemporary of the European Enlightenment and the French Revolution, but it would be difficult to imagine two more irreconcilable points of view. Two centuries later, their ideological heirs continue to clash on such improbable battlefields as the schools of the French Republic. In these institutions—offshoots of the Enlightenment— the presence of young women in veils is the contemporary manifestation of Wahhabism's astonishing momentum.

Abdul Wahhab's specific intellectual contribution to Islamic theology is not very significant, and his disciples reject the term "Wahhabite," which was originally created by the movement's detractors. They prefer "salafist," which evokes their effort to imitate their "pious forefathers" *(salaf)*, companions of the Prophet who led an exemplary life. Abdul Wahhab made his mark by teaching the vigorous implementation of injunctions pronounced by medieval jurists, of whom the best known is Ibn Taymiyya (1263–1328). Starting in the 1950s, religious institutions in Saudi Arabia published and disseminated new editions of Ibn Taymiyya's works for free throughout the world, financed by petroleum royalties. These works have been cited widely: by Abd al-Salam Faraj, the spokesperson for the group that assassinated Egyptian President Anwar Sadat in 1981; in GIA tracts calling for the massacre of "infidels" during the Algerian civil war in the 1990s; and today on Internet sites exhorting Muslim women in the West to wear veils as a religious obligation.

Ibn Taymiyya and Abdul Wahhab counseled the strictest possible application of sharia in the most minuscule aspects of daily life and the use of coercion on subjects who did not conform to dogma. As Wahhabism began to exert its influence, a religious militia, the *mutawwaa*—bearded men armed with cudgels (and, today, riding in shiny SUVs)—was organized in Saudi Arabia to close down shops and offices at prayer times five times a day. Similarly, the Taliban's vice and virtue police, feared by foreigners and Afghans alike, used violence to "command good and forbid evil" when they reigned over Kabul. These militias were also responsible for applying "Islamic penalties"—stoning adulterous women, beheading criminals, amputating the limbs of thieves—in public squares or sports stadiums. In a macabre replay of the circus games in ancient Rome, crowds gathered to watch the spectacle of spurting blood.

Independent reasoning and critical thinking are abhorrent to this school of thought, which always sees heresy lurking. Individual reflection is, by definition, an interloper between Allah's injunctions and the believer's duty to obey them. Wahhabism prefers to seek the solutions to current problems in books and in the literal implementation of the unimpeachable corpus of sacred text, divine revelation, and the sacrosanct tradition of the Prophet— the supreme incarnation of Islamic virtue, who must inspire automatic imitation on the part of the true believer. Because the sacred texts, revealed fourteen centuries ago, cannot provide clear replies to contemporary questions, Wahhabism places utter faith in the words and deeds attributed to the Prophet, even those disqualified as apocryphal by a consensus of the ulema, based on their analysis and collating of the sources. These paradigmatic sayings *(hadith)*, however improbable, are infinitely preferable, according to the disciples of Ibn Taymiyya and Abdul Wahhab, to the intrinsic weakness of human reason. The *hadith* specialist Nasr al-Din al-Albani, who died in 1999, took undiscriminating reverence for *hadith* to its logical extreme. Legal scholars hesitate to attribute unsound *hadith* to the Prophet and have therefore marginalized them in Muslim intellectual history. The Wahhabites, on the contrary, use the Prophet's sacred example to justify, for example, behavior motivated by extreme hatred, such as exhortations to denounce "infidels"—Christians, Jews, Hindus—but also "bad" Muslims.

Such denunciation—in Arabic, *takfir*, to condemn as an apostate—was practiced with unbridled fanaticism soon after the alliance concluded in 1744–1745 between Abdul Wahhab and the tribal chief Muhammad bin Saud, who ruled over the oasis of Diriyya (near today's Riyadh) in the Nejd, the peninsula's central desert province. (In Arabic, *nejd* is any area where water disappears into the sand.) A Hobbesian state of perpetual war pitted Bedouin tribes against one another for control of the scarce resources that could stave off starvation. In exchange for Bin Saud's adherence to the strict dogma of Ibn Taymiyya, Abdul Wahhab offered to consecrate the Saudi tribe's raids on neighboring oases by renaming those raids *jihad*—holy war to promote, by the sword, Islam's triumph over unbelief. In place of the instinctive fight for survival and appetite for lucre, Abdul Wahhab substituted *fath*, the "opening" or conquest of a vast territory through religious zeal.

From the booty of every raid, Saudi warriors put a part aside for Allah and those who served Him, following the canonical rules of jihad, which dictate the distribution of spoils and regulate their management. In the space of two decades, jihad had conquered the entire Nejd, followed by the eastern coast, a rich source of pearls (and of a few naphtha deposits, used to patch up the pearl divers' and pirates' boats when nothing better was available). When the cities of Mecca and Medina succumbed to Saudi domination in 1803, the pilgrimage and its material and symbolic resources fell under the Wahhabites' control.

The force of the Wahhabite word transformed belligerent Bedouins into mujahedeen for whom devotion to the *umma* transcended tribal affiliations. This Wahhabite epic replicated the feats of the Prophet's companions as they rode across the Arabian peninsula at the birth of Islam, and provided an adventurous myth with which young Saudis in religious schools could identify. Later, the heroic conquest of the peninsula by the book and the sword would be invoked to indoctrinate others via television, the Internet, and Webcams. The Wahhabite-Saudi alliance thus brought together forces that had been separate and mutually destructive. It was the catalyst for a rigorous community, the paragon of the mounted "vanguard" conjured up by Bin Laden in Al Qaeda's propaganda and by the vivid title of Ayman al-Zawahiri's manifesto, *Knights under the Prophet's Banner.*

The founding myth would be replayed yet again in the Afghan jihad, the Algerian civil war, and the jihad in Chechnya. Great feats from these battlefields were broadcast to Muslim workers on the outskirts of Western cities and to the dispossessed in the slums of North Africa, the Middle East, the Indian subcontinent, and Southeast Asia. They would also reach the air-conditioned compounds where young men, spoiled by the oil rent, whiled away their time dreaming of a virile, frugal, spiritual ideal.

While Abdul Wahhab was alive, his strong personality assured the dominance of his family over the Al Saud clan. After Abdul Wabbab's death in 1792, relations between his progeny—the Al Sheikh clan—and the Al Saud clan vacillated. In times of stability, the dynasty generally managed to eclipse the preachers; in exchange for revenue that allowed them to live well and exert their spiritual authority, the preachers legitimized the rulers' authority in Allah's name. Whenever young zealots dared to preach revolt against a powerful king, he usually liquidated them. But during times when the dynasty was weakened by crisis, the religious leaders took advantage and extended their dominion over education, morality, and the social and political structure. Their extremism, with its antisocial excesses, would then become yet one more threat to the stability of the Saudi government.

The kingdom of Saud was overrun twice by external forces. At the beginning of the nineteenth century, after their conquest of the holy cities, the Wahhabites reorganized the pilgrimage to Mecca. This caused great distress to the Ottoman sultan in Istanbul, whose caravans were stopped and pillaged and whose pilgrims were harassed if they refused to conform to Wahhabite austerity. The sultan ordered his viceroy in Cairo to reclaim the holy cities. Muhammad Ali's troops landed in 1811, crushing the kingdom of Saud and, in 1818, laid waste to the oasis of Diriyya, the dynasty's birthplace. The Egyptian invaders killed the local Wahhabite clerics and deported the ruler, Abdullah bin Saud, to Istanbul, where he was beheaded.

An attempt to reestablish the Wahhabite state later in the nineteenth century ended in confusion. In 1902 Abd Aziz Ibn Saud, who lived in exile in Kuwait, started his conquest anew. He brought his house to power in a manner comparable to the founding of the first state in the eighteenth century. Once again, an alliance between the ruling family and Wahhabite preachers was the key to success: belligerent, rapacious tribes were brought into line through the creation, around 1912, of a religious militia, the Ikhwan ("the brothers").

The Ikhwan were former Bedouins who could be mobilized at a moment's notice and bivouacked in farming settlements that served as training camps. These camps were called *hijar* (or Hegirae), a term suggestive of the Prophet's Flight to Medina, where he settled while fighting the infidel Meccans. Wahhabite doctrine found in the reiteration of the Prophet's experience a crucial symbolic resource. During the initial phase of the Saudi conquest, the preachers invoked Allah's name to inflame the Ikhwan's rage against all the rival tribes: the Shiite farmers of the eastern coast, the mountain tribes of Asir, and the cosmopolitan inhabitants of the holy cities, then under Hashemite rule. They portrayed these peoples as infidels against whom jihad was permissible, whose blood could be legally spilled, and whose goods and women were legitimate spoils of war.

Still, there was a difference between the jihad of the 1910–1920 period and its forerunner in the eighteenth century: the presence of the British. Standing at Ibn Saud's side, Captain William Henry Irvine Shakespear, sent by the India Office, discreetly encouraged the family's territorial appetites. And in 1924–25 Whitehall helped the Saudis conquer Mecca and Medina by expelling the Hashemite dynasty, whose pan-Arab ambitions had been extolled, in vain, by T. E. Lawrence, the legendary Lawrence of Arabia.

With the holy cities once again under Saudi control, the seesaw of power tilted back from the preachers to the royal family. But for the Ikhwan, the presence of British infidels on Islamic land was a greater abomination than the presence of "bad Muslims" in the holy cities, and so they rose up in revolt. Pragmatism and the lessons of history led Ibn Saud to exterminate these rebels in 1929, with help from the Royal Air Force's bombardiers. The Wahhabite preachers, deprived of their most enthusiastic disciples, lost influence with the royal family, which relegated them to roles as educators and monitors of public morality—a move that would prove to have far-reaching political consequences.

For many lesser preachers, the memory of the Ikhwan's annihilation remained vivid. Though compelled to rally behind a dynasty that fed and clothed them while allowing them a degree of influence, they stood ready to fan the embers of religious rebellion against the royal family's corruption. Jihad was prohibited on Saudi territory from the 1930s onward, however, on the presumption that Saudi Arabia, which adhered to sharia, was the perfect Islamic state. Yet as an integral part of the kingdom's founding myth, jihad as practiced by the Ikhwan between 1912 and the 1920s was still taught in schools. It appeared in textbooks that made no effort to impose historical distance, and the young Saudis who absorbed this epic adventure dreamed of imitating it within their own lifetimes. Thus, a gap opened up between the ideal of jihad as taught by religious instructors and the reality of a state controlled by a ruling dynasty that forbade jihad at home. The royal family would attempt to reconcile religious teaching with state practice by projecting jihad outward, toward foreign arenas, starting with Afghanistan in the 1980s.

In 1964 the kingdom's most efficient monarch, Faisal, came to power. Recognized as the intellectual among Ibn Saud's sons, he had traveled widely, lived abroad, and educated his children in English and French. His ability to combine extensive and detailed knowledge of the international milieu with extreme personal piety allowed him to establish his religious legitimacy while bypassing the blessing of the Al Sheikh preachers. Under Faisal's rule, modernization of the nation's infrastructure went hand in hand with a public discourse emphasizing austerity and religious devotion. The 1973 oil embargo conferred upon King Faisal an aura of resistance to the United States in the Arab and Muslim world. Even if

that aura was more theater than reality, it worried the U.S. administration enough that, as the October War unfolded, plans were
made in Washington to station troops in Saudi Arabia, where they
could take control of the oil fields by force if necessary.

King Faisal was assassinated in 1975 by one of his young cousins.
The assassin, who was promptly beheaded, took the secret of his
motivation to his grave, but his action exposed weaknesses that
would force the dynasty to rely more heavily on the Wahhabite
ulema. In the wake of the oil embargo, Saudi Arabia was drowning
in petro-dollars. Its revenues swelled by a factor of twenty-five in
seven years, rising from $4.3 billion in 1973 to $22.6 billion in 1974,
to $102.2 in 1980, before falling again to $21.2 billion in 1986. (In
2003, revenues would rise again above $85 billion.) Yet disparities
in wealth among the different classes only grew wider during that
period. To prevent implosion from the weight of such rapid and
extensive change, the kingdom desperately needed a means of social control. King Khalid, Faisal's half brother and successor, was
forced to turn to the Wahhabite clerics, who would demand a stiff
price for their loyalty.

The Islamic Revolution in neighboring Iran, which resulted
from mismanagement of a similar boom in crude oil revenues,
sounded a warning bell. In February 1979 the Ayatollah Khomeini
returned to rule Tehran, and he was no friend of the royal family.
The following December the Red Army invaded Afghanistan. But
most important, on November 20, 1979, several hundred radical
young Saudi Wahhabites, joined by foreign Islamists, took over the
Great Mosque in Mecca, Islam's holiest site, and held thousands of
pilgrims hostage in the sacred enclosure.

The leader of the uprising, Juhayman al-Utaybi, was an activist
who had fallen under the influence of Sheikh Abd al-Aziz bin
Baz, dean of the Saudi Grand Ulema Authority. The group made
another of its members, Muhammad al-Qahtani, the mahdi—a

"messiah" who, according to tradition, appears to renew Islam once every hundred years. Utaybi and Qahtani were from tribes with several hundred thousand members each, occupying a territory between the central deserts where the Saud dynasty was born and the coastal region where the two holy cities lie. Many of the Ikhwan's warriors had emerged from their ranks; perhaps as a consequence, these two tribes had been marginalized as oil revenues were distributed throughout the kingdom.

Tribal members who nurtured resentment against the royal family for these slights began to consult with Sheikh bin Baz, who had launched his career in the 1940s by reprimanding King Ibn Saud for allowing American infidels to exploit oil and agricultural resources in the Nejd. Bin Baz based his criticism on the Prophetic *hadith* to "expel the Jews and the Christians from the Arabian peninsula, until only Muslims remain there." (This saying of the Prophet would also become Al Qaeda's motto.)

Today, some "moderate" clerics, like Sheikh Yusuf al-Qaradawi, interpret that saying with considerable circumspection. Qaradawi, who lives in Qatar, surrounded by non-Muslims who provide crucial labor power in the emirate's oil fields and who work for Al Jazeera, where he hosts the weekly Islamic talk show *Al Sharia wal-Haya (Islamic Law and Life)*, explained to me that the term "Arabian peninsula" should be interpreted as the sacred enclosure or forbidden area *(haram)* of Mecca and Medina, where non-Muslims cannot go.

Bin Baz's fatwa, pronounced in the 1940s and included in a collection still on sale in the kingdom in 2001, interpreted the *hadith* more literally:

> It is illicit to employ a non-Muslim servant, whether male or female, or a non-Muslim driver, or a non-Muslim worker in the Arabian Gulf, for the Prophet—peace

and blessings be upon him—commanded that all Jews and Christians be expelled, and that only Muslims remain. He did that at the moment of his death, when he ordered that all polytheists be expelled from the Arabian Gulf, because the presence of infidels, male or female, poses a danger to Muslims, their beliefs, their morality, and their children's education. For that reason, it must be forbidden.

Summoned to a royal audience and ordered to recant, since in fact the Prophet himself had employed foreigners, Bin Baz let it be known that his recantation was without conviction. He paid for his insolence with a prison term, but he was set free after a discussion with the monarch, who persuaded him that publicly expressed dissent threatened the stability of the Islamic state.

From this episode, Bin Baz derived a reputation for independence and was sought after not only by the ruling family—as a person who could exert influence over the dissidents and could pass them conciliatory messages at critical moments—but also by the radical Wahhabite insurgents, who would praise his courage, revere his knowledge, and count on his tolerance toward them. Named dean of the Grand Ulema Authority, which established religious norms on all matters, he was eclipsed for a time by Faisal's personal religious charisma. But after Faisal's assassination, he took advantage of King Khalid's lesser legitimacy to increase his own influence. When the king asked him to discredit the rebels who occupied the Great Mosque in November 1979 (and who were dislodged only when elite squads of French police were called in), he condemned the rebellion—since it brought *fitna*, anarchy and discord, to a Muslim country—but he refused to pass a sentence of apostasy on the insurgents, among whom were several of his disciples. Sixty-four rebels, including Juhayman al-Utaybi, were beheaded in January 1980.

This crisis came as the Muslim world was plunged into chaos by the Ayatollah's call for overthrow of the Great Satan's (the United States') Saudi Arabian lackeys; by Saddam Hussein's invasion of Iran; and by the jihad heating up in Afghanistan. King Khalid and his successor in 1982, King Fahd, were forced by these circumstances to meet the ulema's demands in exchange for their support. Austere standards of public morality were enforced, and social life became increasingly difficult, especially for women. For the government, these concessions to the most retrograde voices within the ulema seemed politically painless in the short term; but in fact they drastically increased the ulema's hold on education, allowing them to go far beyond the strict dissemination of religious teaching and indulge in unbridled indoctrination. Funds set aside for Islamization and managed by the Wahhabites grew as fast as oil revenues and were not subjected to cuts when crude prices fell in the mid-1980s. Bearded preachers who formerly excoriated television and radio as vectors of debauchery and perdition were now permanent fixtures on programs broadcast throughout the peninsula, where they expressed their views freely and enjoined believers to obey them or face unimaginably horrible punishment in this world and the next.

In Mecca, at the Islamic university of Umm al-Qura, founded in 1949, a young generation of zealous preachers was educated during the 1980s by the most intransigent of these clerics and a few foreign Muslim Brothers. During the 1990s, those preachers spread throughout the peninsula and the world, from Muslim neighborhoods on the outskirts of European cities to Indonesia's rice paddies. Transplanted without adaptation outside the kingdom's specific context and generously subsidized, these pious salafists pitted themselves against infidels wherever they were found, multiplying the strict criteria by which proper believers were defined and advocating jihad against anyone who sought to depart from their dogma.

Within the kingdom itself, a third of the school day at the elementary level was given over to religious education. The ratio fell to a fourth during the middle years of grade school, and ranged between fifteen and thirty-five percent in high school. At the university level, nearly half of the social science curriculum was made up of religious subjects; the proportion was a fifth in applied science, petroleum studies, or medicine. A few years ago, a young Shiite from the eastern part of the kingdom, having finished school with a brilliant record, applied to medical school. His examiners guessed his religious identity and, during the entrance interview, asked him to summarize and comment upon the last Friday sermon he had heard. When he could not do so, since Shiites do not attend the Friday sermons of Wahhabite preachers, he was rejected. Eventually, the decision was overturned through recourse to higher authorities, but this type of incident, which has no equivalent elsewhere, reveals the ulema's exceptional influence over society's core values, as expressed in the education dispensed to younger generations.

The rise of salafist influence in the peninsula cannot be separated from the population explosion of the 1980s. Among wealthy beneficiaries of the 1970s hike in crude prices, family size skyrocketed, while the state developed an official pro-birth policy. It had long published inflated population statistics, fearing that a low population and fabulous wealth would tempt the Saudis' overpopulated, underprivileged neighbors in Yemen or even Egypt to immigrate. Even worse, it might encourage notions of equity, which might force elites to share their wealth with other needy

Muslim countries. The solution was for Saudis themselves to produce more children. The ulema encouraged polygamy, in a literal application of the sharia's precepts.

These factors came together in the early 1980s to create an astonishing population explosion. Fertility rates peaked at 8.26 children per Saudi woman, and the birth rate of 50 births per thousand people approached world records. In 1981, thanks to oil revenues, per capita gross domestic product (GDP) in Saudi Arabia was about the same as in the United States—$28,600. During the mid-decade downturn in the oil market, living standards declined, and by 2000 the per capita GDP in the kingdom stood at under $7,000, while in the United States it had risen to over $35,000. Even though the fertility rate had also been cut almost in half over that time (at 4.37 children per Saudi woman in 2000), because of the baby boom of the early 1980s, 600,000 young adults were arriving on the job market—or swelling the ranks of jihad—each year. By the beginning of the new century, the Saudi population reached fifteen million nationals and five million foreigners.

Wide swings in population and wealth are nothing new to the peninsula. In the past, the vagaries of rainfall have been responsible for the greatest upheavals. On rare occasions when torrential rains swelled the riverbeds and groundwater reserves, causing the desert to bloom and creating green pastures for grazing sheep, well-fed tribes experienced phenomenal population growth. But these extra mouths to feed became a curse when resources were exhausted and water sources ran dry. Driven by hunger, tribesmen from the peninsula launched raids on neighboring lands, crossing the Red Sea to ravage North Africa, Arabizing the peoples they conquered, and pushing them toward the least fertile lands. In the Upper Egyptian countryside, inhabitants remember the most recent conquests by Saudi tribesmen, and the peasantry differentiates between "Egyptian" and "Arab" villages. Tradition prohibits inter-marriage between these two groups, although nothing in their appearance serves to distinguish one from the other.

In North Africa, invasions led by the Hilali tribes in the eleventh century lived on in the Berbers' collective memory as a case of forced Arabization, of flight from the fertile plains to the steep mountainsides of Kabylia, the Rif, or the Atlas, where the invaders' dromedaries refused to go. But in the fertile imagination of desert Bedouins, raids such as these became the stuff of legends. The re-telling of these raids, along with doctrinal exhortations from salafist teachers and the sermons of the Wahhabi ulema, may have fed the frenzy that pushed thousands of young Saudi Arabians to leave their native land for jihad in Afghanistan, Bosnia, and Chechnya.

LEFT TO ITS own devices, Wahhabism probably would not have prospered worldwide in the last quarter of the twentieth century, even with the assistance of oil revenues. Adapted to an arid tribal ecosystem, it lacked the intellectual tools necessary to take on the challenges of the modern world, or even to impose its dogma within established schools of Islamic thought, which held it in low regard until the 1960s. Compared with the richness of Muslim civilizations, their renowned dynasties, the mighty empires to which they had given birth, the flowering of arts and sciences they had nurtured for fourteen centuries, from Cordoba to Samarkand, Fez to Delhi, Istanbul to Damascus and Cairo, Isfahan to Baghdad, the modern-day peninsula where Islam had first been revealed was, within the great sweep of Islamic history, forgettable.

By the early 1950s, Wahhabite Islam had triumphed over "heresies" within Saudi Arabia, but it seemed politically maladapted to reach beyond this closed society. It had vanquished the Shiites of Hasa and the Sunnis of the Red Sea coast, who adhered to the liberal Shafiite interpretation of Islam, which held reasoning in high esteem. These Sunnis also harbored many mystical brotherhoods—Sufi organizations that Wahhabism abhorred as heretical because they worshiped holy figures alongside Allah. When King Ibn Saud died in 1953, Wahhabite homogenization in Saudi Arabia seemed, on the surface, almost complete.

The challenge came from without. In 1952, on the other side of the Red Sea (a channel of communication and influence easily crossed), Nasser's socialist regime came to power. The Saudi authorities and their American partners began to worry. The Saudis were particularly concerned by the gradual transformation of Al Azhar, Cairo's thousand-year-old Islamic university which enjoyed unparalleled prestige throughout the Muslim world. It was becoming a progressive institution for training doctors of Islamic law, including young Saudis who went to study there at a time when the kingdom's universities were still in their embryonic phase and when Nasser's prestige was at its zenith. In October 1954 an assassination attempt on Nasser, who was making a speech in Alexandria, was attributed to the Muslim Brothers. Their leaders were hanged, and cadres who were not imprisoned were forced to flee the country. Many found refuge in Saudi Arabia, and some in Kuwait. They were welcomed by the Saudi rulers and, especially in Jeddah, by a society in which many marriage ties linked prominent families on the two banks of the Red Sea.

The arrival of the Egyptian exiles, most of whom were from educated, pious, often multilingual families and were familiar with relatively open societies, was a blessing in the short term. Their antisocialist credentials gave them access to positions of rank and responsibility in the kingdom, on condition that they refrain from any political or religious proselytizing. The first wave of Egyptian refugees, who arrived in the 1950s, was joined during the following decade by an influx of Syrians and Iraqis, on the run from Baath regimes that had seized power in Damascus and Baghdad. Then yet another contingent of Egyptians arrived, fleeing a campaign of repression against the Muslim Brothers which culminated in Sayyid Qutb's execution by hanging in the summer of 1966.

Along with these strictly political refugees came ambitious young men attracted by rumors of oil wealth and access to employment through affluent but conservative Islamic institutions. Religious Palestinians who were uncomfortable with Arab nationalism and the left-wing politics of the PLO immigrated as well. Abdallah Azzam, a Palestinian who would mentor Osama bin Laden in Jeddah before going on to lead the Afghan jihad, was the most famous of them. Algerians who opposed Boumedienne's socialist regime also gathered in salafist circles. One of them, Abu Bakr al-Jazairi, was the author of a salafist manual, *The Muslim's Path*, which became a best-seller and could be found piled on tables in Islamist libraries across North Africa and Europe. Thousands of other Islamists converged in Saudi Arabia, for all of these reasons and others.

They staffed the offices of the Muslim World League, which opened in Mecca in 1962 to oppose Nasser's reform of Al Azhar University. They found jobs at the World Assembly of Muslim Youth, headquartered in Jeddah, which sought to federate Islamist youth organizations throughout the world, through internships, meetings, and charity work in Africa that would rival the Christian NGOs. They cooperated with Muslim Brothers in Kuwait, who had established a political party, the Association for Social Reform (Jamaat al-Islah al-Ijtimai) and, more importantly, a weekly newspaper, *Al Mujtama (Society)*, to serve as the movement's international mouthpiece. They joined the International Federation of Islamic Student Organizations, which translated texts into every language spoken throughout the *umma* and published the essential works of Sayyid Qutb, Sayyid Abul Ala Mawdudi, and Hassan al-Banna—a homogeneous corpus of doctrine.

The movement's international activists, beneficiaries of America's tolerance for anti-communists of any stripe, circulated freely among these groups. One of the most discreet and most active of these militants was Said Ramadan, an Egyptian refugee in Geneva and Banna's son-in-law. His sons, Hani and Tariq Ramadan, French-speaking Swiss citizens, went on to become star preachers, appearing on television talk shows from Geneva to Casablanca and Paris to Dakar, during the first years of the twenty-first century.

The Muslim Brothers grafted their political interests onto the Saudi oil pipeline, even though Kuwait offered them greater freedom of movement than they enjoyed in the kingdom. Muslim Brothers residing in Saudi Arabia rose to international influence alongside the dynasty by adding intellectual value to Islamist thought at a time when Wahhabism was not exportable. Through the international organizations they ran for the dynasty and those they controlled directly, the Brothers quietly carried out their own program of global expansion, sending their message into the West, where they hoped to win the hearts of young Muslim immigrants who had settled there.

Within the kingdom itself, the Muslim Brothers obeyed the prohibition on proselytizing to Saudi subjects. Still, they contributed to discussion circles and frequented the salons held by princes and wealthy commoners in enormous rooms lined with highly wrought gilt armchairs that Egyptian wits lampooned as "Louis Faruq." In these gatherings, ideas and information circulated freely; business deals were concluded informally; careers took off or foundered; and individual destinies were decided. Methodically but without fanfare, the Brothers took control of Saudi Arabia's intellectual life, publishing books that extended their influence among educators and generally making themselves politically useful while obeying the orders that kept them away from the pulpits.

In the late 1960s, two members of this movement began to expose younger generations of Saudis to the Muslim Brothers' influence, alongside Wahhabism's more traditional dogma. The first was the well-known writer Muhammad Qutb, brother of Sayyid Qutb, whom Nasser's regime had hanged in August 1966. The second was a Syrian, Mohammad Surur Zayn al-Abidin, known today on Islamist websites by the moniker Surur. His adversaries describe his disciples as Sururists and his ideas as Sururiyya.

Muhammad Qutb settled in Saudi Arabia after his release from an Egyptian jail in 1972. Sadat, Nasser's successor who became a friend of the United States, freed the Muslim Brothers so that they could serve as his allies against the left. Muhammad Qutb had not been active in the organization, but he had written a few books, the best-known of which was entitled *Jahiliyya in the Twenty-First Century*. The term evokes the period of "ignorance" that prevailed in Arabia before the revelation of Islam. His brother Sayyid had used *jahiliyya* as the criterion for judging the modern world, the benchmark against which to evaluate whether a country was truly Islamic or was just presenting a pious veneer.

Debates over the meaning of Sayyid Qutb's books were raging: the most radical of the jihad ideologues laid claim to his thought for their own agenda, while the mainstream Muslim Brothers rejected it as extremist. Muhammad Qutb endeavored to smooth away these differences by showing his readers that his adopted country of Saudi Arabia was certainly not among the states feigning to be Islamic and therefore was not damnable as *jahiliyya*. While advancing his brother's thinking, he attempted to preserve its place within the doctrine of the Muslim Brothers and distance it from the most violent interpretations promulgated by zealous young self-proclaimed Qutbists.

To that end, Muhammad arranged for the publication of new editions of Sayyid's books, especially *Signposts (Maalim fil-Tariq)*, which served as a manifesto for radical Islamism in the last quarter of the twentieth century. In going over his brother's texts and toning them down before handing them over to Mohamed al-Muallim, the head of the Lebanese-Saudi publishing house Dar al-Shorouk, Muhammad Qutb endeavored to reconcile the Muslim Brothers' doctrine with the salafism that prevailed in his host country. He also certified the authenticity of his edition on the Arab book market, where very different versions of *Signposts* had been published, some excising or emphasizing a given passage or chapter according to the aims of those dealing with the text. Authors' rights are flouted routinely in this market, and unauthorized editors do not hesitate to abridge, amend, and embroider—as I observe regularly when I thumb through pirated Arabic translations of my own books being sold on Cairo's sidewalks.

Muhammad Qutb's reputation and his family's famous name attracted young readers who sought a confrontation between Islam and *jahiliyya* and yearned for invigorating, modern ideas for their battle against secularism, socialism, and the West. Qutb found a job teaching at Mecca's Umm al-Qura University, and there he began to attract students seeking this kind of inspiration.

Highway 15, which links the poor, rocky region of Asir to Jeddah, goes through Mecca. One of Muhammad Qutb's most famous students, Safar al-Hawali, took that road out of Hawala, a town belonging to the Ghamdi tribe. Born in 1950, Hawali wrote a master's thesis on (or, rather, against) secularism, and in 1986 defended his dissertation under Muhammad Qutb's supervision. His defense was so impressive that the latter declared in public that the student had surpassed his teacher. He became one of the two main figures of the *sahwa*, or Islamist awakening, which mingled radical Wahhabism with Sayyid Qutb's ideas. Hawali was already famous in 1985, however, thanks to the school he led every Sunday at a mosque near Jeddah University following afternoon prayers. Crowds of students from the kingdom's coastal regions flocked to receive his instruction, and cassette recordings of his teachings began to spread throughout the peninsula.

The other figure, whose name is always associated with Hawali's and whose life would follow a parallel course until the turn of the century, was Salman al-Awda. Born in 1955 to an affluent family near the city of Burayda—the main urban agglomeration in Qasim, a vast oasis in the northern Nejd—he was known for his religious severity and had grown up in the environment where Mohammad Surur taught. Surur was born in 1938 in the Hawran in southern Syria, on the border with Jordan—"an artificial border in the heart of the *umma*, traced by French and British colonialism at the time of the Sykes-Picot deal," as he reminded me during a 2003 interview in London, where he lives in exile. The Sykes-Picot Agreement, signed in 1916, divided up the Middle East into French and British mandates. Asked if this region corresponded to the Jabal Druze, he expostulated: "It is a region cultivated by Arab tribes that came from Iraq. Jabal Druze is just a name invented by the French Mandate to divide Arabs and Muslims." Already a Muslim Brother militant as a teenager, he studied law at Damascus University but left before obtaining his degree.

In 1965, when he was twenty-seven, two years after the secular, socialist Baath Party had consolidated its grip on Syria and at a time when the Muslim Brothers were targets both as a religious organization and as reactionaries, Surur fled to Burayda. He spent eight years there, teaching religion and related subjects at "scientific institutes" that combined primary education with night classes for adults and which did not require that their instructors hold a doctorate. He was thus able to extend his influence simultaneously over two different generations. In 1968, he left the Muslim Brothers and established his own path. He adhered to a salafism consistent with the Muslim Brothers' political ambition of seizing power and enforcing sharia through state authority. In 1973 he was asked to leave the kingdom for reasons he will not talk about even today. His writing, which is highly critical of the Wahhabite ulema's compromising attitude toward the royal family, is far more explicit.

Surur spent seven more years in Kuwait, during which he became an editor at *Al Mujtama*, the mouthpiece of the Muslim Brothers; he demonstrated thereby that he was still a fellow traveler. In 1984 he moved to London, where visitors to his semidetached house in northern London find a quiet man wearing a long gray beard and dressed in a Damascus-style jellaba over woolen long-johns, for protection against Britain's cold and humid weather—an attire typical of the salafists rather than the Muslim Brothers. He cordially invites his guests to take part in a Syrian meal. They eat seated on the floor, in the manner of the Prophet. In this peaceful context, it is difficult to understand the uproar his writings have aroused on the Internet. Surur does not remember having taught Salman al-Awda directly, but there is every reason to believe that Awda, who attended Burayda's scientific institutes as a teenager, was influenced by the mixture of salafism and the doctrine of the Muslim Brothers that Surur was trying out and that can be found in the thoughts and deeds of the *sahwa*'s young orator and activist.

This religious "awakening" of the first half of the 1980s was inspired by the attack on the Great Mosque in 1979, for which sixty-four insurgents were decapitated. Lesser rebels were encouraged to leave the kingdom immediately and quench their thirst for jihad in Afghanistan. Observers used the term "neo-salafist" to describe these spiritual heirs to Juhayman al-Utaybi, who took Wahhabite doctrine to its logical extreme by reviving the original violence that had simultaneously expanded the Saudi kingdom and religious advocacy. These neo-salafists were immune to the influence of the Muslim Brothers, particularly the Qutb brothers, who were not certified doctors of Islamic law and were therefore unqualified to pass judgment on society's core values. Later on, however, their stay in Afghanistan would forge bonds between these two traditions, especially after Osama bin Laden and Ayman al-Zawahiri joined forces in 1986.

While Saudi authorities executed or exiled those rebels who posed an immediate threat, it offered the remaining militants, ideologues, and preachers of the awakening considerable latitude. Safar al-Hawali and Salman al-Awda were the standard-bearers, but a plethora of young radicals—Ayid al-Qarni, Mohsen al-Awaji, Abd al-Aziz al-Qasim, and many others—were free to preach and write. Their words revealed as never before the influence of the Muslim Brothers and the Qutb brothers over an entire generation of young Saudis. The government, which had been careful to separate the Brothers from the kingdom's Wahhabite subjects, reversed course because neo-salafist extremism among its nationals had grown so strong. Neither King Khalid nor King Fahd had a reputation for piety sufficient to contain the movement solely on the strength of his exemplary behavior. In 1986 King Fahd even went so far as to replace the title "majesty" with the honorific "custodian of the two holy places" *(khadem al-haramayn)* in Mecca and Medina, but this did little to amplify the dynasty's religious legitimacy.

The royal family needed the *sahwa*'s support to maintain political control.

In return for buttressing the monarchy, these ideologues intensified their religious teaching in the schools and their exhortations on morality, emphasizing especially prohibitions aimed at the social life of women. This was in keeping with a pattern dating back to the alliance between the royal family and tribal clerics, in which the ulema occupy center stage in times of crisis and turn the situation to their own advantage. But in the 1980s iteration of this tradition, the religious leaders called upon by the royal family to reestablish moral order were not Wahhabite clerics but were rather *sahwa* militants whose belief system was a hybrid of salafism and Qutbist thought and whose allegiances lay outside the Saudi kingdom.

The government made this about-face for two reasons. First, the main danger encountered in 1979, when Juhayman al-Utaybi occupied the Great Mosque in Mecca, had been posed by extremist Wahhabites linked to the dean of the Grand Ulema Authority, Sheikh bin Baz (despite his assertions to the contrary). This brought the Wahhabite movement as a whole under some suspicion; and from the point of view of the dynasty, there was no harm in fostering a little competition, if only to encourage it to fall into line.

Second, the Iranian Revolution was igniting political passions across the region. Its discourse combined a traditional vocabulary, which emerged from the ancient Shiite corpus, with modern syntax, tinged with Third World values and anti-imperialist rhetoric. It was imperative that Saudi Islam come up with an equally modern argument, capable of countering the verbal assaults Tehran was launching on Riyadh, which the revolutionary mullahs portrayed as a lackey of the United States.

This task was all the more essential because the population explosion Saudi Arabia was undergoing had increased the ranks of the shabab—restless, dissatisfied young men thirsty for new ideas who no longer seemed content with the Wahhabites' effete preaching alone. A new vision was urgently needed to avoid the collapse of the social system under the pressure of so much wealth so disparately distributed. Failure to manage just this kind of political tension had swept away the shah of Iran.

In the decade following the events of 1979, therefore—the storming of the mosque in Mecca, the Iranian Revolution, and the Red Army's invasion of Afghanistan—the kingdom entered one of its recurrent phases of controlled re-Islamization. Public manifestations of piety multiplied, and a large portion of oil revenues was invested in what amounted to a politico-religious insurance policy. The most turbulent insurgents were evacuated to the Afghan war, and the young preachers of the *sahwa* were given free rein to wage a domestic war for Muslim minds.

Over the course of the 1980s, the monarchy's religious legitimacy rose because of its support for the ongoing Afghan jihad. The simultaneous waning of the Iranian Revolution relieved some of the pressure for rebellion from that quarter. At the high point of its influence, Tehran had managed to disrupt the pilgrimage to Mecca by fomenting demonstrations that left several hundred dead. But the mullahs' power had been weakened by Iran's eight-year war with Iraq, in which Saddam Hussein enjoyed the backing of the Arab monarchies and the West. Khomeini was forced to sign an armistice in June 1988, and he died the following year.

With its prospects looking up, the dynasty considered itself strong enough to tolerate the *sahwa* preachers. Then, on August 2, 1990, after his bloody war with Iran ended in a stalemate, Saddam Hussein invaded his neighbor to the south, Kuwait. This act of aggression brought Iraqi troops to the Saudi border, within range of the Eastern Province's oil fields. On August 7, King Fahd called in the debt that his father had negotiated with FDR on board the *Quincy* on February 14, 1945, by requesting that troops of the U.S.-led coalition be stationed in the kingdom to protect its vital interests.

This move stretched religious tensions within Saudi Arabia to the breaking point. Ideologues of the *sahwa*, who had been prose-lytizing among native Saudis with the consent of the dynasty, now dissented openly. The king urgently needed the Wahhabite clerics to sanction his initiative, which violated a widespread feeling (en-couraged by the government) that the kingdom should be an Is-lamic sanctuary and not a battlefield where infidel troops could roam at will. The Wahhabite establishment issued a fatwa approv-ing the decision, but these clerics demanded in return that the regime grant them new measures of social control in the name of Islam. With that exchange, the kingdom fell into bottomless Islamization.

But before the ulema pronounced their support for the king, an astonishing event took place. Prince Sultan, minister of defense and the king's half-brother, received Osama bin Laden, who had been unable to leave the kingdom since the beginning of 1990 when he was deprived of his passport. Bin Laden had come under suspicion of conspiracy following the mysterious assassination in Peshawar of Abdallah Azzam, the Palestinian jihad commander who had been one of the royal family's main contacts in the murky world of international jihad fighters. In his meeting with Prince Sultan, Bin Laden allegedly offered to man the Saudi border with his jihadist fighters, to face the armored divisions of the apostate Saddam Hussein (a reference to the Baath Party's secular ideology).

The most surprising aspect of this incident was not Prince Sul-tan's refusal of the offer—he was probably reluctant to entrust the kingdom's protection to shady jihadists, and dubious about their military prowess. The surprising fact is that the Saudi minister of defense, at a time of such grave crisis, should find the time to meet Bin Laden at all. Their failure to reach an agreement probably fueled Bin Laden's resentment of the dynasty, leading him away from the state-sanctioned Islamist establishment and down the path of terrorism.

IN ALLOWING THE IDEOLOGUES of the "awakening" to speak out publicly and proselytize openly during the 1980s, the royal family had hoped that this fringe group of radicals, mostly students, would fall in line with the dynasty's interests. The doctrinal foundations on which the *sahwa* rested, however, made such an alliance impossible.

The aim of the dissertation that Safar al-Hawali defended in 1986 was to expose and refute *irja*, which, according to Islamic doctrine, consists of deferring conformity of one's actions with the injunctions of Islam. Those accused of *irja* believe that actions cannot compromise the purity of one's faith. This attitude originated during Islam's formative period, when the Kharijites (for whom everyone outside their group, including the Prophet's companions, were infidels) fought the Shiites (who venerated Ali, the Prophet's son-in-law) and the Sunnis (who backed Muhammad's successors, the caliphs, as heads of the *umma* after the Prophet's death in 632). The *murjia* were those people who refused to take sides, "deferring" a decision to join a political faction in order to maintain the unity of believers against Islam's enemies for as long as possible.

All those who had initially taken sides, whether their party won or lost, retrospectively condemned the attitude of the *murjia*. The Sunni majority denounced them as traitors and opportunists, accusing them of separating faith from action, of accepting authority unquestioningly without challenging the validity of its Islamic credentials. The Kharijites, a fanatical minority persecuted by the Sunnis, systematically excommunicated all those who claimed to be Muslims but who did not conform strictly to the injunctions of their dogma. They saw the *murjia* as the embodiment of a tepid Islam, always ready to compromise and worthy only of death by the sword.

In his dissertation and the texts he derived from it subsequently, Safar al-Hawali sided with the Sunni tradition, citing its great authors to expose the heresy of the *murjia* throughout the *umma's* history. He named those whom he considered to be contemporary *murjia* only in a footnote, to avoid political repression. But his target was the Grand Ulema Authority, which placed the preservation of the Saudi dynasty above any criticism. In Hawali's view, sovereignty *(hakimiyya)* is Allah's alone and cannot be claimed by men, who have merely usurped it. This reading of Islam, which takes the recognition of Allah's sovereignty as the supreme criterion in distinguishing between Islamic states and the world of unbelievers *(jahiliyya)*, emerges directly from the Qutb brothers' writings, inspired by the Pakistani Islamist ideologue Mawdudi, who died in 1979, and is foreign to the Wahhabite tradition.

The awakening that spread with the Saudi authorities' blessings during the 1980s was based on the idea that the dynasty did not govern according to divine *hakimiyya* but according to its whims and its financial and political interests. Still more serious was the claim that those who do not govern according to what Allah has commanded are infidels *(kafirin)*. This line of radical Islamist discourse took on greater meaning when Hawali formulated it in his dissertation written at Mecca University, entitled "The Phenomenon of *Irja* in Islamic Thought" *(Zahirat al-Irja fil-Fikr al-Islami)*. Under his pen, an obscure debate between medieval clerics and jurists became a weapon against the Wahhabite doctors of law who controlled religion in Saudi Arabia. It was a sword of Damocles suspended over the dynasty's head; yet the authorities seemed unconcerned by statements that they believed could be controlled. The text was quickly popularized through numerous sermons and cassette tapes, however, and by the late 1990s it was available to anyone with access to the Internet.

When Iraqi troops appeared on Saudi Arabia's border in 1990 and King Fahd called in American troops, the organized coexistence between the *sahwa*'s young Qutbist-salafist ideologues and the Wahhabite ulema shattered. The dynasty turned in desperation toward its traditional backers, the only group that would give Islamic approval to the presence of foreign troops on Saudi soil. Sheikh bin Baz and the Grand Ulema Authority issued two fatwas, the first on August 14, 1990, authorizing deployment on Saudi Arabia's sacred land (in Operation Desert Shield) and the second in January 1991, allowing Muslim soldiers to join the attack on Iraq (Operation Desert Storm). The Wahhabite establishment discredited itself in the eyes of the *sahwa* activists with this endorsement. The rift between the two factions would only widen during the 1990s, as unrest increased.

Three major sources of tension can be identified. The first was an offensive by the militants challenging the Saudi rulers in two petitions presented in May 1991 and March 1992. The latter (a "Memorandum of Advice") upped the ante and was condemned by the Grand Ulema Authority. As well as demanding the complete Islamization of legislation, the petitioners called for the dynasty to be accountable. Around the same time, the government came under attack from liberals, especially Saudi women, some of whom broke the taboo against driving automobiles by taking the wheel.

The second source of tension was repression by the authorities. The main *sahwa* activists, including Hawali, were rounded up and put under lock and key from 1994 to 1999. The arrest of Salman al-Awda in Burayda almost caused a riot. Two attacks were carried out in Riyadh in November 1995 and on the American base at Khobar in June 1996, in the petroleum zone. These were attributed to radical salafists influenced by the Afghan jihad, though given the available information, this claim must be regarded circumspectly.

During the period of repression, Osama bin Laden, who had been living in exile in Sudan for four years, was stripped of his Saudi nationality. He subsequently made two announcements foreshadowing his terrorist activities: a "declaration of jihad against Americans occupying the land of the two holy sites" on August 23, 1996; and a proclamation of the World Islamic Front against Jews and Crusaders, issued in February 1998, which called for the killing of Americans worldwide and was co-signed by Zawahiri and a few others.

This period of repression was also marked by the first in a long series of attacks carried out by the Al Qaeda network: the twin bombing of American embassies in Nairobi, Kenya, and Dar es Salaam, Tanzania, on August 7, 1998. These attacks acquired enormous symbolic value because they occurred on the anniversary of the day on which King Fahd had invited U.S. troops onto Saudi soil. With that fateful decision, the salafist-jihadist theories that Ayman al-Zawahiri had mulled over for years in Egypt were unleashed upon the world. Terrorism sprang forth and would spread around the globe, striking at the faraway enemy in New York, Bali, and Madrid.

The third source of tension began with the freeing of the *sahwa*'s standard-bearers in the summer of 1999, followed immediately by Bin Baz's death in May of that year. Bin Baz had become the grand mufti of Saudi Arabia at the beginning of the decade. Along with Sheikh Muhammad bin Uthaymin (who died two years later, in January 2001), he had become a figurehead for institutional Wahhabism. Still, thanks to his immense religious erudition and his reputation for intransigence, Bin Baz enjoyed great prestige among the population and could reinforce the Saud family's policies through his influence with the masses of believers. At his death, the dynasty found itself staring into a vacuum, for within the Wahhabite clergy there was no great figure who could fill Bin Baz's shoes. The mufti who followed him, Abd al-Aziz Al Sheikh (from Abdul Wahhab's lineage), did not enjoy comparable authority.

Around this time, the Saud family itself experienced a major problem in assuring its dynastic succession. The founding monarch, Ibn Saud, had had a great number of sons by dozens of wives, often from tribes that had pledged allegiance to him. Through a rapid series of marriages and divorces, he had ensured his own genetic proliferation without breaking the rules of sharia, which limit polygamy to four wives at a time. This large, cohesive network of brothers and half-brothers controlled the political system and benefited from exclusive access to oil wealth. By transmitting power laterally, from brother to brother, rather than lineally, from father to son, he guaranteed solidarity between brothers from different mothers over the personal ambitions of a monarch keen to ensure that his own children would succeed him.

Since Ibn Saud's death in 1953, four of his sons have taken the throne: Saud, Faisal, Khalid, and Fahd. King Fahd, who is in his eighties, was crippled by a series of embolisms, most seriously in 1996, and his half-brother, Crown Prince Abdullah—also in his eighties—became the kingdom's de facto ruler. If Abdullah dies before Fahd, power will remain under the control of Fahd's full brothers, three of whom hold high office: Sultan is minister of defense; Nayef is minister of the interior; and Salman is governor of Riyadh. Salman, significantly younger and well regarded by many in the kingdom, is father to two reform-minded princes, Abd al-Aziz, vice minister of oil, and Faisal, a Ph.D. in political science who runs the London-based daily *Al-Sharq al-Awsat*. If Fahd dies before Abdullah, the latter will become king, but since he has no full brothers, Sultan stands in line to follow him. Nothing, however, prevents Abdullah from choosing another crown prince.

Many of the princes who might follow Abdullah or Sultan are quite old, and thus the political system invented by the founding king has been struck by a sort of Tchernienko syndrome, a necrosis that prevents the renewal of the generations at the top of the power pyramid. Furthermore, if anyone attempts to break the rules of power distribution—that is, if a given subclan of full brothers attempts to take over, or if anyone seeks to impose a power transfer in favor of someone in the next generation—the family pact will become vulnerable to those members who were excluded.

Thus, as it entered the twenty-first century, the Saudi royal family was caught between a need for absolute unity and the urgency to modernize its system of succession. At risk was the dynasty's dominion over the country and its control of oil wealth. This dilemma of succession did not make the family stronger when renegotiating the terms of its alliance with the Wahhabites, an alliance on which it had based its title to govern legitimately. Furthermore, it encouraged the other subclans to form external alliances—with commoners, the masses, foreign powers, perhaps certain activists —awaiting the day when a vacancy at the top would allow the best-prepared contenders to impose their candidate.

The uncertainties at the summit of the power structure are illustrated by the curious situation of the titular king, Fahd, who, though weakened by disease and incapable of governing, preserves his status in order to strengthen the influence of his full brothers and his eldest son, who controls access to the king's signature. Crown Prince Abdullah, who is next in line and exercises many of the functions of a monarch, cannot claim the title of king until Fahd's death, and in the meantime he must endure restrictions on his prerogatives and initiatives.

In such a context, reform is difficult. Long procedures to ensure consensus among the family's dominant members must be exhausted before any action can be undertaken. This practice goes back to tribal tradition, and its advocates boast that it guarantees the cohesive, efficient implementation of carefully weighed decisions. But in a national and international context where the monarchy is brought face to face with fast-moving, creative enemies— whether these enemies are radical Islamists from Bin Laden's camp or the most adamant anti-Saudi neoconservatives in Washington and their allies in Israel—this modus operandi constitutes a handicap. The consensus that is supposed to result from slow deliberation is rarely reached, and the deadlines imposed by the age of the king and the crown prince, both in their eighties, encourage the maneuvers of rival clans, each of which controls part of the state. The arrests of political opponents routinely carried out by the security forces under the orders of Prince Nayef, minister of the interior, therefore appear to have placed before the crown prince a fait accompli. For his part, in January 2003 Abdullah reminded a delegation that came to present him with a petition for reform that political decisions in that domain did not depend on him alone.

It was this aging, divided ruling family that found itself obliged to renew its pact with the clerical establishment after Bin Baz passed away in 1999. The *sahwa*'s two most prominent activists, Safar al-Hawali and Salman al-Awda, whose names had always been cited together, began to go their separate ways after release from prison in the summer of that year. Awda seemed fairly receptive to the government's overtures. He made frequent television appearances, especially on Al Arabiyya, the Dubai-based satellite channel financed by Saudi capital, and aroused America's ire when he hosted fund-raising telethons for the families of Palestinian suicide bombers who died in the second intifada. Casting aside his Qutbist extremism, he presented a new profile intended to make him appear suitable to occupy the space left empty by the deaths of Bin Baz and Bin Uthaymin. But his relative youth (he was forty-five in 2000) and his lack of expertise in religious studies (he did not obtain his PhD until the beginning of 2004) precluded his enjoying the same authority as Bin Baz.

Those who looked askance at Awda's compromises with the ruling family soon dubbed his website, Al-Islam al-Yawm ("Islam Today"), "Al-Istislam al-Yawm" ("Capitulation Today"), a play on the Arabic root *s-l-m*, which denotes the general concept of submission (to Allah in the case of Islam). This evolution became particularly visible in October 2001, when on his website Awda condemned the attacks on the United States and identified himself as a bulwark against terrorism. Subsequently, he played a central role in writing a manifesto entitled *How We Can Coexist*, which was published in May 2002 and written in cooperation with liberals and other secular figures. It constituted a response to the manifesto penned by American intellectuals defending U.S. policy in the Middle East, the war on the Taliban, and the attack that had been announced on Iraq, in the name of promoting liberal ideals in the region and emancipating civil society.

In October 2001 Safar al-Hawali also condemned terrorism, which he considered to be a reprehensible deviation from the framework of a just clash of civilizations between Islam and the "lands of unbelief." He, too, signed the manifesto on coexistence but preserved a far more distant attitude toward the government's entreaties than did Awda. Hawali, who was five years older than his colleague and had obtained his PhD in 1986, enjoyed a more solid intellectual reputation and was in a stronger negotiating position with the royal family. He could thus take his time and improve the price of his eventual cooperation with the authorities. His cautious approach was strengthened when all sorts of radical sheikhs began to emerge, from the "old man in Burayda," Hamud al-Shuaybi, to the young cyber-sheikhs who applauded the raids on New York and Washington and had nothing but contempt for lukewarm Muslims and their sympathy toward the victims. Safar al-Hawali was reluctant to abandon his radical discourse entirely to these dissidents or contenders, but he was walking a knife-edge.

Shuaybi, an eighty-year-old sheikh, belonged to the radicalized Wahhabite faction. He had studied with the most prestigious doctors of Islamic law in his day and had mentored not only his "compatriot," Salman al-Awda, but also the grand mufti of Saudi Arabia as well as other members of the religious establishment. In the 1990s, he gained media celebrity by praising the Taliban "emirate" unreservedly, which he went so far as to describe as the sole existing Islamic regime. This opinion did not go down well with the rulers in Riyadh. He was jailed in the mid-1990s and then released. The message prerecorded by Ahmad al-Haznawi al-Ghamdi, one of the September 11 hijackers, and broadcast by Al Jazeera on April 16, 2002, cited Shuaybi as a religious authority who had approved the attacks.

During the war against the Taliban in November 2001, Shuaybi publicly lamented the fall of Kunduz, crying out, "But where are the Muslims?" at the sight of Arab jihad fighters imprisoned with barbed wire and turned over to the Americans by their Afghan captors. His disciples began to fear for his life, and indeed on January 20, 2002, to the great chagrin of his spiritual sons, he died of sorrow, a broken old man. Jihadist websites throughout the Muslim world mourned his passing.

Galvanized after 9/11 by the attacks Al Qaeda was carrying out all over the world, salafist-jihadist networks proliferated in Saudi Arabia. In March 2003 the Saudi government showed the world clearly where its own loyalties lay, by producing oil at maximum capacity to support the U.S. invasion of Iraq. But inside the country, the government opted for a policy of accommodation toward the most radical jihadist sheikhs, like Nasir al-Fahd, Ali al-Khudayr, and Ahmad al-Khalidi, who made themselves very visible on their websites even as the police limply staged manhunts for their arrest. Any remaining hope that jihadist passion could be channeled to the kingdom's political advantage was dashed when three suicide attacks killed thirty-five people in Riyadh, nine of them Americans, on May 12, 2003, the day of a visit by U.S. Secretary of State Colin Powell. Mass arrests ensued, and the three sheikhs were rounded up. But another attack in the capital, on November 8, claimed seventeen more victims, all Arab.

Deploring the deaths of these "innocent Muslims," the jihadist sheikhs made televised shows of contrition from their prison cells. They feared that their financial backers and contacts on the xenophobic fringes of the population would disappear, perceiving that the serpents they had handled so deftly had now turned to bite them. Just this kind of retrenchment had occurred in Morocco in May of the same year, after the Casablanca attacks in which all the victims killed were Muslims.

This bombing on its own territory forced the Saudis to admit the futility of the strategy that had begun with the export of jihad activists to Afghanistan after the November 1979 attack on the Great

Mosque in Mecca. Crown Prince Abdullah slowly began to implement reforms. His goal was to involve certain sectors of civil society in political decision-making and the exercise of power, under conditions that were still closely controlled. The founding pact between the Al Saud and Al Sheikh families was enlarged to integrate the *sahwa* militants, fresh out of prison, in the hope that they could be co-opted to help the royal family control the most turbulent sectors of society. At the same time, within Saudi civil society and in opposition to terrorist extremism, "moderate Islamists" and "liberals" attempted to narrow their differences, expressing themselves in a series of petitions that called for more daring reforms, with the ultimate goal of limiting the dynasty's grip on power and placing checks on the distribution of oil wealth.

The government also endeavored to provide these initiatives with a new institutional framework. At the crown prince's instigation, the first such "national dialogue forum" took place in June 2003—an initiative that would perhaps lay the groundwork of a new Saudi social contract. The goal was to substitute nationalism *(wataniyya)* for the concept of jihad, on which the alliance between the Saud dynasty and Wahhabism had been built. The first conference brought together thirty representatives of Saudi Islam in Riyadh for four days. A third of the participants were from the *sahwa*, a few were from the Wahhabite establishment, but there were also representatives, given equal weight, of Sunni Shafiite and Malikite Islam from the Hijaz and the Asir regions, Sufi mystics and Ismailis from the Najran (the zone abutting Yemen), as well as Shiites from the Eastern Province. Until that time, the Wahhabite preachers had considered the Shiites abominable and had issued fatwas damning them as unbelievers. As for non-Wahhabite Sunnis, they were supposed to have disappeared in the wake of the Ikhwan militias in the 1920s. Their reappearance and official recognition constituted a noteworthy political advance. At the conference's end, Salman al-Awda was photographed inviting the Shiites' spiritual leader, Hassan al-Saffar, into his car—and ostensibly marking the path he was ready to follow to help establish national unity. Safar al-Hawali, on the other hand, was just as ostentatious in refusing such a reconciliation.

After the traumatic attacks of May 12, 2003, Saudi Arabia enjoyed a brief "Riyadh springtime." The most daring of the liberal papers—like *Al Watan*—a daily published in Abha, the capital of Asir province, whose governor is Prince Khaled al-Faisal—ran articles with such titles as "The Nation Is More Important than Ibn Taymiyya," which explicitly broke the taboos of Wahhabite doctrine. More serious still, three days after the attacks a political cartoon was published which showed two identical bearded figures dressed in short jellabas, with sandals on their feet and white scarves on their heads, indicating salafist piety. One, however, had a belt of explosives around his waist, while the other, wearing enormous spectacles on his nose, had a belt made of fatwas. The caption read: "A terrorist. And the one who issues fatwas inciting to terrorism is a terrorist too." The most conservative clerics put pressure on the interior minister to get the editor-in-chief of *Al Watan*, Jamal Khashoggi, fired. He later became adviser to the Saudi ambassador in London, Prince Turki al-Faisal.

Crown Prince Abdullah's quiet revolution, backed by certain branches of the royal family against the will of some others, may be able to put in place symbolic measures that break taboos and indicate the way in which the society must evolve. But symbolic gestures are no substitute for real political reform, which will necessarily force the Saud lineage to enlarge the circle of power. Reform will also force the rulers to rethink the way that the nation's wealth is distributed, and it will demand that respect be paid to the dignity (and memory) of all components of the kingdom's population—the cosmopolitan merchants of the Hijaz, the sedentary peoples of the Asir, the Shiites of Hasa, and women of all sects—who feel that their identity has been denied under Wahhabite ideology. The project is daunting, and the obstacles numerous, but if it is not undertaken there will be no way to ensure the kingdom's survival, now that centrifugal forces are at work in Washington, London, and Tel Aviv—not to mention jihadist cells all around the kingdom.

Perhaps the biggest challenge facing the kingdom of Saud is the status of women. Bowing to pressure from the ulema, the government has restricted Saudi women to a few "feminine" jobs. Most Saudi women are forced to remain idle, despite a handful of exceptions, epitomized by such examples as Reem al-Faisal, a photographer, or Lubna Olayan, one of the wealthiest businesswomen in the world. The star of the Jeddah Economic Forum held on January 17, 2004, Olayan inaugurated the event with a radical speech broadcast nationwide: "Without real change, there can be no progress. If we seek to advance, in Saudi Arabia, we have no choice but to embrace change."

I was in Riyadh on that day, and like most viewers in the kingdom, I was struck less by what she said than by the smart suit she wore. She made no effort to adjust the light scarf on her head as it gradually slid off, exposing her hair and giving immediate substance to her message. Lubna Olayan could well afford this inattention: in a country where anxiety over unemployment is the primary source of political instability, economic players like herself who can provide jobs cannot be silenced by the clamor of conservative zealots who would be hard put, even with heaven's help, to solve the problem of joblessness among young people. Three months after the Jeddah Forum, its organizer was promoted to head the Saudi Arabian General Investment Authority, which manages foreign investment in the country.

The kingdom's liberal press soon took up Olayan's unprecedented challenge to the commandments of the ulema, which demand that Saudi women wear the *abaya* (a long black robe) and
the *hijab* (Islamic veil). Olayan's speech fueled more than a few
conversations in the lounge at Riyadh Airport, where I was awaiting my flight to Asir. Mature men, seemingly well established,
were commenting on the event between prayers and seemed at a
loss for words harsh enough to criticize the woman who had dared
behave so provocatively—by uncovering her hair!

Perhaps in order to please them, or to satisfy the preachers appearing on television at the same time to condemn the French law
that prohibits schoolchildren from wearing markers of religious
identity, the Saudi government carried out a raid on outspoken liberals. Some weeks later, a handful of intellectuals and academics
found themselves in prison.

DURING MY TRIP to the province of Asir in January 2004, I stopped
on Highway 15, not far from Safar al-Hawali's native village, to have
lunch with a member of the Ghamdi tribe, to which many of the
September 2001 attackers belonged. I was afforded a small glimpse
of the Saudi dilemma: in this magnificent region of sedentary
mountain-dwelling farmers, where Bengali or Egyptian immigrants now till the fields, I saw few young people, because there are
no jobs for them. They have all gone to Jeddah, where they scratch
out an existence on the city's fringes, along with poor foreigners. As
my host and I toured the region in a jeep, we passed Bedouin
camps at the desert's edge, their inhabitants recognizable by their
long hair. The young women, heads covered by scarves, left the
camps to watch over the herds. Men from the village drove to the

pastures in four-wheel-drive vehicles to stare at the women from afar. The wives of these men were forbidden to leave their homes. The Wahhabization imposed on the region in the 1920s made non-Bedouin women all but invisible. In Jeddah, rumor has it that Muhammad bin Laden, Osama's father, who died when his plane crashed in this area, loved the Bedouin women of Asir. When the billionaire's arrival was announced, these women would dress in their finest, in the hope of a request for marriage that would bring wealth to the tribe.

From atop a promontory one views a vast panorama, thick with history: such and such a 9/11 attacker was from that village, over there in the distance; farther down, toward the south, is Hawala, where Safar al-Hawali was born. The inhabitants now live in functional, charmless concrete buildings on the outskirts of abandoned town centers. There, one can find beautiful old houses of painted stone, with doors of carved wood topped by sculpted lintels. But these dwellings, which bear witness to the Asirs' sedentary civilization, have been abandoned to troops of baboons, which howl from behind the barred windows at nostalgic visitors breathing in the grandeur of the past. The males, with their fan-shaped beards, stand guard as the females scurry to safety, their young clinging to backs and breasts. On one terrace the wrist bone of a baboon is fastened to a wall by a skein of hemp—all that remains after birds of prey swooped down to attack the defenseless monkey, providing morbid amusement for a few youngsters with nothing better to do.

In Jeddah, among wealthy families, the name Ghamdi always provokes sly smiles. Long ago, the Ghamdis were gardeners, cooks, or drivers. They disappeared once Filipinos and Pakistanis took over those jobs. A few people from the tribe managed to have illustrious careers, but as a whole the tribe made its name in the world through the events of September 11, 2001.

6

The Calamity of Nation-Building in Iraq

On March 20, 2003, President George W. Bush launched a military invasion of Iraq intended, in his mind, to conclude the war on terror by dislodging Saddam Hussein. Deploying the United States' military arsenal against an appropriate enemy (which Bin Laden was not) would, in the view of his neoconservative advisers, inspire shock and awe among terrorists around the globe and erase from memory the American failure to liquidate Al Qaeda, which had continued to claim credit for terrorist attacks. Toppling the Baathist regime would also obscure the inability—despite an ongoing manhunt unprecedented in U.S. military history—to locate and capture Al Qaeda's ringleaders, Osama bin Laden and Ayman al-Zawahiri. The administration's new message, honed for public consumption by Fox News Network and in *The Weekly Standard,* seemed to be that the hunt for Al Qaeda could not eradicate terror, because Bin Laden and his Taliban hosts were mere puppets. The man pulling the strings was in fact Saddam Hussein.

Destroying the rogue regime in Iraq would eliminate the true sponsor of global terror, the neocons claimed, as well as a monster who had oppressed, tortured, and murdered thousands of his own people. Two birds, one stone: with the fall of the Iraqi despot, tyranny in the region would decline, and terrorism, its nefarious offspring, would vanish. A democratic, pro-American democracy in Iraq, pumping out five million barrels of oil every day, would put economic pressure on Saudi Arabia to heed U.S. demands for political and religious reform and end its indulgence of terrorists. Iraq would become the keystone in a New Middle East, a region now free of its demons and eager to join the New American Century.

The imagination of Bush's advisers did not stop there. Proportionate representation for Iraq's Shia majority, which had been marginalized and oppressed under Saddam Hussein, would provide a model for post-Khomeini Iran. Following in the footsteps of its former enemy, Iran would push its most fanatical mullahs aside and reestablish ties with the United States. The holy sites of Najaf and Karbala, restored to their former grandeur, would shine forth on a hundred million Shia, spread between Lebanon and India and preponderant along the Gulf coast, who would serve as a counterweight to the Sunni petro-monarchies. Finally, and most important, routing Saddam would deprive Arab nationalists in Palestine and elsewhere of their last hero, and sap their will to continue their vendetta against the state of Israel. From a new position of strength, Israel would reenter the regional system, under conditions far more favorable to its economic interests and national security.

In sum, neoconservative theoreticians and their followers in the White House dreamed that a virtuous circle of missiles and tanks, liberation and democratization, would eradicate the sponsors and promulgators of terror. It would, as the title of Richard Perle's December 2003 book suggested, bring about "an end to evil."

Despite a few passing setbacks as U.S. troops advanced across the desert, Operation Iraqi Freedom, directed from Central Command headquarters in Qatar, demonstrated that the U.S. military could launch a coordinated, invincible assault by land, sea, and air. But just as Spain's Invincible Armada was overcome by a tempest that King Phillip II's admirals had not foreseen, the strategists behind America's well-oiled military machine had not anticipated the perils of occupation. Whether one uses the word "resistance" or "terrorism" to describe the attacks on U.S. troops after May 1, 2003—the date of Bush's triumphant tailhook landing aboard the aircraft carrier USS *Abraham Lincoln*—these strikes were far more violent than anything the Pentagon had predicted or prepared for.

Convinced that the speed and spectacle of its military conquest would result in a similarly swift and spectacular political and social victory, Washington neglected to secure the means to restore public order or to repair Iraq's social fabric, torn by Saddam's violence but also by the ten-year embargo imposed by the United Nations. The 135,000 soldiers on the ground after military action ended were poorly trained for peacekeeping and too few in number to provide security for Iraqi civilians. Problems in the military chain of command would become obvious when the degrading treatment of Iraqi prisoners at Abu Ghraib prison was revealed in April 2004. The torture and sexual humiliation of inmates, graphically displayed in photographs taken by the perpetrators and circulated via the Internet throughout the Muslim world, would force President Bush and members of his administration to apologize for the actions of American soldiers and their superiors.

When U.S. forces entering Baghdad in April 2003 pulled down the colossal statue of Saddam Hussein in Paradise Square—in a media event that recapitulated the fall of the giant statue of Stalin in Prague—they created an ideological shortcut between Ronald Reagan's "evil empire" and George W. Bush's "axis of evil." The expected sequence of events—the tyrant is crushed, Iraqi civil society emerges—was supposed to follow the script of the post-Communist transition in Eastern Europe. But once the enthusiasm of the first weeks of freedom had passed, events of the next year would demonstrate that democratization in Iraq would not follow the path taken by the former Soviet bloc after the fall of the Berlin Wall, nor that of Germany and Japan after the Second World War. Nowhere had the U.S. army confronted such violence on the part of those it came to liberate from tyranny.

The recurrent insurrection in the Sunni triangle northwest of the capital was perhaps understandable. The fallen dictator had lavished payments upon this stronghold to ensure the loyalty of Arab Sunnis, who make up barely seventeen percent of the Iraqi population. The Shia (who in Iraq are mostly Arab, with a few Kurds) account for about sixty percent, and Kurds (who are mostly Sunni) account for twenty percent; a handful of Christians, Turkomans, and Yazdis make up the rest. But when Shia militia fighters of the Mahdi Army rose up in April 2004, under the command of Moktada al-Sadr, a young zealot and the scion of a line of prestigious ayatollahs, Washington was taken aback by this show of ingratitude. The Shia population had been coddled by the American liberators as the backbone of any future Iraqi civil society, and their leaders were promised a major role in the New Middle East order. When I visited Paul Wolfowitz in his Pentagon office in July 2003, after passing through countless security checks to enter the immense blockhouse, I was asked to wait in an anteroom where I was surrounded not by crew-cut military men speaking English with Midwestern accents but by civilian Shia dignitaries and clerics wearing turbans and speaking Arabic with Mideastern accents.

In the worldview of most neoconservatives, the fate of the Jews and that of the Shia are linked. Both are persecuted peoples who owe the preservation of their identity to a visceral attachment to their sacred texts, and both place high value on the role of clerics—rabbis and ayatollahs—as guarantors of their threatened survival. At the beginning of the twentieth century, as the tide of secularism rose, both groups transferred their high regard for scriptural knowledge from clerics to intellectuals, from messianic theologians to militant activists. Sons of rabbis and ayatollahs were disproportionately represented among the communist leadership, and in the Middle East—with the exception of the Levant, where a few Christians, especially from the Greek Orthodox community, played a role in bringing communism to maturity—Marxists were mainly Jews or Shia. When Jews left Arab states at the creation of Israel following World War II, the region's only substantial Communist Party developed in Iraq, and it was overwhelmingly Shia. Saddam persecuted and finally destroyed it, but many of its exiles ended up—a good deal older—by the side of the very Americans whose imperialism they had denounced in their youth, working this time to overthrow the Iraqi tyrant and democratize their country.

The Middle East was only partially heir to these conflicts of past decades, however. The population explosion of the 1980s produced multitudes of young people with no historical memory, who were struggling to survive in a region where violence and arbitrary power had stripped established regimes and official parties alike of any popular legitimacy and where everyone knew that wealth and jobs go to those who prevaricate, swindle, or coerce. These frustrated young people made up the overwhelming majority of the population in Iraq, and their presence would foil the forecasts made by the occupation's planners in Washington.

Even the capture of Saddam Hussein himself turned out to be a disappointment. Represented as the long-awaited apotheosis of the invasion, delayed repeatedly by the complicity of clan members as the fallen dictator fled from one safe house to the next, the takedown finally came about in his tribal stronghold, Tikrit, on December 13, 2003. U.S. forces staged the event carefully, but in the end they produced only a few images of Saddam—shaggy, dirty, bearded, and a bit dazed—resembling nothing so much as a haggard drifter. The sight of the humiliated despot having his hair and teeth examined by a military physician was intended to show his remaining partisans that there was no point in resisting the democratic transition.

Unfortunately for the occupation, the arrest of Saddam Hussein had no effect on daily violence in Iraq. Indeed, it was almost forgotten in the storm of renewed attacks, as if Saddam, despite the enormity of his crimes and the millions of Iraqis, Iranians, Kuwaitis, and Kurds for whose deaths he would be indicted belonged irrevocably to the past. History was racing forward, and in the ferocious struggle for immediate power, where the equilibrium between religious communities, ethnic and national groups, age cohorts, cities, countryside and suburbs was still undecided, the discovery of Saddam Hussein in a spider hole in Tikrit had little impact.

In only a year, America's military triumph had turned into a political quagmire, compromising all the objectives that were supposed to result from Iraq's liberation: eradicating terrorism once and for all, bringing Iran back into the fold of civilized nations, disciplining the Saudi system, and integrating Israel into the region while guaranteeing its security. To understand this unexpected twist of events, we must begin by separating the true aims of the war from the pretexts the Bush administration invoked to hide them.

THE OBJECTIVE of President Bush's State of the Union speech on January 29, 2002, was to build a rhetorical arsenal for the war against Saddam Hussein. The hunt for Al Qaeda was virtually ignored, as the president accused Iraq, Iran, and North Korea of constituting an "axis of evil, arming to threaten the peace of the world." On September 12, in a speech to the fifty-seventh session of the U.N. General Assembly, the president singled out Iraq as a target and enjoined Saddam Hussein to "immediately and unconditionally forswear, disclose, and remove or destroy all weapons of mass destruction, long-range missiles, and all related material." Twelve days later, Tony Blair revealed a British Secret Service report indicating that the Iraqi government was still developing weapons of mass destruction and would soon have nuclear capabilities. On these grounds, the U.S. Congress voted, by a very large majority, to allow unilateral recourse to force against Baghdad.

The war machine revved up immediately: soldiers, ships, and fighter planes began moving en masse toward Iraq, surrounding it. The call to arms was loudest in Colin Powell's presentation before the United Nations on February 5, 2003. Using diagrams and models, the secretary of state demonstrated that Saddam Hussein posed an imminent threat and that it was therefore necessary to eliminate him forthwith. Photographs of aluminum tubes, supposedly intended for use as part of a nuclear weapon, were the centerpiece in a production designed to persuade the majority of U.N. Security Council members to throw their support behind the invasion. Powell's attempt met with skepticism from France and Russia, as well as from most of the other member nations.

Now that specialized American, British, and Australian inspectors have combed occupied Iraqi territory in vain for weapons of mass destruction (WMD), it is widely accepted that Saddam in fact had no nuclear arsenal and that his armed forces were incapable of using chemical or biological weapons. As the head of the American inspectors, David Kay, declared before the Senate on January 28, 2004, "We were almost all wrong." He thereby confirmed conclusions already reached by the International Atomic

Energy Agency (IAEA) and the U.N. Monitoring, Verification and Inspection Commission (UNMOVIC), created on December 17, 1999, and on the ground in Iraq from November 25, 2002, to March 17, 2003. Between January 27 and March 7, 2003, their respective directors, Mohamed el-Baradei and Hans Blix, prepared several reports showing that no sign of nuclear activity had been detected in Iraq, nor was there any indication that it possessed WMD. In 1998 inspectors from IAEA and UNSCOM (U.N. Special Commission on Disarmament, created April 3, 1991) had clashed with Saddam Hussein and left Iraq, but by that time the operational WMD that the dictator possessed had already been dismantled or destroyed. Their testimony was disregarded, even ridiculed, in Washington and London. The inspections, they said, only proved, once again, that the U.N.'s incompetence made it obsolete, not to say dangerous, now that America's hegemony was global.

A year after the war, it is clear that the U.S. president and the British prime minister deliberately used the bogus threat of WMD to gain support for the Iraq War at home and among Western allies. In the United Kingdom, the first evidence came from a BBC journalist, who reported in May 2003 that the Blair government had told its intelligence services to "sex up" the dossier on Iraq WMD and to state that such weapons could be ready for use within forty-five minutes. His report was based on statements made to him by David Kelly, a Ministry of Defence specialist on questions of nuclear proliferation. On July 17, in the face of denials by the Blair government, Kelly committed suicide.

In the United States, about fifty days after the invasion of Iraq, Paul Wolfowitz explained to *Vanity Fair*'s Sam Tannenhaus why Iraq's WMD had been placed at the heart of the mobilization effort. The Machiavellian thinking was worthy of Leo Strauss—even of Plato, who counseled the philosopher-king to lie to his people for their own good. When Wolfowitz was asked about the place given Iraq in the strategy-planning meeting President Bush held at Camp David on the first weekend following September 11, 2001, the deputy secretary of defense stated:

> There was a long discussion during the day about what place if any Iraq should have in a counterterrorist strategy. On the surface of the debate it at least appeared to be about not whether but when. There seemed to be a kind of agreement that yes it should be, but the disagreement was whether it should be in the immediate response or whether you should concentrate simply on Afghanistan first . . . To the extent it was a debate about tactics and timing, the President clearly came down on the side of Afghanistan first. To the extent it was a debate about strategy and what the larger goal was, it is at least clear with 20/20 hindsight that the President came down on the side of the larger goal.

Later on in the interview, to a question about the links between the U.S. attack on Iraq and Al Qaeda's attack on the World Trade Center and the Pentagon, Wolfowitz gave an ambiguous answer that has intrigued (and angered) many of the administration's critics:

> The truth is that for reasons that have a lot to do with the U.S. government bureaucracy we settled on the one issue that everyone could agree on which was weapons of mass destruction as the core reason, but—hold on one second [pause: Kevin Kellems, Wolfowitz's special adviser, interrupts]. There have always been three fundamental concerns. One is weapons of mass destruction, the second is support for terrorism, the third is the criminal treatment of the Iraqi people. Actually I guess you

could say there's a fourth overriding one which is the connection between the first two. Sorry, hold on again [pause: Kellems interrupts again]. To wrap it up. The third one by itself, as I think I said earlier, is a reason to help the Iraqis but it's not a reason to put American kids' lives at risk, certainly not on the scale we did it. That second issue about links to terrorism is the one about which there's the most disagreement within the bureaucracy.

These statements have been dissected and commented upon extensively, since they implied that the WMD issue had been put forth for purely opportunistic reasons. Of the other two themes that Wolfowitz brought up, one was universally recognized—that Saddam Hussein was a criminal—but did not justify the deaths of American "kids." The other—the causal links between Iraq and Al Qaeda, which should have given the American invasion its greatest legitimacy as part of the war on terror—seemed insufficiently convincing to certain sectors of the Bush administration, according to Wolfowitz. This last admission is surprising, because the Bush advisers who were in disagreement are rather hard to find. Although the neocons dismissed the State Department under Colin Powell as too accommodating, not to say archaic, it was Powell who defended the invasion before the United Nations by citing the presence of a safe haven on the border of the Iraqi Kurdish zone for Kurdish Islamist members of a terrorist organization (Ansar al-Sunna) whose cadres had undergone training in Pakistani camps under Bin Laden's authority.

As early as the autumn of 2001, *The Weekly Standard* was making much of the rumor that Mohammed Atta, head of the 9/11 terrorists, had met an Iraqi intelligence agent in Prague in June 2001.

Gary Schmitt, executive director of the Project for a New American Century, wrote:

> The United States is now engaged not in legal wrangling but in a deadly game of espionage and terrorism. In the world where we operate, the Prague meeting is about as clear and convincing as evidence gets—especially since our intelligence service apparently had no agents-in-place of its own to tell us what was in fact going on. This much, however, is beyond dispute: Regardless of the differences between their visions for the Middle East, Saddam Hussein and Osama bin Laden share an overriding objective—to expel the United States from the Middle East. Alliances have been built on less.

American intelligence services remained cautious about the truth of the Prague rumor, however, and in June 2004 a U.S. bipartisan commission created to investigate the events of 9/11 reported that it was false; Atta was in Florida on the day the meeting was supposed to have occurred.

Richard Clarke, former head of antiterrorist coordination at the National Security Council, testifying before the 9/11 commission, revealed that the overthrow of Saddam Hussein's regime had been a priority for the Bush administration as early as January 2001, when the president took office. He went so far as to claim that advisers to Bush had used the September 11 strike as a tragic opportunity to unleash a war on terror in which the hunt for Al Qaeda was merely a secondary goal. The primary objective was to destroy the Iraqi regime and replace it with a pro-American democracy.

By spring 2004 some skeptics had renamed the war on terror the "war on error." Their criticism often focused on the most visible neoconservatives—especially Richard Perle and Douglas Feith

—who had contributed to "A Clean Break: A New Strategy for Securing the Realm," a report written to support Benjamin Netanyahu's successful campaign in the 1996 Israeli elections. The document set regime change in Baghdad as a mid-range objective, intended to stabilize the Middle East around Israel while guaranteeing the latter's security. Setting aside notions of various government conspiracies and "secret agendas"—historians will sort out the truth of those—the main concern here is to understand why, if overthrowing Saddam Hussein was the United States' clear goal since September 2001, it did not affirm that intention clearly, instead of resorting to dubious causal links between Saddam's state terrorism and Bin Laden's global terrorism. And why, above all, did it build its propaganda effort prior to the invasion on the fiction that Saddam Hussein possessed operational WMD—a fabrication that was sure to be discovered eventually, to the administration's embarrassment, once inspectors were back on the ground in Iraq?

Padding out the empty dossier on Iraqi WMD was intended, first of all, to ground the overthrow of the Iraqi regime in the irrefutable moral logic of the war on terror. That logic was based on the right of reply by civilized nations to the barbarism of September 11. This grounding was necessary because the near-universal coalition that had supported the U.S. attack on the Taliban in October 2001 had fallen apart over the course of the next year. In addition to Arab states, whose leaders were suspicious of any attempt by external forces to overthrow a despot, many European states—first among them Germany and France—failed to see the purported link between Saddam Hussein's criminal regime and the actions of Al Qaeda. Nor did they understand how eliminating the Baathist regime in Baghdad would make it easier to deal with the root causes of Islamist terrorism.

The threatened invasion and occupation of Iraq fueled suspicions in Europe that the United States was promoting the birth of

Arab democracy simply to mask its own strategic and energy interests in the Gulf. The WMD dossier was designed to overcome this skepticism by presenting Saddam as the ultimate terrorist and an imminent threat to world peace. It was also used to justify the U.S. decision to ignore the United Nations, which, in the administration's view, was now dilapidated and bankrupt. In his March 17, 2003, address to the nation, President Bush suggested that the White House was stepping up to a responsibility that the U.N. had proved incapable of fulfilling: ridding the planet of the leader of a rogue state who was determined to terrorize the world with his weapons of mass destruction at the earliest possible opportunity.

The violence that broke out in Iraq within weeks of the American victory suggested that the skeptics had been right. Neither Saddam's overthrow nor his capture a few months later could eliminate the root causes of terror in the Middle East. Guerrilla attacks in the Sunni triangle to the northwest of Baghdad forced the United States to launch Operations Peninsula, Desert Scorpion, and Desert Rattlesnake, but none had any lasting effect. Not only was there no cutback in American troops, as President Bush had promised on the flight deck of the USS *Abraham Lincoln*, but reinforcements had to be sent in by some U.S. allies: Spain, Italy, Poland, and a few former Soviet states whose leaders were actively courting Washington. As of May 1, 2004, six hundred American soldiers had been killed in Iraq since the end of "major operations"—as against one hundred forty-three during the invasion itself.

To understand what went wrong with the occupation, we must look more closely at the political and religious factions that confronted American troops and their civilian commanders after the triumphal march into Baghdad.

ON JULY 13, 2003, U.S. proconsul Paul Bremer, head of the Coalition Authority, set up an Iraqi Governing Council. Made up of twenty-five members representing the country's varied religious and ethnic groups, it symbolized the first steps toward democratization in Iraq. Simultaneously with their participation in the Governing Council, however, these groups were making every effort to seize power on the ground, using methods very much at odds with democratic institutions.

In the northern part of the country, where an autonomous Kurdish regime under international protection had been in place since April 1991, the two Kurdish parties, the KDP (Kurdistan Democratic Party, led by Massoud Barzani) and the PUK (Patriotic Union of Kurdistan, led by Jalal Talabani), pushed to extend their territory and reclaim oil fields in parts of the country where, prior to 1991, the majority of the population had been Kurdish. The roots of this expansion go back to 1968, when the Baath Party took power definitively and Kurdish guerrillas responded by attacking the oil fields in Kirkuk using money and weapons provided by the shah of Iran. After negotiating with the rebels in order to gain time, Saddam regrouped and launched an ethnic cleansing operation in September 1971 designed to drive the Kurds from this oil-rich region. Several tens of thousands of Kurds were expelled by force and replaced by Arabs. The fearsome Peshmerga guerrillas retreated to the mountains, and Baathist control over Kirkuk's oil resources was thus secured.

But Iraq had been weakened, and in 1975 it was forced to sign an agreement with Iran that restricted its navigation rights on the Shatt al-Arab waterway—the confluence of the Tigris and Euphrates rivers and the country's only outlet to the sea. In September 1980 Saddam launched an eight-year war against Iran. Some of Iraq's Kurdish regiments deserted, and in early 1988, when the war had exhausted both Iran and Iraq, Saddam, fearing that Kurdish separatism would jeopardize the Kirkuk oil fields, launched a genocide against the Kurds.

The number of men, women, and children massacred was estimated at 180,000; another quarter of a million fled to Iran or Turkey. The atrocities reached their peak when Iraqi forces, under the command of Saddam Hussein's cousin, Ali Hasan al-Majid (thereafter known as Chemical Ali), used poison gas against Kurdish civilians in the town of Halabja. Over five thousand people died on a single day in March 1988. The ethnic cleansing operations, combined with the Baath Party's forced Arabization policy since 1963, left over three hundred thousand Kurds dead and destroyed four thousand villages.

For these reasons, in April 1991, after the Gulf War, the Kurds were granted autonomous status, though their zone did not include the Kirkuk oil fields. Just as it had done after World War I, when the Treaty of Lausanne between Turkey and the victors ignored the Kurds' claims to independence, the international community turned a blind eye to Kurdish demands. President George H. W. Bush had his hands full trying to stabilize the Middle East and convene the Madrid peace conference between Israel and its Arab neighbors. It was impossible to think of reopening the Kurdish question and thereby inflicting separatism upon all the countries with territories populated by Kurds: not only Iraq, which had just been beaten, and Iran, which was openly hostile to the United States, but also Turkey, an old ally, not to mention Syria. The administration chose to preserve Iraq's territorial integrity at the expense of the Kurds' nationalist ambitions. Its main fear was that a dismembered Iraq would become a safe haven for terrorism, even more dangerous than stateless Lebanon had been during the previous decade.

The world had looked on indifferently as the Kurds were massacred in 1988. In 1991, the survivors could see that their fate was still second to international geopolitical interests and the logic of the oil market—two domains in which they were taken into account not as players but as potential troublemakers. They were caught in the pincers of two nations hostile to their cause: Iraq, where Saddam was still the dictator, however diminished his power might be by the U.N. embargo, no-fly zones, and sanctions, and Kemalist Turkey, where the government was dealing with its own rebellious Kurdish minority. While engaging in intense exchanges with Iranian Kurdistan, which Tehran encouraged, the Kurds found themselves torn apart by disputes between their two parties, the KDP and the PUK. In 1996 the KDP called in troops from Baghdad to help weaken its enemy, but when the Iraq army crossed the border into the autonomous zone on August 31, intense U.S. bombing pushed it back.

Over the years the Kurds managed to de-Arabize the autonomous zone to a large extent, and since the fall of Saddam's regime their opponents have accused them of discreetly practicing ethnic homogenization of the mixed population south of their zone. By pushing to expand their territory since the Iraq War, the Kurdish parties have attempted to create facts on the ground that will foment tension between Washington and the Sunnis and Shia. Having learned painful lessons in the past, they have tried to build a strong position that will force the Western powers, neighboring states, and oil companies to treat their interests with respect. As long as the Iraqi situation is unstable, they will likely be content to push for maximum autonomy while remaining a part of the nation. But the Kurds are keeping all their options open and attempting to expand into oil-rich territories, as a precaution against the uncertain future of a region where the only currency, as far as world order is concerned, is oil.

From Washington's perspective in May 2003, the Kurdish nation qualified as democratic *ipso facto* because Peshmerga guerrillas had fought alongside U.S. troops and special forces in northern Iraq during the invasion. But in fact, the long-range political strategy of Kurdish party leaders differed little from that of their counterparts among the Shia and Sunni—only their tactics diverged. As the immediate beneficiaries of an occupation that reconfirmed their autonomy, the Kurds avoided confrontation during the first year following the invasion. But today they stand ready to take up arms in defense of their interests if they perceive a threat—which is to say, if a centralized Iraq, moving toward unification, takes control of all the country's oil resources.

When the Governing Council's interim constitution, approved on March 8, 2004, provided for the creation of an autonomous Kurdistan, it upset many parties besides Turkey. Arabs were also concerned, seeing this development as encouraging Kurdish independence. Even among Kurds themselves, the most ardent separatists objected to the attempt to disarm Peshmerga militias and threatened to secure the oil fields by force. The conjoined interests of the United States and the Kurds—celebrated on both sides during the military invasion of Iraq—will not necessarily coincide in the coming years.

America's Kurdish collaborators stood at one extreme of the Iraqi political-religious spectrum during the first year of American occupation. At the other extreme was the Sunni Arab minority, slightly less numerous than the Kurdish population and spread mainly throughout central Iraq. Before Saddam's fall from power, Sunni Arabs were a dominant minority, with a history of shifting alliances to maintain their fragile power. Until the collapse of the Ottoman Empire in World War I, Sunnis shared the religion of the Turkish sultan and received benefits as a result. But the Sublime Porte (the Ottoman government) knew how to play minorities off against one another, within a hierarchical, Sunni-dominated system, and it maintained a lively pluralism. Jews and Christians were well represented in urban areas, especially Basra and Baghdad. (These two minorities would emigrate to Israel or the United States after World War II.)

When the British took over from the Ottomans at the end of the war, Britain's colonial cartographers merged the three Ottoman provinces of Basra, Baghdad, and Mosul to create a country that was practically landlocked. Its meager outlet to the sea was a 46-kilometer stretch on the Gulf between Iran and Kuwait. In order to export oil, the nation would have to make agreements with Turkey, Syria, Iran, and Saudi Arabia—all states whose relations with Iraq were fraught with perpetual border disputes. The invasions Saddam Hussein launched to the east, against Iran, and to the south, against Kuwait, cannot be ascribed solely to the madness of a bloodthirsty tyrant. They also had geostrategic implications that could be compared with the Third Reich's desire for *Lebensraum*.

British occupation forces imposed a federal government on Iraq, drawing on support from local urban elites. These elites proved wanting, however, and a nationalist uprising in 1920 instigated by the Shia forced the British to call in troops from India. The repression left many dead. Once colonial authority was reestablished, the Shia, now marked by the stigma of treachery, were relegated to the margins of power. The British placed Hijaz-born Faisal, a non-Iraqi Sunni Arab, on Iraq's new throne, backed by Sunni officers of the former Ottoman Empire and protected by Whitehall. Faisal and his brother Abdullah, king of newly-created Jordan—sons of Hussein the Hashemite, *sharif* of Mecca—embodied T. E. Lawrence's dream of the Arab kingdom (which would pay homage to London).

In 1958, in a swift and bloody coup led by General Abd al-Karim

Qassem and supporters in the officer corps, the Hashemite monarchy fell and the Republic of Iraq was born. Power passed to a group of Sunni officers around Qassem who were steeped in pan-Arabism. In a frenzy of murder and mayhem, on July 14 an enraged crowd dragged the mutilated body of the regent, Abdulillah, through the streets and then strung up the corpse from the gates of the Ministry of Defense. The officers went on to liquidate or exile the traditional urban middle classes and use their oil wealth to subsidize the upward mobility of members of their own tribe. Among the victims of this policy were religious dignitaries, Sunnis and Shiites alike, who lost their land and other "clerical benefits." Rumor had it that some clerics ended up in the furnaces of locomotives.

After five years of growing turmoil, a small group of Baath officers overthrew Qassem's government in yet another bloody coup —one that would last only a few months. In an attempt to consolidate their power, they displayed on television the body of the general who had overthrown the king, his corpse riddled with bullets. Only in 1968 was the Baath Party finally able to seize control of Iraq. From that point on, torture and murder would become instruments of government. The party's strong man behind the scenes was Saddam Hussein. A decade later, in 1979, through a series of bloody purges, Saddam would became the uncontested leader of a regime that Iraqi dissident Kanan Makiya has described as a "republic of fear."

The fact that power in Iraq was held for so long by a minority group helps to explain the violence, extraordinary even by regional norms, that has convulsed Iraq since its inception. Fear, engendered by public displays of atrocities and rumors of unspeakable torture, was the force that kept the Sunni Baathists in control. Iraq was the only Muslim country where Sunnis, who make up a majority of Muslims worldwide, were in the minority but nevertheless held absolute power. Kurds were also Sunnis, but ethnic issues between Arabs and Kurds were so divisive that the two groups could never unite and provide a counterweight to the much more populous Iraqi Shia.

Fear was not the only instrument of power at Saddam Hussein's disposal, however. Like other rulers in the Middle East, he had so much oil money during the second half of the 1970s that he could buy allegiance far beyond his circle of direct supporters. Journalists at Arab papers published in London or Paris, poorly paid novelists and essayists from Morocco to Yemen, and over-the-hill filmmakers in Cairo all benefited from Saddam's generosity. He bought the services of secular nationalists in the same way that Saudi Arabia bought those of religious clerics. (The publication of account books and receipts found in Baghdad after March 2003 was a temporary source of embarrassment for some of the beneficiaries.) Businessmen, oilmen, weapons manufacturers, and contractors from around the world flocked to Iraq's modernizing, solvent leader, who was busy erecting his country's civilian and military infrastructure.

In 1979, when monetary reserves reached $35 billion in a country with only fifteen million inhabitants, Iraq's standard of living became the envy of the rest of the Middle East, with the exception of the Arabian peninsula. As long as Iraqis acquiesced to Saddam Hussein's total monopoly on power, shared only with a small coterie of political, religious, ethnic, and tribal loyalists, they received a share of the oil wealth, in proportion to their proximity to the regime. Saddam's family members were at the top of the list of beneficiaries, followed by his tribesmen, natives of Tikrit, Sunni Arabs, high-ranking Baath Party cadres, and loyal officers. After May 2003, all of these former Sunni beneficiaries were still around, along with the officers who had been demobilized by the provi-

sional authority. Their frustration at being deprived of their liveli-
hood and status, and the ensuing violence they turned against their
American "liberators," in the form of bombings, murder of hostages, and desecration of corpses, were all well-practiced and pre-
dictable responses.

During the affluent 1970s, Saddam's secular pan-Arabism was in
tune with the times. But when he declared war against Iran in September 1980, he was forced to legitimize his regime on a new basis.
He began to downplay secular references and retool Sunni religious discourse for his own purposes. In order to contend with
Khomeini without allowing Iran's revolution to monopolize the
political discourse of Islam, Saddam began to mix Sunni pan-
Islamism with his standard pan-Arabist rhetoric. With the help of
his propaganda services and xenophobic Arab writers on his pay-
roll, Saddam denigrated Khomeini as a Persian, the heir of the
Sassanids whom the armies of the first Arab Muslim caliphs defeated at Qadisiyya in 637. Mosques sprang up throughout Iraq,
and religious leaders were reinstated to promote Saddam's brand
of Sunni Islam as the true source of the nation's "cultural authenticity." A movie, *Qadisiyya*, commissioned from the Egyptian film-
maker Salah Abu Seif, glorified Iraq's ruler as a hero fighting for
the faith.

In the eight-year war with Iran, Saddam's regiments were made
up of many Arab Shia volunteers, attracted by wages paid with oil
revenues. These impoverished young men, drawn from Revolution
City (renamed Saddam City in the despot's honor) and the desti-
tute marshlands of the south, were the first foot soldiers sacrificed
to the bullets of their Iranian co-religionists. The elite Sunni regiments of the Republican Guard were equipped with state-of-the-
art weaponry specially adapted to crush revolts among the Shia
and any other opponents.

During the 1980s, Saddam reconciled with the "reactionary"

Arab regimes of the peninsula, whose funds he needed for the war effort. Saudi Arabia in particular was happy to supply Iraqi soldiers willing (or forced) to fight the Islamic revolutionists in Iran. As the war progressed, Saddam also garnered support from the West, particularly France and the United States, and subsidies provided by the Gulf Cooperation Council, whose members were terrified that the Iranian Revolution would spill over into their underpopulated countries. In Bahrain, Shia constituted a significant majority, making up seventy percent of the population. In Kuwait, at one quarter of the population, they were an influential minority. And in Saudi Arabia, where they made up only ten percent of the population, they were strategically situated in the oil-rich Eastern Province.

The war against Iran ended in the summer of 1988 with a cease-fire that left the adversaries exhausted and devastated. Nevertheless, Saddam lost little time before turning his army against Kuwait, Baghdad's most tenacious creditor. The invasion on August 2, 1990, garnered applause from much of the Arab public. But it posed a direct threat to Saudi Arabia's nearby oil rigs, and the United States responded to King Fahd's distress by raising an international coalition to drive Saddam back across the border.

For Saddam, the propaganda war now moved inside Arab Sunni space. His opponent was no longer Iran's revolutionary Shiism but the "custodian of the two holy places" in Saudi Arabia who controlled important Wahhabite contacts in mosques and Islamic associations around the globe. To counter this new enemy, the Iraqi president organized Islamic conferences in Baghdad, where insults rained down upon the Saudis: they were hypocrites, impostors who had sold themselves to the United States and Israel, unworthy of controlling the holy cities. Rival conferences were held in Mecca, where the Sauds' clients reviled the impious secularism of Saddam's Baath Party. Muslim Brothers from the Middle East, Asia, and Europe, seeing an opportunity to return to the mission field in Iraq, shuttled back and forth between the two camps, tendering their good offices and emphasizing their role as the *umma*'s "mediators." They reestablished the organization's old networks, which had been set up in the 1940s in Mosul but broken by Baathist repression.

Saddam inaugurated a Saladin revival, invoking the hero immortalized in the Arab-Muslim ideological imagination for having defeated the Crusaders. As part of the show, during the Gulf War he launched a few Scud missiles against Israel, which he portrayed as a modern Crusader state. During and after the Iraqi army's rout in Operation Desert Storm, the country was subjected to intense "faith campaigns" *(hamlat al-iman)* intended to present the military defeat as a travail inflicted by infidels, and resistance to the embargo as a symbol of the cultural and religious tenacity of Muslims persecuted by the West. This tack made it easier for Saddam to exonerate himself of responsibility for his society's suffering.

Saddam thought he could manipulate Sunni Islam for his political purposes, but it followed a logic of its own. During the 1990s, Islamists invested their energy in repairing the social fabric, torn by repression and embargo. Charitable activities called for the veiling and seclusion of women, along with other Islamic virtues aimed at strengthening religious control of all aspects of daily life. Iraq's Islamists followed the example of the Palestinian Muslim Brothers in the occupied territories, who prospered as pietistic charity associations with Israeli encouragement until the first intifada broke out in December 1987. At that point, they mobilized their flocks behind Hamas, which was expressly created on that occasion.

Muslim Brothers and salafist militants in Iraq, whether they were linked to the movement's Saudi or Kuwaiti networks or followed Mohammad Surur, extended their social presence among

Sunnis during the 1990s, with encouragement from the ministry of religious endowments *(waqf)*, which, like other Baath Party social structures, was undergoing thorough Islamization. At mid-decade, all the women who had been party members or political officials, as well as the female academic and scientific researchers whom Saddam was fond of showing off to demonstrate the degree of women's emancipation in Iraq (like Huda Ammash, known in the West as "Doctor Germ," a biologist educated in the United Kingdom who obtained her nickname thanks to her research on biological weapons), were appearing on state television in veils.

In 2003 when the regime fell and its social control networks were dismantled, along with the party and intelligence services, Islamist associations moved in to replace them. An Iraqi television preacher who had enjoyed a few minutes of fame on the Gulf's Arab television channels, Ahmad al-Qubaysi, returned to Baghdad, where he gave impassioned sermons against the U.S. occupation, organized demonstrations outside Sunni mosques after Friday prayers, and provided the religious inspiration that the fallen regime's former beneficiaries needed to regain their pride and resolve.

Soon after, the first clashes with American troops took place in the conservative Sunni city of Fallujah, which controls the main road to Jordan and the bridge over the Euphrates. Insurgents drew on a multitude of small groups, some of which had Baathist or nationalist loyalties but most of which claimed Islamic attachments. The occupation forces were completely out of their depth in reacting to these developments. They were convinced that the emergence of a democratic symbol such as the transitional Governing Council, set up on July 13, 2003, would restore order. But democratic representation was not the issue in Fallujah. The issue was power.

With the situation continuing to deteriorate, the American army laid siege to the city in April 2004. It was a partial failure. On May 1, exactly one year after President Bush declared an end to major combat, a U.S. Army general handed the keys of the city to a former general in Saddam's Republican Guard, in a symbolic gesture. The new governor, a Sunni, was now responsible for pacifying the insurrection among his co-religionists that Abrams tanks had been unable to contain.

Persuaded before the war that the transition between military victory and democracy would be smooth, the U.S. administration had failed to take into account the possibility of a grassroots insurgency rising from a segment of the population now cut off from its former source of revenue. By demobilizing the Iraqi army, which he saw as the noxious residue of the regime's repression, Paul Bremer not only left approximately 350,000 regular soldiers unemployed and ready to join the protesters' ranks, but he also deprived tens of thousands of officers and NCOs of their wages. These military elites, who no longer had anything to lose and had been trained in the ways of the intelligence services, brought to the insurgents their superior experience in urban guerrilla warfare and in the manipulation of violence for political ends. The combination soon made itself very visible in Fallujah.

The U.S. expeditionary force on the ground was neither specifically trained nor sufficiently numerous to win a counter-guerrilla war in an Arab country on a massive scale. Even if one allows for the difficulty in apportioning responsibility for violence among Iraqis and foreign jihadists who saw Iraq as the next Somalia, the violence deployed by Sunni insurgents was deadly. On August 7, 2003, an attack devastated the Jordanian embassy. On August 29, the U.N. secretary-general's special envoy, Brazilian diplomat Sergio Vieira de Mello, was killed, along with twenty-three other people, when a booby-trapped truck targeted the Canal Hotel, where the U.N. services were gathered. In the same month, saboteurs cut the pipeline channeling Iraqi oil to the Turkish port of Ceyhan, on the Mediterranean, then hampered reconstruction efforts. The guerrilla fighters thus showed, early on, that they were capable of hijacking the country's main political and economic resource; they would threaten it time and again.

November was the deadliest month of 2003, with over a hundred coalition troops killed, including nineteen Italians. Both October and November witnessed suicide bombings, booby-trapped car attacks on the U.S.-trained auxiliary police, and assaults on the Red Cross and on barracks housing foreign soldiers. The fighters, displaying a degree of professionalism and access to heavy weaponry that suggested a source beyond the stockpiled supplies of demobilized officers, began to fire missiles at American helicopters. U.S. soldiers became easy targets for systematic attacks by Sunni militants. This tactic resembled the one used by the Afghan jihad in the 1980s, when mujahedeen—assisted by the CIA—ensnared the Soviets' artillery, attacked their patrols, and killed off many in the Red Army's ranks. But this time, it was more harmful to the adversary, because television immediately broadcast the events around the world.

On October 26, Paul Wolfowitz, the prime proponent of state-of-the-art military technology and smart weapons, was in Iraq on an inspection tour when the Al Rashid Hotel, where he was staying, came under fire from a salvo of artillery rockets, launched from a donkey-drawn cart. The deputy secretary of defense emerged unscathed, but it would be difficult to dream up a more potent symbol to express the limits of a U.S. geopolitical strategy that had been mugged by the reality of occupation in a Third World Muslim country.

Triangulating the calculated collaboration of the Kurds and the explosion of Sunni violence is the attitude of Iraq's Shia—the highest stake, and the least-known factor, in the U.S. war on terror. By placing its bets on Iraq's Shiite community, the Bush administration sought to achieve several goals: weighting the distribution of oil revenues in favor of the Shia, who are more numerous than Sunnis on the shores of the Gulf; shifting the center of gravity in the Shiite world toward Iraq; and in so doing, drawing Tehran back into Washington's sphere of influence for the first time since 1979. By trying to settle this new geostrategic account in the currency of oil, the United States was betting on the gratitude of an oppressed population who had been emancipated from its Baathist persecutors in Iraq and would be free of the mullahs' grip in neighboring Iran.

But this is a complex negotiation, based on the assumption that forces within Iran's civil society will successfully pressure the regime to forsake its pan-Islamist and anti-American bias for the sake of restoring Tehran to its role as a major regional power—a role lost in the revolutionary turbulence of 1979. From that perspective, the evolution of Iraqi Shiism in the near term is a critical variable. If most of the community shifts toward the democratic, pro-American, and generally pro-Western pole, the magnetism of this move may align elements in Iran very quickly. But if chaos continues among the Iraqi Shia, the Iranian middle class, still traumatized by the revolution's violence and threatened by disorder west of the Shatt al-Arab, will remain cautious about any change. In the meantime, the hard-liners in Tehran may seize the unrest as an opportunity to intervene politically in their Iraqi neighbors' affairs. Once in Iraq, Iran's agents—the Pasdaran (Revolutionary Guards) and mullahs—will have their say, while the United States stands by, bewildered and vulnerable.

The Shia in Iraq and Iran are inextricably linked and yet profoundly different. While the clergy of the two groups, especially ayatollahs at the summit of the hierarchy, are closely intermingled, the faithful are motivated by powerful national and ethnic allegiances. The strength of this indoctrination became clear during the 1980–1988 war, when young Arab men signed up to kill young Persian men, and vice versa, without regard for their shared religious beliefs. The senseless bloodletting of that war did not reduce the patriotism of these groups; it seems only to have reinforced it. Gigantic mural frescoes exalting the "martyrs" fallen in battle decorate the walls of Iran's cities, drawing references from the Shia doctrine of martyrdom.

In both countries, Shiism is a relatively recent phenomenon. Iran converted in the fifteenth century, when the Safavid dynasty adopted this belief system as the state ideology, in opposition to the Ottoman Empire's Sunnism, and the population followed their leader. Iranian intellectuals have debated the question to what extent adherence to Shiism represented a way to reaffirm, in a different guise, an ancient Persian Indo-European identity, as against the Semitism of Arabs, or even a way to rediscover the Zoroastrian clergy's strict hierarchy. As a rule, the Iranian intelligentsia believe passionately that their five-thousand-year-old culture is superior to that of the "lizard-eating" Arabs or "peasant" Turks and Afghans.

Conversion of Iraqi Arabs to Shiism is even more recent. For the most part, it occurred in the nineteenth century, when some Sunni tribes, after centuries of pastoralism, settled down on the fertile lands of Mesopotamia. The great shrine cities of the Shia imams, Najaf and Karbala, provided these newly sedentary peoples with a system of social regulation overseen by a clerical hierarchy. (Ali, who died in 661, is said to be buried in Najaf; Hussein, killed in 680, is entombed in Karbala.) The Shia clerical hierarchy evolved into a very cosmopolitan corps, in which access to the highest rank (the *marja al-taqlid,* or "source of imitation") was open to very few men only after long years of study. Unlike the Catholic pope, the leader of this group is limited by the need to negotiate and achieve consensus with his peers. Vast erudition earns certain learned men the title of *bahr al-ulum* (literally, "ocean of knowledge").

If Najaf is a sort of Vatican of Shiism, Karbala is its Golgotha, the place where Hussein's martyrdom is commemorated in the ceremony of Ashura, a manifestation of piety and allegiance on the part of the faithful toward the community of great, infallible ayatollahs. Forty days after Ashura comes a second ceremony, still more important: the Arbaïn. In 1977 the procession organized for this occasion turned into a riot against the Baath Party, with the crowd shouting slogans hostile to Saddam. A harsh crackdown restored order, and the leaders of the riot—young men from Najaf with no political affiliation—were executed or tortured to death.

The ceremony was banned until April 2003, following the U.S. invasion, when three million pilgrims arrived, in a remarkable demonstration of the social control the Shiite clergy exercise over the faithful. By comparison, the pilgrimage to Mecca, under Saudi Arabia's aegis, brings together only two million people. Karbala was instantly recognized as a counterweight and a challenge to the annual *haj* taking place in Mecca. When I mentioned this astounding turnout to a member of the Saudi royal family in late April 2003, he responded that no one in Saudi Arabia had failed to notice it. Representatives of the kingdom's Shia, who make up ten percent of the total population, seized the opportunity to present Crown Prince Abdullah with a petition demanding equality and an end to the discrimination that Wahhabite intolerance had fostered.

Traditionally, the power and independence of the Shiite clerical hierarchy was the result of a pact made with their rulers. The clerics, citing Hussein as the "first martyr" and his death as a symbol of the defeat of Good on earth, counseled withdrawal from struggles in this world of shadow and injustice and encouraged the faithful to seek spiritual perfection, which can open the doors of Paradise. They preached patience—or quietism—until the End of Days heralded by the return of the messiah *(mahdi)*, who will fill the universe with light and justice. The ruler was considered a mediocre man, not the embodiment of sovereignty, and for this reason the Shiite clergy discouraged the faithful from attending congregational Friday prayers, which were traditionally said in the name of the ruler.

Still, subjects should demonstrate surface allegiance *(taqiyya* or *kitman,* "dissimulation") to the secular authorities and not seek to overthrow them. In return for this pacification, the clergy was allowed to exact a tax from the faithful: the "fifth" *(khums),* which day after day flowed into the vast treasury of the mullahs. The mullahs channeled this immense wealth into foundations, charitable works, and endowments. They used the treasury's revenues to carry out mediations and regulations that maintained social order, to the ruler's benefit as well as their own.

In modern times, this system was thrown off balance in Iraq and Iran, but in opposite ways. Baathist socialism in Iraq sought to dismantle the clerics' empire by nationalizing their wealth and replacing religious jurisdiction with a secular legal code. In Iran, Khomeini broke with the doctrine of quietism and seized political power for the clergy.

The leader of the July 1958 coup in Iraq, General Qassem, was the child of a mixed marriage between his Sunni father and his Shiite mother. Qassem relied for political support on Iraqi communists, who recruited members mostly from among the poor

Shia in Baghdad and the south. The Communist Party's secretary-general was a *sayyid* (one of the Prophet's descendants) from Najaf, and many of the Central Committee's members and the party cadres were also from the Shiite community. Qassem's regime harbored no ethnic hostility toward the Shia, though they clashed over agrarian reform of the clergy's vast landholdings. Grand Ayatollah Mohammad Baqir al-Hakim, seeking to avoid a head-on confrontation with the regime, let his office leak the opinion that agrarian reform was contrary to the laws of Islam, as was the regime's family code that granted equal rights to women. But then he personally issued a fatwa declaring membership in the Communist Party an act of unbelief *(kufr)*—a move that escalated the ideological war for Shiite souls.

The putsch of 1963, which put the Baath briefly in power, and the final coup that consolidated Saddam's regime in 1968, marginalized the Shia. They enjoyed little or no representation among Saddam's officers, and repeated nationalizations undermined their merchant class. The Communist Party, to which many Shia belonged, was annihilated in a ferocious repression campaign. Najaf remained a clerical training center for the transnational Shiite world; the Ayatollah Khomeini—exiled there by the shah between 1963 and 1977—developed his thoughts on Islamic government in conferences of seminarians in Najaf. But Saddam's policies of secularization, property confiscation, and financial sequestration considerably reduced the religious hierarchy's influence over its flock.

This is the context in which Iraq's Islamist Shiite political party gained ground. Formed in the late 1950s, when the monarchy was ousted, it recognized as its first ideologue a cleric born around 1930 to a great family of ayatollahs but a man still too young to impose himself on the religious hierarchy: Baqir al-Sadr. The founders of Dawa, as the new party was known (its name taken from "the call to Islam"), were inspired by the Communist Party's organization—partly out of concern about the attraction it exerted for young Shia—but they also borrowed from the Egyptian model of the Sunni Muslim Brothers. The founders' goal was to create a totalitarian Islamic state, in which the party would be the guardian of Sovereign Good as expressed in Islam. This state would come about through a revolutionary struggle to defeat the impious secular regime, after a phase of consciousness-raising and mobilization among the masses. While awaiting the return of the infallible messiah, the new state would impose the rule of Islamic law through *shura*, the consensus of the ulema.

This hybrid mix of revolutionary Marxism and Islamic messianism at first sowed confusion in the party. The religious hierarchy opposed it, and the Baathist regime repressed it. Baqir al-Sadr was forced to renounce his affiliation and return to the fold of his clerical family. But in 1959 and 1961, he published two books in a style very different from the pedantic writing of the ulema. Entitled *Our Philosophy* and *Our Economy*, they were steeped in Islamist ideology, but with socialist accents. The second one especially became immensely popular in the Arab and Muslim world, even among Sunnis. *Our Economy* is still the reference work for advocates of an Islamic banking system.

Since the 1960s and continuing to the present, the Shiite religious movement in Iraq has been still torn between its clerical and militant poles. Each side sought to win over the seminarians and low-ranking clerics, *khums* collectors, and preachers who made popular mobilization possible. When Grand Ayatollah Muhsin al-Hakim died in June 1970, the office passed to Abu Qasim al-Khoei and then, when he died in 1992, to Ali Sistani. Both men were of Iranian origin (Sistani speaks Arabic with a very pronounced Farsi accent) and followed the "quietist" branch of Shiism. While cultivating their images as religious leaders in rare public appearances, they remained relatively detached from Iraqi politics and kept their distance from the Iranian Revolution and Khomeini, whom they considered inferior in erudition to them. Opposing them were two clerics of Iraqi extraction, Baqir al-Sadr and his cousin Sadiq al-Sadr, who embodied the militant, radical wing of Shiism and who were eventually assassinated by Saddam's secret service (Baqir in April 1980 and Sadiq in February 1999). Their mantle was taken up by Sadiq al-Sadr's son, Moktada, a young man who burst upon the scene in April 2003 as the representative of Shiite opposition to the American occupation.

The militant wing had experienced ups and downs, linked to the Iraqi regime's repression but also to its ambiguous relations with Khomeini and the Islamic Republic. During his fourteen years of exile in Najaf, Khomeini associated very little with his Iraqi colleagues, but as the uprising in Iran developed in 1978 and the radical clergy took control, those in Iraq who supported the Islamic Revolution could not remain silent. Baqir al-Sadr renewed his association with militants of the Dawa Party who had survived Saddam's executions and now pledged allegiance to Khomeini. By contrast, Grand Ayatollah Khoei merely sent him a telegram of congratulations, addressing him as *hujjat al-islam*—the equivalent of a lecturer, as opposed to a tenured professor.

Demonstrations of support for Khomeini, organized in Najaf around Sadr's house, led the regime to arrest him in June 1979, after violently killing the party workers. At a time when Saddam was purging the Baath Party of rivals and tightening his iron grip on Iraq, Islamist activists were launching a terror campaign and attempting to assassinate government officials. On April 4, 1980, Sadr and his sister, Bint al-Huda, were kidnapped, and on April 9 his body arrived at the cemetery in Najaf. In September, Saddam invaded Iran.

Eight long years of war, following the assassination of Baqir al-

Sadr, sent the Iraqi Shiite opposition into decline. It was poorly organized and wary because of its collusion with the enemy at a time
when hundreds of thousands of young Shia were dying in the
trenches. In 1982 opposition activists exiled in Iran created the Supreme Council of the Islamic Revolution in Iraq (SCIRI), led by
Mohammad Baqir al-Hakim, a cleric from a prestigious Najaf family. It managed to raise a militia of a few thousand men (dubbed
the Badr Army), recruited from among Iraqi Shia POWs but
equipped and funded by Iran and structured by the Pasdaran. But
before they saw action, Khomeini reluctantly signed a cease-fire on
July 18, 1988, while declaring he was "drinking the poison chalice."
Iraq's militant Shiites, who had dreamed of their country's becoming the first conquest of the global Islamic revolution under the
guidance of Tehran's imam, saw their hopes evaporate.

At a loss for what to do next, the militants backed Saddam when
he invaded Kuwait in August 1990, in the name of a jihad against
America. Consequently, they were unable to benefit politically
from the Iraqi army's retreat under coalition bombing in late January 1991. The Shiite uprising in the south in early March—which
the United States encouraged but then failed to support—was a
leaderless revolt that massacred Baath Party members and government officials. The Republican Guard quickly avenged their dead,
drowning the uprising in its own blood. Among the Shia, memory
of these events is both sharp and ambivalent: while Saddam's
guards set about their business of murderous repression, the
United States chose not to intervene, although American troops
were massed nearby and could easily have stepped in. The Bush
Sr. administration sacrificed the Shia uprising to its own global interests in the region.

Those interests included, first, maintaining and leveraging the
integrity of the coalition in order to force a settlement between Is-

rael and the Palestinians. The second interest was to keep a "neu-tralized," weakened Iraq intact, under Saddam's leadership. The administration feared that a dismembered, leaderless nation would devolve into a vast, unpredictable zone of Shiite turbulence in the Gulf under the aegis of Iran, which had not yet abandoned its revolutionary ways. A weakened, "contained" dictator was deemed preferable to a leap into the void. The third interest was to reward the conservative Sunni petro-monarchies that had allied themselves with the United States against a rogue Arab nation. The drastically curtailed oil production in Iraq—where damaged and antiquated infrastructure prevented Saddam from prospecting and drilling, and the embargo limited the benefits of selling any oil he produced—kept crude prices high, raising revenues for Saudi Arabia and Kuwait. These beneficiaries showed their gratitude, in turn, by signing a host of contracts on very lucrative terms for American firms. A wide circle of family and friends of the Bush administration realized huge profits. But there was a price to pay. When high energy prices inhibited economic recovery and job creation in the United States, George H. W. Bush, having defeated Iraq, was himself defeated in the November 1992 election by a young, upstart governor from an economically depressed state— William Jefferson Clinton of Arkansas.

In Iraq itself, these geostrategic interests concerned the population—particularly the impoverished Shiite majority—only to the extent that they intensified its suffering. A dictator's folly still ravaged the country, and the U.N. embargo was stifling economic recovery from over a decade of almost continuous war. The larger world showed little interest in Iraqi civil society, let alone its democratization. Ironically, the neoconservatives were among the most vocal outsiders offering a moral critique of this international cynicism, and around the middle of the decade they began to lobby for a change of regime in Baghdad that would target Saddam instead of holding the Iraqi population hostage.

During a period when, for their daily survival, every Iraqi relied on a network of corruption and contraband controlled by Saddam and his clan, the dictator adapted his legitimating discourse to accommodate the misery of the Iraqi people, by leaving considerable space open for religious activists. Sadiq al-Sadr took up the task of mobilizing poor Shiites, whose situation was made more precarious by a population explosion and mass migration to the ramshackle housing projects of Saddam City on the fringes of Baghdad. The welfare associations and charitable networks Sadr developed resembled those in Lebanon created by another of his cousins, Musa al-Sadr, who founded the Movement of the Dispossessed (Harakat al-Mahrumin) to deal with a similar crisis: rapid population growth, civil war, and mass migration from the south of the country toward the Dahiyya, the poor southern suburb of Beirut.

Just as the regime in Beirut had regarded Musa al-Sadr favorably, since his advocacy of piety channeled the Lebanese Shia population's volatile sentiments away from political unrest, so did Saddam encourage Sadiq al-Sadr, at least in the beginning. Although the Iraqi ruler had ordered the assassination of Baqir al-Sadr in 1980, he recognized this new Sadr as an Arab ayatollah who could stand up to the Persian Sistani, who had nothing good to say about a regime that had butchered so many Shia in the war with Iran and during the subsequent uprising. Against the grand ayatollah's "silent seminary" *(hawza samita)*—a retreat from worldly matters—Sadiq al-Sadr created a "talking seminary" *(hawza natiqa)* that became actively involved in social issues. His network of neighborhood preachers, grassroots mullahs, and *khums* collectors worked to lighten the burden imposed by the embargo and U.N. sanctions.

Following the measures Khomeini had taken when he seized power in Iran, Sadr encouraged Iraq's Shia to attend congregational prayers on Friday. In the Islamic Republic, this innovation had strengthened the clerics' new political power because prayers were, by tradition, pronounced in the name of the Muslim leader (that is, Ayatollah Khomeini). In Iraq, however, Friday prayers strengthened Saddam Hussein, which delighted the tyrant for a while. They gathered large crowds, but as the years went by the Friday sermons grew increasingly hostile to the regime. Punishment was not long in coming: like his cousin Baqir, Sadiq al-Sadr was assassinated by Saddam's thugs in February 1999, along with two of his sons. Only one son remained: Moktada, then twenty or so, who was receiving his clerical education at the time of his father's death. Deprived Shia had idolized Sadiq al-Sadr and brandished his portrait on every possible occasion. Four years later, when the U.S. invasion created a power vacuum in Iraq, the young cleric, scion of a beloved and famous family, stepped forward to fill it.

Such was the state of Iraqi Shiism, on which so many hopes in Washington were pinned, when U.S. troops marched on Baghdad. Its many exiles were scattered among a host of nationalist, Marxist, secular, or religious groups with very little in common apart from the goal of eliminating the Baath regime—so many that the U.S. administration had difficulty keeping them straight. The Pentagon and the neoconservatives fervently backed Ahmad Chalabi, a Shiite businessman with a checkered past who headed the Iraqi National Congress (INC), a coalition of nineteen Iraqi and Kurdish organizations, created in the 1990s and bankrolled by the U.S. government to "gather information, distribute propaganda, and recruit dissidents" for the overthrow of Saddam Hussein. The State Department favored Ayatollah Baqir al-Hakim and his Tehran-based

SCIRI, which, according to American diplomatic circles, enjoyed greater popular support.

But both the Pentagon and the State Department had bet on the wrong horse. In a society where the Baath had killed off every possible form of association and where the embargo had broken the resilience of civil society, the postwar political void among the Shia was mainly filled by two groups, neither of which was represented in the INC and neither of which had ties with the provisional government or the State Department. The first group consisted of the Shiite hierocracy at Najaf under Grand Ayatollah Sistani, and the second consisted of followers of Moktada al-Sadr. These two forces, which first clashed a few months after the fall of Baghdad, structured the competition for power within the Shiite world after the fall of Saddam Hussein.

For anyone paying attention, the strength of Sistani's networks was clear in March 2003 when U.S. forces reached Najaf on their way to Baghdad. The supreme *marja* told his followers not to stand in the troops' way, but at the same time he forbade the U.S. soldiers from approaching the *hawza*. American troops retreated, their guns in the air, as a turbaned mullah from Sistani's headquarters communicated instructions to their commander. In television images of this confrontation, the mullah's power over the tense crowd is palpable. Najaf immediately became the main stake for those who were struggling for control of the Shia community.

The strength of Moktada al-Sadr's faction was demonstrated on April 10, when Abd al-Majid al-Khoei, an ayatollah who had returned from exile in London and who represented the most rationalist, liberal, and pro-Western faction in the clerical community, ventured into the mausoleum of Imam Ali. An enraged crowd tore him from the mausoleum and led him, bound, to Sadr's nearby home. Then—according to subsequent accusations—they stabbed him to death before dragging the corpse through the streets. This act marked the eruption of Sadr's party onto the Iraqi political and religious scene and demonstrated the violence potential of interests linked to sacred power. Moktada was willing to use hit men to assert his political presence, and U.S. forces were powerless to protect the only ayatollah who would have welcomed Iraq's democratization as conceived in Washington.

Moktada al-Sadr's march to power passed through Baghdad's vast Shiite suburb, formerly Saddam City, which his supporters had renamed Madinat al-Sadr (Sadr City). By marking the territory of liberated Iraq with the name of his martyred father, supporters simultaneously conferred legitimacy and visibility upon the son. The change took place as Baghdad spiraled into anarchy and U.S. troops stood by as the city was looted. By contrast, the imams at the Shiite mosques in Sadr City, where many of the looters lived, collected stolen goods in order to return them to their owners, thus demonstrating their role in restoring morality to social relations. They immediately extended their control to dispensaries and hospitals, where female nurses and doctors were ordered to cover their hair. The so-called Mahdi Army, Sadr's newly formed militia, performed critical municipal tasks such as collecting garbage, regulating traffic, and "commanding good and forbidding evil" in the zones it patrolled.

Moktada al-Sadr turned to social activism and, as necessary, violence against his adversaries to compensate for his youth and relative lack of erudition—major handicaps among the Shia—as well as his total ignorance of the outside world, which he saw through the narrow prism of his religious convictions. He had left Iraq only once, to travel to Iran. His militancy worried the Shiite middle classes as much as the Sunnis and Kurds. His style of leadership stood in sharp contrast with that of the State Department's favorite, Ayatollah Mohammad Baqir al-Hakim, the spiritual guide of SCIRI. On May 10, 2003, after twenty-three years of exile in Iran, he tried to stage his return to Iraq as an echo of Khomeini's triumphant entry into Tehran on February 1, 1979. The crowds greeting him were a disappointment. Baqir al-Hakim presented himself as the leader capable of uniting the Shia and as a candidate to lead an Islamic Iraq, where different ethnic and religious groups would be recognized and where multiparty politics would prevail. He was the political choice between the poles of Sistani's quietism and Sadr's militancy.

Mohammad Baqir al-Hakim was assassinated on August 29 in a car bomb explosion in Najaf that claimed over a hundred victims. Sunni jihadists and U.S. forces accused each other of complicity with the assassins. His brother, Abd al-Aziz, was elected to the leadership of SCIRI two days later, but this could not compensate for the death of the organization's charismatic leader.

Moktada al-Sadr's path was now clear. He tried to undermine Sistani's influence among Shia while sending out numerous feelers to radical Sunnis, professing his loathing of the American occupiers and the West in general and revealing his intention to solidify his power base throughout the country. In January 2004, when Islamist preachers were appearing on Arab satellite television to protest the French law against the display of religious symbols in schools, Sadr, who does not have the vaguest ideas about France and the world in general, spoke out violently against Paris, attempting to intervene in a debate that supposedly transcended exclusively Shiite interests. In March 2004, as violence committed mainly by radical militants in the Sunni triangle was reaching unprecedented levels and the Provisional Governing Council was adopting an interim constitution for Iraq over Sistani's protests, Israel assassinated Sheikh Ahmed Yassin, the spiritual leader of Pal-

estinian Hamas. This provided Sadr with the opportunity to orga-
nize a very visible demonstration of solidarity with that Sunni
organization. By identifying Hamas's struggle against Israel with
the Mahdi Army's fight against the United States, Sadr strengthened the tendency of many in the Muslim world to identify Tsahal
with the U.S. army—a message constantly conveyed by images on
Arab satellite television—and attempted to rise above the antagonism between Shia and Sunnis.

Moktada's movement grew wider when the Sunni uprising in
Fallujah on April 5 coincided with demonstrations Sadr organized
on April 4 to protest his formal conviction in the assassination of
Abd al-Majid al-Khoei the previous year. The riot spread to the
Shiite strongholds of Basra and Kufa, where Sadr retreated, surrounded by his poorly trained and equipped Mahdi Army, and
challenged the U.S. forces to arrest or kill him. This dare threatened to ignite the community and to put Sistani and the Shiite
leaders who advocated conciliation with Washington in an untena-
ble position. The United States was forced to accept the existence
of autonomous enclaves that it could no longer control—Fallujah,
Kufa, and parts of Madinat Sadr.

In the same month, Sadr sent detachments of the Mahdi Army
into Najaf to take over the mausoleum of Imam Ali and dislodge
Ayatollah Sistani's followers. Sistani resisted, but their opposition
was now out in the open.

AROUND THIS TIME, evidence of brutality toward Iraqi prisoners
surfaced and further damaged U.S. credibility around the world.
The moral arguments that the neoconservatives had used to advocate the invasion of Iraq—establishing democratic institutions and

ending the practice of torture—were undermined by these revelations of humiliation and abuse in the very prison where Saddam Hussein had tortured so many Iraqis for so long. These photos were new and gripping, and they distracted Arab viewers from recent images of Iraqi insurgents murdering and desecrating the bodies of American civilians. On March 31, 2004, agitated young men in Fallujah had beaten the corpses of their victims to a pulp with shovels, doused them in kerosene and set them on fire, then suspended the decapitated, burned bodies from the metal truss of a bridge over the Euphrates. The killers brandished their Kalashnikovs, grinning widely for the cameras. And shortly after the Abu Ghraib photographs came to light, insurgents captured and murdered Nicholas Berg, an American businessman; a video of his decapitation circulated widely on the Internet.

Rather than bringing an end to terror, the demobilization of Saddam's army opened up Iraq's borders to foreign jihad fighters, and their presence on the ground was now being felt. The size of the problem is difficult to measure on the basis of current evidence, but the number of Sunni Arabs from neighboring countries who have been arrested and the ceremonies being held at mosques in Saudi Arabia, Kuwait, Syria, and elsewhere in honor of jihad "martyrs" fallen in Iraq suggests a significant contingent. Also suggestive (but to be read with caution) were two letters circulating in Iraq that bore Bin Laden's signature. They incited "Muslim brothers in Iraq" to fight a continuous jihad against the "incursion of Crusaders and Jews" into one of Islam's ancient capitals, and encouraged young mujahedeen in Yemen and neighboring countries to join the battle. The letters condemned and sentenced to death as an apostate any Iraqi Muslim who collaborated with the U.S. occupation or sought to establish democracy—the "religion of unbelief and *jahiliyya*."

In a memorandum intercepted by Kurdish forces in January 2004 and attributed to the mysterious Jordanian-Palestinian jihadist Ahmad al-Khalayleh (known as Abu Musab al-Zarqawi), the putative author laid out his vision of Iraq as the new heart of global jihad, "in the depth of the Arabs' land, a stone's throw from the land of the holy sites [Saudi Arabia] and Al Aqsa [Jerusalem]. We know, by Allah's religion, that the true, decisive battle between unbelief and Islam occurs on the land of the Levant [*al-Sham*, or Greater Syria]." The text went on to say that unbelievers (Jews and Americans) wage this battle with the help of local allies: the Kurds, first and foremost, among whom Islam has been extinguished, and especially the Shia, which the text describes contemptuously as *rafidin* (heretics). Assisted by "their Jewish friends," they seek to establish "a state of heresy [*dawlat rafd*—a Shiite state] that will extend from Iran to Lebanon, via Iraq and Syria, ending in the cardboard states of the Gulf." This project consists in attacking (Sunni) Islam from the rear, just as—according to the author—the Shiites attacked Baghdad while the Ottomans were laying siege to Vienna in 1683 and thus forced the sultan to call back his troops from Europe. The Shiites prevented the sultan "from seizing this stronghold, which would have made it possible to spread Islam by the glorious sword and extend jihad to the four corners of Europe."

Citing lengthy extracts from Ibn Taymiyya, the text praised resistance in the Sunni triangle, where foreign jihad fighters were making inroads. In contrast, Iraqi Sunnism was crippled by popular piety (sufism) that had intoxicated the people and caused them to forget jihad. The Muslim Brothers were no better, according to the author of the manifesto: they, "as is their custom, buy and sell the blood of martyrs" while pretending to represent the Sunnis. Claiming responsibility for twenty-five suicide attacks at the time of its publication, the author designated four targets: the Americans ("easy prey"); the Kurds; the police forces, soldiers, and agents; and especially the Shia, "far more dangerous than the Americans."

Abu Musab al-Zarqawi was allegedly the masked man who slit the throat of Nicholas Berg and that of a Korean hostage in June 2004. It is difficult to know whether this document attributed to him is authentic, but if it is borne out by operations, it will provide one more damaging piece of evidence against the argument that Saddam's fall would automatically purge Iraq of jihadists from Al Qaeda and similar organizations.

So worrying was the threat of terror that the transfer of power was advanced by 48 hours. Paul Bremer left Baghdad on June 28 without fanfare. The new government, hand-picked by the United States and U.N. Special Envoy Lakhdar Bramini, immediately restored the death penalty just before Saddam Hussein and eleven top leaders were finally delivered to an ad hoc Iraqi court by their U.S. captors on June 30.

Particularly problematic for the United States and Europe was the taking of hostages from Western countries for the purpose of blackmailing their governments. After the Madrid attack of March 11, 2004—which demonstrated that terrorism was capable of striking a European capital directly and intervening in the democratic process by changing the outcome of elections—an Italian hostage was taken captive in the Sunni triangle and eventually assassinated. During the ordeal, his kidnappers demanded that Italians take to the streets to force their government to call back its troops from Iraq. This troubling development showed more clearly than ever that the war on terror did not end with the fall of Baghdad. On the contrary, it had escalated. While the United States was focusing attention on fending off the insurgency in Iraq, jihadists and their fellow travelers were staging a new attack from the rear: on the battlefield of Europe.

7

The Battle for Europe

The bombings in Madrid on March 11, 2004, established Europe as the new frontline for terrorist attacks. Before 9/11, Europe had provided a sanctuary where Al Qaeda's planners could complete preparations for the world-shattering operation they had conceived in the mountains of Afghanistan. But with events in Madrid in spring 2004, Europe emerged as the primary battlefield on which the future of global Islam will be decided.

In Germany, Mohammed Atta (an Egyptian), his flat-mate Ramzi bin al-Shibh (a Yemeni), and other conspirators from North Africa or the Middle East had formed the "Hamburg cell" that became the main operational base for 9/11. Their points of contact were mosques whose imams were fascinated by the Afghan jihad and especially the charismatic Bin Laden. The German security forces' ignorance of Arab Middle Eastern networks (as compared to their familiarity with Turkish and Kurdish organizations, since those regions provide most of Germany's Muslim immigrants) benefited the jihadists, who were able to go about their activities relatively undisturbed. Consequently, Germany became a favorite site for settlement of Muslim activists in the years preceding the attacks on the United States. The German legal system, in which a very strict burden of proof protects those accused of a crime (a precaution against any possibility of a return to fascism) seems to have worked to the advantage of a number of shadowy figures.

In Spain, financial and operational coordination meetings were held in Tarragon in July 2001 during the final planning phase for September 11. In November 2001 Abu Dahdah, a naturalized Spaniard of Syrian origin who had peacefully plied his trade as a second-hand clothes salesman and traveled throughout the world during the 1990s, was jailed on suspicion of having been in contact with Al Qaeda's activists. Spain harbors a large Moroccan population, partly illegal, whose networks, hiding places, and contacts made the country an important crossroads for jihadists. Clandestine immigrants crossed the Strait of Gibraltar at night on flimsy wooden boats to try their luck in Europe. In the 1990s, during the Algerian civil war, Islamist militants of the GIA (Armed Islamic Group) and the AIS (Islamic Salvation Army) used the Iberian peninsula as a stopover on the way to safe havens in Britain and Canada.

In England, Londonistan became a sanctuary for global Islamist extremism beginning in the 1980s. It was the place where a letter of recommendation was forged for two Tunisians from Belgium who, on September 9, 2001, in a prelude to Al Qaeda's attack, assassinated the Afghan commander Ahmed Shah Massoud, a much-feared opponent of the Taliban. One of Londonistan's leading figures at the time was the Syrian Abu Musab al-Suri, who, like Abu Dahdah, acquired Spanish citizenship by marriage. He was, along with his colleague Abu Qatada, another character on the salafist jihadist stage.

In Belgium, the GIA set up several cells in the 1990s that were immune from investigations of the French intelligence services. Since 9/11, many militants, especially of North African origin, have been arrested there. Police operations were also undertaken in

France, Italy, and the Netherlands to dismantle branches of Al Qaeda, and authorities in those countries have made many arrests. A French national of Moroccan origin, Zacarias Moussaoui, was imprisoned in the United States. Among the prisoners at Guantanamo Bay are dozens of Europeans—young men from immigrant families of North African, Middle Eastern, Turkish, and Indian origin—who were captured in Afghanistan by the U.S. army during the first phase of the war on terror. Since their encounter with the military operation that the Bush administration hopefully named "Enduring Freedom," they have been detained in secret without being officially charged with any crime or allowed access to lawyers.

Several young European converts to Islam have been placed on trial. The most notorious was the shoe bomber Richard Reid, a British citizen arrested for attempting (unsuccessfully) to blow up his sneakers on a flight between France and the United States in December 2001. These arrests and sentences have drawn attention to a hitherto neglected phenomenon: the conversion to Islam of growing numbers of European young people from working-class backgrounds. In France alone, the number of converts is estimated at around fifty thousand. Even if jihadist militants make up a tiny minority of this fresh group of enthusiasts, converts are of great concern to security services, because insurgents who choose not to display their new faith overtly can easily elude authorities. For this reason, conversion is an intense focus of terrorist networks.

Before Al Qaeda existed, Europe faced Islamist terrorism on its territory. France was the victim of two successive waves. The first, during the 1980s, originated among Lebanese Shia linked to Khomeini's Iran, and the second, in the 1990s, originated among the Algerian GIA's local contacts. But the source of this terrorism was foreign, and the Islamist constituency in France, which was small at that time, had only minimal interaction with the militants. In the past twenty-five years, the French government has taken an uncompromising attitude in combating terrorism, by consistently refusing to grant political asylum to radical Arab Islamist leaders. The goal has been to prevent them from proselytizing among France's mostly North African Muslim population, which is the largest Muslim group in Europe. What French officials fear is that the social malaise felt by Muslims in the suburbs of major cities, living for the most part in below-standard housing projects and experiencing relatively high rates of unemployment, will be expressed as religious extremism, leading eventually to violence and terrorism. The French political model seeks to promote—with varied success so far—a policy of integration, individual by individual, that will lead to upward social mobility among the relevant populations, just as it has for the republic's other citizens. This policy does not discriminate—either positively or negatively—for or against persons based on their religious affiliation. Islam is granted the same rights and duties as other faiths. Its free exercise is guaranteed on condition that it respects the public order. It receives neither recognition per se nor funding from the French state.

Britain has adopted a diametrically opposed policy. In the last decades of the twentieth century, radical ideologues of global Arab Islamism, hunted down in their home countries, found refuge in Londonistan. Today, they continue to benefit from political asylum and freedom of expression, no matter how extreme, as long as they do not implement their ideas on British territory. Underprivileged classes of Muslims in Britain, most of whom are from the Indian subcontinent, share neither a language nor family ties with the Arab ideologues of North Africa and the Middle East, and Scotland Yard therefore has been less concerned than French intelligence services with the possible contagion of extremism among these groups. Although Tony Blair's cabinet went along with the Bush administration's war on terror in the Middle East, British territory was in fact considered immune to attack—until worrying signs led Her Majesty's Government to contemplate a radical overhaul of its policy.

In November 2003, while President Bush was visiting London, terrorist attacks in Istanbul targeted British banks and a consulate—a first for Islamist terrorism. Then, in March 2004, stocks of ammonium nitrate fertilizer, used in explosives, were discovered in a London suburb, leading to the arrest of several young Britons of Pakistani background. These events shook up many accepted notions of Britain's invulnerability. The terrorist movement's fragmentation—as evidenced by the Casablanca and Madrid attacks, which were carried out by relatively unsophisticated fanatics who, though inspired by Bin Laden, had no organizational ties for the most part to Al Qaeda, nor training in the camps of Pakistan or Afghanistan—set off alarm bells. Free agents are not concerned with the refugee status of jihadist ideologues in their British sanctuary, and therefore feel no restraint on their actions. This fact invalidated the security calculation on which Londonistan's existence was predicated.

British multiculturalism has traditionally celebrated distinct ethnic or religious groups of foreign origin and has empowered community leaders to promote law and order through activities centered on mosques, temples, and other houses of worship. Following the March 2004 discovery of explosives in London, a first step was taken away from this doctrine when the president of the United Kingdom's Commission on Racial Equality—a body that had made multiculturalism its cornerstone—declared to the media that "the word is not useful, it means the wrong things. Multiculturalism suggests separateness. What we should be talking about is how we reach an integrated society, one in which people are equal under the law, where there are some common values—democracy rather than violence, the common currency of the English language, honoring the culture of these islands." During demonstrations in support of the young Muslim men incarcerated in connection with the explosives, bearded co-religionists in traditional Pakistani Islamic attire, also British subjects, reacted to the crackdown by burning the Union Jack in the middle of London, shouting "Allahu akbar!" for the cameras.

While this unrest was brewing in Great Britain, in France various Islamist groups and television preachers on Arab satellite channels protested the new French law that prohibited the wearing of religious symbols in schools—and in particular (though not exclusively) the Islamic veil. The bearded and veiled demonstrators who took to the streets four times between December 21, 2003, and February 14, 2004, brandished the tricolor. The women draped themselves symbolically in a great display of red, white, and blue, to invoke their rights as French citizens. Liberty, equality, and fraternity were the rallying cries raised to defend the right to wear veils at school.

Thus, for political purposes, Islamists on either side of the Channel took advantage of their citizenship in a European state with a liberal tradition, but in opposite ways, according to opportunity: the national flag was burned in one country, brandished in another. In both cases, however, fundamental questions about the contract of citizenship were being raised, with integration and separatism for Muslims in Europe hanging in the balance.

WHEN TERRORISM LINKED to Al Qaeda erupted in the heart of Madrid in March 2004, the Islamist movement took advantage of the crisis to increase its visibility among European young people of Muslim background and to blackmail European governments.

One statement on the Internet, attributed to Zawahiri, threatened France, which was considered an enemy of Islam since it forbade Muslim girls to wear the veil at school. Another, attributed to Bin Laden, suggested a three-month truce *(hudna)*, starting on April 15, 2004, with "[our] neighbors to the north of the Mediterranean" if the states that had sent troops to Iraq alongside the United States pulled out, "following the positive signs shown by recent events and the opinion polls indicating that most of Europe's peoples desire peace." Probably referring to the decision of Spain's new socialist government, elected after the March 11 attacks, to withdraw from Iraq, the statement proposed *sulh.* In traditional Islamic geopolitical discourse, that term means "treaty" between Muslims and parts of the "land of unbelief," which are therefore no longer targets of jihad.

The day before Bin Laden's statement was posted an Italian hostage, kidnapped along with three of his compatriots in Iraq, was executed by his captors, who identified themselves as the Green Phalange of Muhammad. The four hostages had been displayed to the world through video images broadcast by Arab satellite channels. In a message issued immediately after the abduction, the kidnappers made three demands: an official, public apology from Prime Minister Berlusconi for the outrages he had committed against Muslims and Islam; a precise schedule for the withdrawal of Italian troops from Iraq; and the release of all the imams and mosque preachers under arrest in Italy. When no response from Rome was forthcoming, the kidnappers, after assassinating one hostage, broadcast a second message on April 26, accompanied by video footage of the three survivors. This second message addressed the Italian population directly and promised to free the surviving prisoners if, five days later, on the occasion of the May 1 celebrations, mass protests forced the government to pull its troops out.

Whether or not Bin Laden's statement was authentic, and whatever the identity of the kidnappers, it was now clear that public opinion among Europeans had become a new weapon in the war on terror. It would be exploited by terrorists who had an accurate understanding of political life in the West and the intention to put pressure on the democratic process at a time of their own choosing: in Italy, on Workers' Day; in Spain, just before the legislative elections.

But the militants' strategy of using Europeans in the war on terror went beyond manipulations of public opinion. The Madrid attacks relied primarily on homegrown Islamist militants of Moroccan background, aided by global jihadists. Most were Spanish residents leading ordinary—even, in some cases, socially well integrated—lives. Without undergoing indoctrination or brainwashing or deprivation in an Afghan training camp—without a transition experience of any kind—grocers, mobile phone repairmen, and real estate agents suddenly became activists bent on waging a jihad of terror, assisted by a few experienced militants who themselves blended into the multivariate Spanish social landscape.

March 11, 2004, sounded an alarm for the French and British security apparatuses. It revealed the flaw in Paris's logic of forbidding entry to activists: in Spain, radical Islamist ideologues were few and far between and those who were present led discreet lives; so turning known activists away at the door was not enough to keep susceptible individuals among Europe's Muslim population from making contact with a jihadist recruitment agent. March 11 challenged London's strategy at a deeper level: granting political asylum to extremist ideologues in Londonistan in return for orderly behavior offered no guarantee that their sympathizers would not be transformed, overnight, into terrorists. In late May 2004, Britain drew a few logical conclusions from this dead-end strategy and began to make changes. Londonistan's most media-friendly denizen,

Abu Hamza al-Masri, an Egyptian salafist-jihadist imam who had lost an arm and an eye in Afghanistan (and whom the British press had dubbed "Captain Hook"), was arrested at the request of an American judge. His extradition to the United States was pending—though it could not be implemented until he was stripped of his British citizenship.

Germany, Spain, Italy, the Netherlands, Belgium, and the Scandinavian countries evolved public policies that fell between the French and British extremes, with regard to both anti-terrorist measures against jihadist activists and the debate over the integration of immigrant populations of Muslim background. Over ten million immigrants from Muslim countries live in Western Europe as a whole. Their children were born in Europe, for the most part, and hold citizenship in a European nation. They were educated in European schools, they speak European languages, and they are accustomed to European social practices. As far as many of these young people are concerned, the battle for Europe is fought by two opposed camps, between which they attempt to find their way, according to their personal identities, interests, and opportunities.

A positive, optimistic vision of the future would see the vast majority of these young people as the ideal bearers of a modernity bestowed on them as Western Europe's newest citizens. By the example they provide, they are potential purveyors of these values to the Muslim countries from which their families emigrated. They offer an alternative to increased religiosity, which has served as both an ideological shield for corrupt authoritarian regimes and as an outlet for the social rage of a dispossessed population. In this reading of the future, Europe's young Muslims will become the international vectors of a democratic project whose success they themselves embody—by blending innate Arab or Muslim traits with acquired European ones. They will participate fully, as Muslims, in the most dynamic, creative dimensions of a universal civilization, while rejecting extremism, along with the violence and chaos that follow in its wake. The first generation of university graduates among Muslim immigrants' children in Britain, France, and Germany have already begun to take their place as educated, activist citizens of Europe and the world. They possess the skills and perspective to build bridges with North Africa, the Middle East, or Pakistan and assist those countries in emerging from the quagmire.

A more negative reading of the future would focus on young people at the opposite extreme, whose rigid Islamic identity leads them to reject cultural integration into the European environment and to embrace cultural separatism. Some—a minority—will pass from voluntary secession into violence, expressing social resentment through hatred that they justify on religious grounds. Others, more numerous, will be satisfied to turn inward, to closed communities, or to dream of emigrating from the land of unbelief back to the land of Islam. Both of these separatist attitudes have their roots in the salafist teachings and influence of some Saudi Arabian preachers.

The first group—adherents of jihad—condemn not only the "impious" regimes of the West but also the "apostate" ruling family in Riyadh. Many of them left the outskirts of Lyon, Paris, Roubaix, or Birmingham for a time to gain experience in the camps of Pakistan, Bosnia, Chechnya, or Georgia, awaiting the right moment to accelerate the Islamization of Europe, as called for in Bin Laden's declarations and Zawahiri's reasoning. In the meantime, they gather with other young sympathizers and look at videos or DVDs of armed jihadists, veterans of war who left their neighborhoods as ragged children and returned as weathered combatants, bearded, crowned in glory, and guaranteed a place in Paradise. These heroes bypassed unemployment, identity crises, and even drug addiction by going off to fight the infidels on one of the frontlines between Dar al-Kufr (the land of unbelief) and Dar al-Islam.

The second group of separatists—also highly influenced by salafism—is explicitly nonviolent and pietistic. Jihadist zealots contemptuously dub it "sheikhist," because its partisans obediently follow the injunctions of Saudi sheikhs who show no hostility to the Riyadh regime. These sheikhs offer instant legal opinions (fatwas) on the behavior of devout Muslims wherever they may happen to be, accessible through telephone numbers and email addresses posted on salafist websites. Opposed to violence—which they combat relentlessly with Quranic verses, Prophetic sayings, and rulings of apostasy—these salafists nevertheless adhere to a version of Islam that imposes complete cultural separation from the West. When a sheikhist imam takes control of the prayer room in a working-class neighborhood on the outskirts of Paris, problems related to veiling often arise in nearby secondary schools in the following weeks and months. The new preacher's injunctions galvanize young male zealots, who reinforce his influence by applying social pressure on the young women in their neighborhood.

Here is an example of the kinds of questions put to one of Medina's principal salafist sheikhs, Rabi al-Madkhali, and the answer he gave on a French website run by the movement (quotidien_madkhali_sounnah.free.fr):

> Q. Is it allowed to take the contraceptive pill in the following case? We live in a country of unbelief and will be able to undertake the hijra [emigration toward a Muslim country] in five years at most. We do not want to have children here, for fear that they receive a bad education.
>
> A. I say to those who use those contraceptive pills for fear of the consequences that were mentioned . . . . : Return to a Muslim

country and do not stay in a country of unbelief, because there, they are vulnerable to many temptations *[fitna]*. Worse yet, many of them begin to lean toward apostasy. And their children are exposed to Christianization, carried out through schools . . . The advice that I give them is this: instead of remedying the problem by unlegislated or legislated [sic] means, if necessary, go back to a Muslim country and be patient if you face poverty there. Certainly Allah promises them prosperity, as the Divine Word affirms: (an approximate translation) "And whoever emigrates in the path of Allah will find on this earth sanctuary and abundance." S4V100 [Quran, sura 4, verse 100]

Such questions, addressed to a sheikh by a believer, are part of the tradition of Islam. But the practice has been transformed by the Internet, with the help of translators. In this example, the French is sufficiently correct to suggest that the author received an average university education. The Quranic citation is considered "approximate" because, in a rigorous interpretation of Islam, Arabic is the inimitable language in which Allah revealed the Quran, and other languages into which it is translated are by definition inferior. The question-and-answer format does away with time and space and creates a direct connection between a precise situation in Europe, "country of unfaith" (the literal salafist translation of Dar al-Kufr), and a legal opinion emitted from Mecca. The fatwa is formulated according to the strictest salafist canon: only the injunctions of Islam's sacred text matter; the European social *con*text is devalued, even demonized, in comparison with that norm.

Another question on the same website addresses the customs of Saudi Wahhabism: a woman who lives in Europe asks the sheikh "whether Muslim women are allowed to drive in a land of unbelief." In a question that returns to the matter of children, a mother asks: is it permitted to send them to nursery school, which "corrupts" them? "There, our children learn singing, dancing, painting, and many other things that Allah does not condone." If not, "can we send them twice a week to mosques led by deviated [sic] groups like The Muslim Brothers, for instance, so that our children can learn only the Quran and the Arabic language?" Conflicts that, in Saudi Arabia, pit pro-regime sheikhist salafists—the "court ulema" that Rabi al-Madkhali embodies so perfectly—against militant Islamists with explicitly political ambitions are thus reproduced in identical terms on European soil.

The "deviant" Muslim Brothers targeted on this website are represented in Europe by the various national sections of the U.K.-based Federation of Islamic Organizations in Europe (FIOE). Its French branch is the Union of Islamic Organizations of France (UOIF), which has been the main element in the French Council of the Muslim Creed (CFCM) since its creation under the auspices of the French Ministry of the Interior in the winter of 2002. Unlike the salafists, who preach self-imposed apartheid or advise believers to isolate themselves in a mental ghetto to avoid contamination by European infidels, the associations emerging from the Muslim Brothers have chosen since 1989 to root themselves in civil society. That year, along with the Berlin Wall, the communist alternative to European liberal society collapsed, and a vacuum opened up for the socialization of classes that had previously identified with Marxism and its offshoots. The Muslim Brothers, always quick to seize political opportunities, rushed into the breach. That same year, the UOIF changed its name to the Union of Islamic Organizations *of* France (formerly it was *in* France). This simple substitution of a preposition spoke volumes about the transformed legal, social, and political environment of French Muslims.

Since that time, the Brothers and their heirs have no longer considered Europe a land of unbelief but a land of Islam: Muslim children have now been born on European soil and are citizens of those countries. In France, in the name of Islamic communalist identity, the Brothers began to champion the socialization of these poor young people who, born in the 1970s as French citizens, had reached adulthood only to face a bleak job market.

The new perception was also manifest in the demand—approved by the European Fatwa Council, an ad hoc Islamic legal organization linked to the FIOE and whose spiritual advisor is Qatar-based Sheikh Yusuf al-Qaradawi—that sharia be applied to Muslims settled on European soil, since Europe was now part of the land of Islam. The movement's theologians called this stipulation "minority sharia." The most immediate and visible result was the struggle over the wearing of the veil in schools. According to these associations' interpretation of sharia, veiling was a mandatory injunction for young women.

Fifteen years later, when terrorism inspired by Osama bin Laden and implemented by his followers and imitators was weighing heavily on Europe, the continent's Islamic organizations split among various factions in a struggle for hegemony. Each brought a different nuance to its interpretation of relations between Islamic identity and the European environment, and each saw the actions attributed to the Al Qaeda network from a different perspective— from fascination (marginal, but present nonetheless) to outright rejection, via denial of its actual existence (these last two attitudes were frequently combined).

Sheikh Qaradawi, whom I met in October 2001 in Qatar, could not find words harsh enough to blame those guilty for the 9/11 attacks. According to him, the terrorists had brought opprobrium upon all of Islam in the West and threatened the progress of conversion and the strengthening of Islamist political action within the community—in other words, the accomplishments of the Islamist movement that had caused preaching to triumph over jihad since 1989. This reading of terrorism's impact on Islam's missionary effort in the West, which fit well with the Muslim Brothers' logic, diverged from that of the salafists, who did not acknowledge the "cultural revolution" in 1989 that transformed Europe into a part of the land of Islam. Both branches of salafism—jihadist on the one hand, pietistic on the other—persisted in calling Europe the "land of unbelief," not land of Islam.

In traditional Islamic political theory, the "land of unbelief" is subdivided into Dar al-Harb, the land of war, where jihad is allowed, and Dar al-Sulh, the land of truce, where Muslims do not instigate violence against unbelievers and infidels. In the pietistic sheikhists' view, Europe is Dar al-Sulh. In the jihadists' view, it is Dar al-Harb. The statement of April 15, 2004, attributed to Bin Laden, offered Europe an opportunity to become a land of truce, on condition that European states conclude a treaty with radical Islamism that includes withdrawing European troops from Iraqi soil.

All salafists preach mental and moral rejection of the surrounding European society, but the jihadists and pietists (sheikhists) have found plenty of grounds on which to wage a merciless battle against one another, especially on the Internet. The pietists devote their efforts to turning young Muslims away from jihad, while protecting them from the "deviant" Muslim Brothers. In every sermon and on every website, their sheikhs demonize the "lost sects" of the Brothers along with the jihadists, whom they lump together indiscriminately. Disciples of the Qutb brothers are ridiculed as "Qutbists," and those who admire Sheikh Qaradawi, the preacher on Al Jazeera, are ridiculed. Partisans of Sheikh Surur, the Syrian exiled in London, are slurred as modern-day heretical "Sururists." Other sects, less known, are not immune from this electronic smear campaign.

The jihadists do their bit as well, heaping insults on their sheikhist rivals, whom they condemn as "fake salafists" and devotees of *irja*—the Islamic heresy that allows Muslims to advocate a rigorous version of the faith without ever holding the ruling regime accountable for its corruption. On websites in every European language, whether jihadist or pietist, "trendy" jargon blends in with an intense polemic founded on obscure religious references to medieval scholars whose work was written in abstruse Arabic. In chat rooms, linguistic shortcuts ("2" for "to" in English; "C" for *C'est* in French) mingle with a profusion of Islamic formulas (*alhamdulillah*—praise Allah; *astaghfirullah*—Allah preserve me). In the midst of an English text one finds PBUH (for "Praise be upon him") in Arabic script, which deeply religious people pronounce after every mention of the Prophet. All of this debate and intensity seems completely unrelated to the social and cultural reality of European Islam as it is lived in the workers' cities. Yet this strange language serves to express some of the tensions that pull the members of these communities to one side and then the other.

The verbal fireworks of the debate highlight how porous the two branches of salafism really are: to pass from one to the other is quite easy. The intense indoctrination preached by the sheikhists reduces their flock's capacity for personal reasoning, which makes these followers easy prey for a clever jihadist preacher. Young people who were born in Europe, tumble into jihad, and are later jailed often follow a typical trajectory. The first stage of brainwashing occurs at the hands of a pietistic salafist imam. Later, they encounter a jihadist recruiting sergeant, who offers to quench their thirst for absolutes through a bracing activism. But this progression is neither systematic nor inevitable, and the intensity of the anti-jihadist polemic preached by pietistic salafists demonstrates their firm determination to protect their flock from incursions by jihadists.

Hostile to participation in any associations or institutions in the land of unbelief, pietistic salafists carefully mark the borders of the territory where the re-Islamization they control takes place. They are similar, in that respect, to certain ultra-Orthodox Jews, such as the Hasidim one might meet in Jerusalem's Mea Shearim neighborhood (or in Brooklyn, for that matter). Both groups preserve their identity through isolation in a ghetto, set off by visible markers. In salafist Muslim neighborhoods, women leave their homes only in a black niqab that covers their faces; men are bearded, with their mustaches shaved, and they wear skullcaps. Because of the shape of their outfits, they are nicknamed "bells": in winter, a huge windbreaker or jacket is zipped up over a white jellaba that reaches to mid-calf, in literal application of the Prophet's saying: "That part of a garment that hangs below the ankles is destined for hell" (Bukhari, 5787). For the most fashionable of the "salafs," that religious injunction gives license to show off their ankles and thus to emphasize the latest model of Nikes, in a marriage of Western consumerism with strict orthodox practice.

One of the bastions of French salafism can be found in the low-income housing projects of Argenteuil, on Paris's northern outskirts. The rigorous Islamic moral order that prevails there, of a type that one does not generally find in Muslim societies of the southern or eastern Mediterranean, is so obvious that it is sometimes difficult to remember one is in France. Salafists of every persuasion live here, turned inward on themselves and away from a state of unbelief whose contagion they fear.

On rare occasions when salafists expose themselves to the public media, their discourse arouses such outrage that it can trigger reprisals. The misadventures of Imam Bouziane illustrate this point. This salafist Algerian preacher, who had lived in France since 1979, gave an interview to *Lyon Mag* in April 2004 in which he asserted his right to bigamy by reference to the Quran. He also appeared on television to make further declarations of his views about relations between men and women. Bouziane, who had sixteen children by two wives on French soil, so infuriated authorities that he was expelled from French territory—a decision later overturned by an administrative court, which allowed him to continue his mission as before.

It all began innocently enough, as Bouziane explained the differences between salafists and Muslim Brothers: "They have very political goals and strategies, which incites them to make concessions in order to gain acceptance in the West. As for us, the salafists, our goal is purely religious. For example: we do not demonstrate in the street . . . In fact, the salafists did not protest the law that forbids veiling in schools, while the Muslim Brothers participated in those demonstrations." The journalist asked him whether he wished for France "to become an Islamist [sic] country." His candid response partook of the logic that devalues the land of unbelief: "Yes, because people would be happier if they drew closer to Allah. Besides, Allah punishes societies that wallow in sin, with earthquakes, diseases like AIDS . . . And I am very happy when I see French people converting to Islam, because I know they are on the right path."

Bouziane rounded off his explanation of his group's position by making clear what differentiated them from the jihadists—while expressing the skepticism characteristic of all salafists with regard to the identity of those who perpetrated the attacks attributed to

Al Qaeda—and finally presented himself as a guarantor of social order:

> I cannot condemn Bin Laden as long as there is no proof that he is really the one who organized the attacks on New York and Madrid. But if someone proves that he did do it, I would condemn him, because these attacks were counterproductive . . . Those who organize attacks are never salafists! I brought salafism to Lyon . . . Everyone knows me here . . . And the DST [Directorate of Territorial Security] knows very well that I have never incited Muslims to organize attacks. That, incidentally, is the reason why some young militants don't like me . . . I firmly condemn terrorism in my sermons, but maybe some people don't hear my advice, especially if they have been victims of manipulation. Unfortunately, I can't do anything about that.

These views, which very clearly expressed the position of sheikhist salafism in the European environment and distinguished it explicitly from its closest enemies, would not have caused Bouziane any problems with the police—indeed, would not even have earned him public disapproval—had he not been equally frank about salafist norms with respect to women: "A Muslim man can have several wives, but no more than four." Asked if he knew that it was illegal under French law to have more than one wife, he replied, "It is licit in the Quran." He then went on to explain that the holy text allows men, under certain circumstances, to beat their wives, and that an adulterous woman should be stoned. His words, which were coldly repeated and clarified with gestures for television cameras and then broadcast at peak viewing time, aroused considerable emotion because they were being expressed unambiguously for the first time. Usually, salafist practice discourages outside curiosity and reserves such comments for sermons at the mosque or anonymous websites. Within their closed community, salafists impose rigorous Islamic norms over state law, but without openly defying it. As one 26-year-old cybernaut noted on oumma.com (French Islam's main website): "Laws made by men are made for them and therefore are always unjust, only Quaranic law is good because it is impartial."

Bouziane was expelled to Algeria under an emergency procedure. But after filing an administrative appeal against the injunction, he returned to France triumphantly a few weeks later, having demonstrated that French law, which had caused his deportation, was fallible. The ordeal only increased his prestige and that of sharia. Bouziane promptly sued the magazine, contending that he did not know what "stoning" *(lapidation)* meant in French and that the word had been put in his mouth by the journalist. Islamist organizations and their media contacts, not to mention the imam's lawyer, maintain that he was tricked into portraying Islam in an unfavorable light, in order to incite Islamophobia. Bouziane's case against the magazine is still pending.

THE EMERGENCE OF SALAFISM within European Islam is a relatively recent phenomenon. In the mid-1980s, when I was conducting research for my book *Les banlieues de l'islam (The Outskirts of Islam),* this trend was not visible at all. Socialization and rigorous instruction were fulfilled mainly by Tabligh, a movement which advocated a return to rigid faith. It was born in India in the 1920s, at a time when, according to some men of religion, the Muslim minority ran the risk of losing its identity to the Hindu majority. Tabligh, meaning "propagation" of the Islamic faith, imposed a highly restrictive orthopraxis: followers must dress like the Prophet, sleep as he did on the ground, on one's right side, and so on. Like pietistic salafism, Tabligh imposed on its followers a separation in their daily life from the "impious" society that surrounded them.

Tabligh had an impressive capacity for indoctrination. Some people who returned to Islam or converted through its influence and then later abandoned it—such as the singer Abdel Malek, of NAP (New African Poets), an Islamic rap group from Strasbourg—denounced the movement in retrospect as "stultifying." Tabligh organized "outings" for advocates who were to preach in neighborhoods and bring a vulnerable population back to the straight and narrow. The longest "outing," to Pakistan, took place when devotees were considered sufficiently mature. Those who wished to deepen their faith attended the madrassas of Pakistan's Deobandi movement—the same religious schools that indoctrinated the Taliban.

Tabligh peaked in Europe between the mid-1970s and mid-1980s, when it focused on marginalized populations—migrant workers deprived of any cultural access to European society, "lost" teens, drug addicts, and others. It declined around 1989, when young people from Muslim families, educated in Europe and now reaching adulthood, began to seek a more intellectual framework for their faith. The movement, unable to respond to their increasingly sophisticated demands, withered, though one of its branches is still represented in the French Council of the Muslim Creed.

Tabligh lost its market share to the pietistic salafists, who concentrated on indoctrination, and the UOIF network, whose organizations focused on charity work. The salafists had first arrived in France as the Islamic Salvation Front (FIS) was emerging in Algeria (1989) and civil war was raging (1992–1997). France at that time had a population of Algerian origin estimated at around two million people. The influence of the great Saudi sheikhists, such as Mufti Bin Baz, Sheikh Bin Utheimin, or their Lebanese colleague Albani, was crucial in convincing many Algerian salafists who had gone underground during the civil war to stop fighting. The Algerian regime, in tacit cooperation with Riyadh, turned to these eminent clerics for fatwas designed to bring armed jihadists back to the apolitical salafist way. The strategy worked, and the civil war ended in 1997.

The salafists' influence spread on French territory through the Algerian diaspora. But a translation of FIS salafism into political action was impossible in France, and so the movement took a mainly pietistic course, requiring isolation from the daily manners and customs of French unbelief. By focusing on a rigorous interpretation of sacred texts, salafism met the demands of a young, educated generation better than the deliberately ignorant Tabligh propaganda.

As Tabligh faded into the background, its charity network in Muslim communities was captured not by the salafists but by the UOIF, an outgrowth of the Muslim Brothers. In 1987, the head of the French Ministry of the Interior's office of religious affairs, who had just finished reading *Les banlieues de l'islam*, let me know that I was overestimating the UOIF's potential (it was still in its infancy) and that I had given it a disproportionate place in my analysis of emerging Islamic movements. By 2002 the Ministry of the Interior had made the UOIF the main prism through which to analyze French Islam, thereby reversing its previous policy. (This move from one extreme to the other is not necessarily a sign of keener understanding.)

In contrast with the salafists, the many groups, influenced by

Muslim Brothers ideology, despite differences in method, collectively sought to collaborate with institutions and nongovernmental organizations. They advocated a gradual widening of Islamic influence in European cities through full participation in political, social, and cultural life. This approach was expressed in a dynamic advance on every accessible domain. Charity networks or Islamist "social workers" (sometimes paid out of public funds) provided structure in economically depressed areas, where they proselytized among the lost and dispossessed. In the Middle East and North Africa, this kind of activity, carried out by Islamist movements and parties inspired by the Muslim Brothers, had been the starting point for the recruitment of a base among the young urban poor; their opposite numbers just transported that strategy to Europe.

Conducted without fanfare, and with some success by the turn of the twenty-first century, this activity was taken up on French outer-city university campuses (which accept almost any high school graduate) by the UOIF's student section, the EMF (Muslim Students of France). That organization offered social services to Muslim students, most of whom were from low-income North African families and were poorly acquainted with the cultural cues that would allow them to identify academic options leading to satisfying jobs. Their experience of "destitution in the student environment" (the title of a pamphlet written in the mid-1960s by a member of the "situationist international") was acute. The EMF thus acted both as a union that responded to an urgent social need and as a resocialization body that aimed to transform poor students from Muslim backgrounds, who were generally indifferent to the politicization of religion, into activists with a new political and religious awareness—in other words, "Muslim Youth."

In 2003, when the vast majority of university students, disenchanted with the left-leaning student unions, were no longer voting, the EMF got its delegates elected to student councils for the first time. This success was reminiscent of the situation in Egyptian and Algerian universities in the 1970s and 1980s, when student associations close to the Muslim Brothers had made a breakthrough on campuses through intense charity work, scholarships, subsidies (awarded especially to women students who had taken the veil), and a panoply of social services.

These activities of the UOIF, while highly effective, were designed to avoid excessive publicity. In other arenas, however, Islamist organizations have sought maximum visibility to stage the plight of European Muslims. The conflict over veiling in schools and the public demonstrations it provoked was one example. By casting Muslims in the role of victims, Islamist organizations caught the attention of the media. Various human rights groups, antiracist organizations, environmentalists, priests, teachers, antiglobalization activists, Trotskyites, and sometimes also fascist groups chimed in with support. Islamist organizations responded in different ways to these new allies, depending on how they defined "concessions" (in Imam Bouziane's terms) that might corrupt Muslim identity or even lead to its being co-opted. Each one weighed the threat of corruption against the benefits of alliances with various state institutions and with non-Muslim political, religious, or social parties and movements, from the far left to the far right of the political spectrum.

This dilemma of corruption (or co-optation) versus manipulation is reminiscent of the internal debates among Western Europe's communists in the twentieth century. On one side, the Popular Front or Union of the Left in France and the "Historic Compromise" in Italy advocated intense participation in institutional and political life. On the other side, a class-against-class party line favored an ideological break with the "bourgeoisie," in order to strengthen the public perception of the party's opposition

to the political establishment. The function of the category "bourgeoisie" provided contrast, in terms of social identity, with the
hated "other," just as the category "unbelievers" provides contrast
for Islamist ideology.

When they were in a position of strength, Europe's communist
parties portrayed themselves as the unchallenged champions of
those who suffered, and this hard line attracted a plethora of fellow
travelers or sincere democrats—less charitably described, in the
intimacy of cell meetings, as "useful idiots." When they were in a
position of weakness, communists were forced to make ideological compromises by associating more closely with noncommunist
democrats, who gradually led them to abandon the dictatorship of
the proletariat and accept democracy. This path ultimately led to
the decline and dissolution of West European communism.

The Islamists also managed to annex useful fellow travelers—
indeed, sometimes the very same individuals the Communist Party
had once captured. This shift of loyalties was made easier by the
fact that some Islamists championed the cause of the lower classes
—which, they claimed, were now for the most part Muslim.
Priests, teachers, sociologists, and other non-Muslims attended the
congresses of movements inspired by the Brothers' ideology, and in
so doing granted them a seal of approval, thus reassuring police authorities and the media of these organizations' good intentions.

The presence of these non-Muslims dissociated Islamists on the
north side of the Mediterranean from their brothers on the south
side, whose rallying cry was the creation of an Islamic state on the
ruins of unbelief (just as the dictatorship of the proletariat was to
be built on the ruins of the bourgeois state—a catchphrase that
served a similar purpose in mobilizing the foot soldiers of communism). Among Europeans, this bellicose slogan would have fright-
ened secularists and Christians.

As was the case with Western communism, it is difficult to know whether changes in Islamist vocabulary accurately track structural transformations in ideology or whether they are merely rhetorical artifice to mask a hidden agenda. This is an important point of contention, not just for the Muslim Brothers' descendants in Europe and America today but also for those betting for and against them. It will determine the movement's evolution and the way it is perceived both from within and from without, by militants, sympathizers, and potential recruits, as well as by Western institutions and public opinion-makers. The basis for such a challenge lies in an ethnic-religious minority in Europe today, but the group is destined to undergo considerable expansion if only because of its high birthrate and foreseeable further immigration. How it manages its relationships with its non-Muslim allies will determine whether Islamist ideology becomes "democratic" in this European context (and as such could be exported to the Muslim world) or, on the contrary, becomes increasingly radical, as strongholds within European society pass on the rigid, aggressive ideology originating on the other side of the Mediterranean.

The galaxy of factions emerging in Europe from the Muslim Brothers' ideology has a more diverse social base, however, than that of the communist movement. For example, one finds a pious intellectual petty bourgeoisie that aspires to the status of social mediator—recognized and consolidated by European states as the manager of the Muslim community it claims to represent, while defining the contours of that community in religious terms. In Britain, the U.K. Islamic Mission, founded by disciples of Mawdudi, the Pakistani ideologue, tries to play this role. It seeks to function as an intermediary while providing the British state with various services, such as awareness training for police officers. In France, the role is taken up by the UOIF.

Starting small in the mid-1980s, the UOIF expanded its social, political, and media visibility gradually by bringing together tens of thousands of people at its annual congress in Le Bourget, a northern working-class suburb of Paris. This event, which blends religious and political speeches with a huge market selling "ethnic" products, books, tapes, and other sundry Islamic paraphernalia, is reminiscent of the Communist Party's annual gathering: "Fête de l'Huma" had become "Fête de l'Umma." Like any movement seeking to derive political capital by controlling the behavior of its popular base, the UOIF needed to resolve the contradiction between the aspirations of its constituency and the tactical constraints imposed upon its leaders as they grappled with state policy. Besides the Moroccans from Bordeaux, who have controlled the organization since the 1990s and whose members are always trussed up in dark suits and ties, appropriate garb for meeting counterparts in the state apparatus, the UOIF includes more populist figures who wear T-shirts or other casual clothing (though never a jellaba, which identifies the wearer as a salafist) and are more in tune with the aspirations of militants and their sympathizers in the organization. The tensions within this diverse group are acutely reflected in a small, popular book by one of the organization's best-liked leaders, who regularly appears on television talk shows, Farid Abdelkrim. Its title is *Naal bou la France?!*

Naal bou is a popular expression widely used in North Africa to curse someone's father, and by extension the son and his lineage. In oral usage, the abbreviation *bou* (for *Abu*, father of) designates any kind of relation to an object: for instance, *bou lihya*, literally "father of a beard," designates a person with a beard, that is, an Islamist or salafist militant. The title of Abdelkrim's book can thus be rendered *Damn France*. It raised objections, especially from Dalil Boubakeur, dean of the Muslim Institute at the Paris Mosque (a rival of the UOIF) and president of the French Council of the

Muslim Creed, who denounced it as a scathing anti-national attack. Written in an easy colloquial style that resembles the slang used among young North Africans, *Naal bou la France?!* is a brutal text that seeks to speak plainly to a country blamed first of all for its colonial exploitation of North Africa a generation earlier.

The cover is illustrated by a double exposure of the author and his father in front of what looks like a shantytown; the book is dedicated "to our mothers, to our fathers." Neither the blood spilled by Muslims from North Africa fighting in French uniforms during both world wars nor the sweat of migrant laborers, living under deplorable living conditions, who rebuilt France (and Europe) for a pittance after 1945, has made their children, as far as the French or indeed Europeans in general are concerned, full fellow citizens. Since they are denied such recognition, the author demands: "Oh sweet France! Are you astonished that so many of your children commune in a stinging *naal bou la France*, and damn your Fathers?" How could one, Abdelkrim asks, be surprised that young people resent those they denigrate as *kuffar* and *gouères* (from the North African colloquial term *gaouri*, which also means infidel)?

According to the author, however, the expression of this social rage—which the book illustrates through numerous anecdotes in which "native" French people ("cheeses") come across as odious or ridiculous and in which their institutions are systematically disparaged—should not lead to self-destructive violence. Rather than casting blame, he believes it is necessary to rebuild one's identity on a political-religious basis that will be capable of sublimating the loss of cultural and social markers, as he explains in a chapter titled "Young and Muslim!"

> Before going further, we are going to put an end to all the names that are used, *zama* ["supposedly" in North

African colloquial], to designate young people "emerging from immigration." Whether you are white, tanned or black, you have to reject slurs and pet names that put you in the category of "we don't know who you are." You are not a North African or an Arab. You are still less a *beur* or the second generation of anything at all. Nor are you an outer-city teen. No, you are none of those things. You are neither an Islamist nor a fundamentalist . . . Yes, in France you are at home. And whether you apply the precepts of Islam or you are non-practicing, if you do not renounce the faith in your heart, you are Muslim. Therefore, you are: a young Muslim. Respect starts here! With the way you see yourself, and who you want to be. Then you will be able to demand respect from others. As far as I'm concerned, in the following pages and forever, you were, are, and will be a young Muslim.

These lines convey the essence of the strategy used by the UOIF to capture a young, popular social base. When *Naal bou la France?!* came out in 2002, Abdelkrim was president of the JMF (Jeunes Musulmans de France, Young Muslims of France, the organization's youth section). According to him, whatever the multiple modes of identity that young North Africans, socialized in France, try out, there is only one truth (even for those who are unaware of it): their identity as Muslims. All the alternatives are belittled as *zama*—pretend. Only Islam engenders self-respect and respect from others. To assert oneself by displaying one's Islamic heritage is the necessary condition for full participation in political life.

This compulsory Islamism—except for those who betray their identity—is an outgrowth of the Muslim Brothers' ideology. In the biographical notes, the author presents himself as someone who escaped life as a delinquent ("mix-ups, fights, dope, hold-ups, robberies, the whole shebang"). A police slip-up that caused the death of one of his friends was his wake-up call, leading him back to the mosque. He became an increasingly religious associative militant, while going back to school, where he eventually received a degree in sociology (traces of this training are detectable in the quotation above). Most important, by frequenting a local branch of the UOIF, he discovered the Arabic language, and "a man, then his thought. Hassan al-Banna! And what a man! I owe him, for what little I know, my way of seeing the world, practicing Islam, and making myself useful."

This paradigmatic itinerary shared traits with Malcolm X's life course and was recounted to turn young people into self-aware Muslims. It also was intended to reinforce the UOIF in its struggle with the salafists and jihadists. Within such a frame of reference, *Naal bou la France?!* targeted the salafists when it made fun of "a bunch of cranks [busy] scrupulously following the letter of Islam while ignoring its spirit just as much." Obeying the Islamist movement's customary principle of precaution regarding September 11, Abdelkrim stated that "no tangible evidence exists as to the true mastermind of the attacks," and "only media repetition designated Bin Laden as their despicable mastermind." His reference work on the question was Thierry Meyssan's *L'effroyable imposture (The Atrocious Imposture)*, which denied that a hijacked plane ever hit the Pentagon.

Paradoxically, both the UOIF and the salafists benefited from the September 2001 attacks. They drew strength from the social base that Abdelkrim and his colleagues, preachers, or lecturers pulled in and which social workers then organized within their charitable associations. They took advantage of the few months during which Al Qaeda had not yet claimed responsibility for the attacks to deny that any sort of blame could be placed on Islam, and to accuse the press of distortion. But more important, they also provided answers that addressed the deep feeling of unease among young people who were suddenly faced with the urgent need to define Islam in a way that would exonerate them from the crimes and massacres committed in its name.

Instead of pushing young people away from Islamist organizations, the explosions of September 11 created a vortex into which some young European Muslims were drawn. Leaders and organizations denounced the carnage from within the movement, while granting a blanket exoneration to any activist who identified with the "correct" Islam. Sometimes these leaders placed the blame for 9/11 on obscure forces, including Mossad or the CIA, and sometimes they blamed a deluded sect of Islam. (The sheikhists, in their conflict with the Muslim Brothers, did not hesitate to suggest that the Brothers were just such a sect.) Attendance at the UOIF's Le Bourget congress, which was stagnating in the late 1990s, took off once more, and the veil became more visible in schools. Many signs indicated that, as a way of coping with the vague and unjust suspicions directed at bearded men and veiled women, a growing need for a deeper understanding of their faith took shape.

The groups that were in a dominant position to supply such a demand were UOIF and other like-minded Islamist organizations, which favored a strategy of visibility, or the salafists, who preferred greater discretion. Less up-market were two other branches of Islam: the more intellectual mystical sects, where confidentiality or the challenges followers must face discouraged a more general audience, and Islamic institutions that were perceived to be associated with a European state, such as the Paris Mosque.

From the 1990s, both the salafists and the UOIF claimed many converts among young people who were not from Muslim backgrounds. Some of these young converts found their way to Islam after having grown up on the streets of poor neighborhoods where Arabs predominate. When young Arab men began to grow beards and go to the mosque, their French, Portuguese, Caribbean, African Christian, or West Indian friends did the same, for fear of becoming marginalized at a time when the urban subculture was becoming increasingly salafist, when Christian names were mocked, and when European culture as a whole was devalued. Others were drawn to Islamist organizations after having been alcoholics or drug addicts. Sometimes their redemption came about in prison, following the Malcolm X model, or in the housing projects where some Islamist groups, such as the Tabligh, specialized in retrieving "strays." But idealistic, intellectually motivated students were also seduced by the proselytism of movements active on outer-city university campuses.

The converts' universe in Europe today is infinitely diverse. Leaving aside those who discovered their new religion through the influence of future in-laws and who, although their numbers are taken into account by the mosques, feel more or less indifferent toward this formality, there are also intellectuals and artists attracted by Sufism, who are more loyal to their brotherhood than to the *umma* and are not concerned with matters affecting the Muslim community as a whole. Some are rigorously ascetic, but others emancipate themselves from common belief. It is difficult to know what proportion these mystics make up among the fifty thousand "native French" converts Islamic organizations claim; but these mystics are hardly representative of the "social Islamism" that has arisen in recent decades.

Recently, there has been a tendency among certain converts to minimize the break in their lives when they embrace Islam. Until the mid-1990s, converts systematically took a second, Muslim, name, seeking to translate their Christian name (Vincent/Mansur, Régis/Abdel Malek) or to achieve an alliterative effect (Roger/ Raja). But today, outside salafist circles, the fashion is to use only one's original name in public. This can be confirmed on all sorts of Islamic websites, where intellectual converts play an important part. Many Muslim participants in chat rooms and newsgroups now sign with European names.

This evolution in naming may be due to a growing concern with the need of law-abiding citizens to distinguish themselves from radicals who have moved into jihad and related activities. Radical converts—such as former GIA supporters who underwent training in Afghan or Bosnian camps, or even combined armed robbery with jihadism, as did the "Roubaix gang" in the 1990s—inspire some people; but most Muslim converts are keen to offset the suspicions that weigh on the majority because of the mayhem caused by a minority. On the other hand, keeping one's Christian name may be, in a few cases (such as that of the shoe bomber Richard Reid), an attempt to deflect the attention of authorities away from militant activities.

PERCEIVING THE RISE of an organized Islamist movement after September 11, the French authorities adopted a two-part strategy. The urgency of the terrorist threat led them to encourage the institutionalization of religious representation for Muslims within France, in order to create negotiators who would receive recognition from the Ministry of the Interior (which is responsible for religious institutions) in return for community policing. The UOIF, which had stayed at arm's length from the government because of doctrinal loyalty to the Muslim Brothers, was chosen to play a leading role, since it seemed more capable than the Paris Mosque of imposing social constraints at a time when law and order were of the essence. The Paris Mosque had traditionally enjoyed a special relationship with the political leadership, especially the right, but it was not attuned to the young people in the outer cities.

By singling out the UOIF, Minister of the Interior Nicolas Sarkozy decided to favor an organization with a public, communalist agenda. Communalism, which is the opposite of integration, stresses belonging to an exclusive communal identity. In doing so, he failed to send any message to the majority of the country's Muslims who had followed the secularist path and had privatized religious observance. All of a sudden, the secularist French state looked as though it had abandoned its citizens of Muslim descent who were imbued with the secular values of the republic; it treated them as a mere flock for bearded communalist shepherds.

At the national level, no deputies or senators came from these communities, although they included many upwardly mobile second-generation immigrants from North Africa who had acquired social, economic, or cultural status and importance. Sarkozy favored one particular religious organization as an intermediary; after a period of time it would transcend its religious function and take over the task of political representation. Critics of this development—whether secularists or UOIF rivals—suspected electoral shenanigans to deliver the Muslim vote. In Britain, by contrast, where the political system has consolidated an explicitly communalist vision of "race relations"—as the British say—several parliamentarians, deputies, or lords of Indo-Pakistani Muslim origin play the role of mediators between their co-religionists and the state. The social and political diversity of elected representatives, former union activists in Labor, and "brown yuppies" among the Tories diminishes the effect of the "Muslim vote."

In December 2002, at the end of a complex process of negotiation, the French Council of the Muslim Creed (CFCM) was finally established. Its representatives were elected on the basis of administrative divisions, each mosque receiving a certain number of votes according to the space it occupied on the ground. This was a totally novel modification of election policy, which favored the UOIF—the only organization that had permeated the fifteen hundred Muslim prayer rooms across the country through its numerous local franchises. To maintain an equilibrium of sorts within the council, the government made sure that Boubakeur, dean of the Muslim Institute at the Paris Mosque, was appointed president of the CFCM. The real power, however, was Vice-President Fouad Alaoui, secretary-general of the UOIF.

One faction was excluded entirely from the council: the partisans and disciples of Tariq Ramadan, a star preacher among young Muslims. In reaction, his spokesman disparaged the CFCM in very harsh terms, drew ironic parallels between the "rigged" elections and those held back home in Algiers, and compared the UOIF to the local North African notables of the colonial period; like them, it had delivered votes and stability to the ambitious interior minister in return for help in consolidating its hegemony over France's network of Muslim organizations. "The French Council of the Muslim Creed and its local representatives," wrote Ramadan, "are to part of the right, and to Sarkozy in particular, what SOS Racisme and Ni Putes Ni Soumises [Neither Sluts nor Slaves, a women's rights group] are to the socialist party . . . private hunting grounds, tools in the new vote collection campaign, the instruments of a fairly crude retrieval policy."

Against the cumbersome maneuvers the UOIF carried out to approach the state, Tariq Ramadan deployed a far different, lighter strategy, one that avoided expending his energy in a laborious effort to garner votes. A charismatic figure whose appeal flowed from his eloquence and his legitimacy as the grandson of Hassan al-Banna, founder of the Muslim Brothers, this Swiss citizen, whose father had fled to Geneva to escape repression under Nasser, was on *Time* magazine's list of the world's one hundred most influential people in 2004. Unsure whether he was an angel or a demon, the press was reduced to stupefied fascination, which reinforced his status, for better or worse, as an international media phenomenon. Unlike the charmless UOIF, he needed no bureaucracy; in Weberian terms, Tariq Ramadan embodied the figure of the Prophet, against the managers of the "goods of salvation" who controlled the CFCM.

Ramadan reached out to make alliances with the far left, working a territory abandoned by his rivals—just as the UOIF had done in its flirtation with the right, as exemplified by Minister of the Interior Sarkozy's keynote speech at the Easter 2003 congress. After having charmed (and then, in some cases, discarded) part of the Catholic Church, secular educators from the Teaching League, and the Third Worldist editorial staff of *Le Monde diplomatique*, Hassan al-Banna's grandson completed his triumphant polarizing march that year by establishing himself as the star of another congress. At the European Social Forum held in mid-November 2003 in northern Paris, he stole the limelight from anti-globalization activists on the extreme left.

The charismatic preacher was propelled to notoriety thanks to a profitable little scandal that pitted him against well-known French intellectuals. He made the front pages of *Le Monde* and *The New York Times* alike and appeared on numerous talk shows, where he deployed all his charm to seduce viewers of all ages, origins, and faiths. The minister of the interior, by failing to invite him to join the CFCM, had closed the institutional door of French Islam, but Ramadan came in through the media window, snatching the extreme left's political capital for himself and achieving the status of a martyr in the eyes of his young disciples and a growing number of sympathizers.

The scandal revolved around the question of Israel and the U.S. occupation of Iraq. On October 3, 2003, oumma.com published an article by Ramadan titled "Critique of the [new] Communalist Intellectuals." The lead explained that the text had been turned down by two prominent French dailies—thereby instantly granting its author victim status in the eyes of frequent visitors to the site. Challenging "French Jewish intellectuals [who], although hitherto considered universalistic thinkers, have begun to develop analyses increasingly oriented by communalist sentiment, on the national and international levels," with regard to the Israeli–Palestinian conflict and the war on Iraq, but also to "Judeophobia" in the outer cities, he singled out the philosopher Pierre-André Taguieff (who is not Jewish, but who found himself under attack because of his name), then drew up a list on which Alain Finkielkraut, Alexandre Adler, Bernard Kouchner, André Glucksman, and Bernard-Henri Lévy appeared.

This carefully calculated provocation reminded some of the "lists" of journalists who could be identified by their Jewish family name and were booed by crowds at a notorious extreme right-wing French leaders' meeting. The uproar this action triggered in the Paris press forced Ramadan to recant, while inadvertently dropping a hint of his media manipulation ("I knew Mr. Taguieff wasn't Jewish . . . I had been told, *and I checked* [emphasis added])." Still, he reaped the benefits of exceptional notoriety. The skill of this provocation forced his targets to react to the unacceptable form of his attack (in effect, a blacklist), rather than to the real question raised by Ramadan in the article.

Ramadan's position struck a chord in a part of the French public who felt increasingly that, in France or Europe, any challenge to Israel's policy in the Middle East—indeed, any rational consideration whatsoever of Israel's place in U.S. foreign policy—was swept aside because pro-Israeli interest groups denounced them immediately as anti-Semitic, though Israel's security, along with guaranteed oil supplies, are the two inseparable pillars of the United States' Middle East policy. Unless this factor is taken into account, the Bush administration's war on terror is inexplicable.

The dexterously preserved confusion between form and content in Ramadan's "scandalous" article allowed his supporters to point out that the press was deliberately evading the main issue. They deplored a benign, formal bit of clumsiness in their hero's mode of expression, a peccadillo that his enemies had magnified and transformed into a cardinal sin. Ramadan thus scored another point: he turned the accusation of "communalism," frequently leveled at the Islamist movement, against "French Jewish intellectuals," while taking over the universalistic position they had abandoned when they became, he claimed, nothing more than the deaf and blind followers of Israel under Ariel Sharon. He deprived Jewish intellectuals of their universalism and took it for himself.

Through participation in the World Social Forum, Tariq Ramadan exchanged his costume as the Muslim Youth's spokesman—an outfit too tight to accommodate his ambitions and talent—for the garb of the universalist intellectual, capable (in the formula Edward Shils uses to describe such an intellectual's function) of "speaking about society's core values." When he intervened in the forum—and in an article published in the mainstream journal *Pouvoirs*, where references to Susan Sontag far outweigh passages from the Quran—Islam became not a condition of the argument but a conclusion, however implicit.

This posture is taken up in Ramadan's carefully studied style of dress. He shuns both the salafists' jellaba with a jacket and sneakers and the UOIF leaders' dark suits and ties. He prefers instead a white shirt with a Mao-style collar, worn slightly open. This attire distances him from the salafists' extravagant oddness and the UOIF's excessive conformism but respects the prohibition on wearing ties, which most exalted Islamists consider a symbol of the cross. Dressed a little like a Revolution-era Iranian government dignitary (the type that also mixed Third World verbosity with religious verve, but in a stronger cocktail), he stands out because his overall appearance references a different system of meaning. While the Pasdaran and Revolutionary Guards expressed their solidarity with the "disinherited" by wearing filthy clothes and roughly clipped beards, Tariq Ramadan cultivates a thin, piously trimmed beard that combines a reference to Islam with seductive elegance. His white shirt belongs at the intersection of several fields of meaning: the revolution (Iranian or Chinese) but also the media-savvy intellectual, a necessary guest on television debates, epitomized by Bernard-Henri Lévy—the first to wear an open-necked white shirt on TV in the 1980s. Tariq Ramadan is playing a faithful variation of that seduction game—all the more faithful because his strategy is to snatch away Lévy's place as a universalist intellectual, after having consigned him to the darkness of Jewish communalism.

Some anti-globalization activists find this posture enchanting, and Ramadan uses bearded young men and veiled young women to fill out meeting halls that would otherwise be sparsely populated by aging middle-class leftists. But his position is somewhat disconcerting to "Young Muslims" who can no longer follow him—as cybernaut "manyielle" wrote on February 15, 2004, in a chat room called forum_islami.com: "*assalamu alaikuom* [sic]. For a long time now Tariq Ramadan has been saying two different things. He tells us Muslims one thing, and he tells *kouffars* [unbelievers] what they want to hear. But the pb [problem] today is that the *kouffars* are aware of this duality in Tariq Ramadan's personality and discourse. He has been stigmatized since he said those anti-Semitic things and it looks like now he wants to correct his mistake! *wa Allah o alam. Assalamu alikom wa RahmatuLah wa barakatuh* [only Allah knows. Allah's greetings and blessings upon you]." (The transcription of Arabic religious phrases is approximate and based on colloquial pronunciation.)

After various messages for or against Ramadan, an erudite contribution posted the same day in the same discussion group and signed "Anas A.L." made a positive evaluation of Ramadan's attitude, comparing him to the Prophet, who tricked infidels in times of weakness. He also judged Ramadan favorably in light of the norms established by the intransigent thirteenth-century jurist Ibn Taymiyya, the ultimate reference for salafists and Muslim Brothers alike, before concluding: "Another thing about TR is that his discourse is very subtle . . . He doesn't tell the *kouffars* what they want to hear, he uses *tawriya* [dissimulation, double meaning]. An example of his subtlety: he suggests multiculturalism, not communalism, for France: neither of these words appears in the Quran and the Sunna, and what counts is . . . the goals he tries to find so that Muslims living in France can practice the maximum expected of them as a Muslim minority in a non-Muslim country . . . The brothers and sisters should go further than just noting that he has said he doesn't want communalism. They also need to consider the rest of his discourse and its content!"

Discussions in this online forum followed an article by Ramadan published in a major daily on February 11, 2004, and posted on oumma.com calling for a demonstration for the right to wear the veil at school, which was to be held on February 14. The Geneva preacher asserted his attachment to universal values, asking "all citizens, without exception, to stand up and say, together, very loudly, that there is no such thing as minority citizenship in France, that these questions are everyone's business, in the same way, and that, after all, the political class itself is encouraging communalism while saying it wants to combat it. *Rights are rights, and to demand them is a right!*"

This text presented the right to wear hijab at school not as the request of a specific community—it would have attracted support only from Islamist groups—but as a question of universal entitlement. This made it possible to include José Bové, the anti-globalization activist, as well as Noël Mamère, the environmentalist and advocate of the right to gay marriage, in the call to demonstrate. (Both refrained from attending, citing previous commitments.) In an attempt at value-switching, similar to the one he had undertaken in denouncing "French Jewish intellectuals," Ramadan turned the accusation of communalism against the French state and its institutions, stripping them of the republic's vaunted universalism and trying to retrieve it for himself, while drawing the basic references on secularism and socialism into his cause: "Voltaire, first and foremost, but also, closer to us, Jaurès, must be spinning in their graves, shaken by the betrayal, twice bruised by the closed-mindedness of those who no longer know how to read them . . . Their words are being used, emptied of their spirit."

As in the case of the UOIF, which must reconcile the conflicting demands of a support base influenced by populist preachers and its leaders' desire to be co-opted by certain French politicians, Tariq Ramadan needs to take responsibility for his growing internal contradictions. For now, he is attempting to flee the inconsistencies of his position by increasing his territory continuously. Geneva, France, even Old Europe are now too small: the world is his new frontier—the New World, dominated by America. Having perfected his English in the 1990s at the Leicester Islamic Foundation (a British Islamist think tank staffed by Mawdudi disciples), in 2004 Tariq Ramadan announced with great fanfare that he had been hired as a visiting professor at Notre Dame University in Indiana. There, he received academic recognition he does not enjoy in Europe; this seal of approval is intended to strengthen his fragile status, in the absence of a structured, hierarchical bureaucracy of the UOIF type.

But he is balanced on a tightrope. Part of his community base accuses him of having betrayed his Islamist affiliation. On the other hand, the television viewers who belong to his universalist target audience were surprised when, in a prime-time debate with Minister of the Interior Sarkozy, he refused to condemn the stoning of women explicitly. He was reduced to requesting a "moratorium" on the question, so as not to alienate the part of his support base that follows a rigorous interpretation of Islam's sacred texts. Unless Tariq Ramadan takes responsibility for his growing internal contradictions, they will propel him, like all shooting stars, into the dark night.

As ISLAMIST MOVEMENTS develop, the issue of gender equality becomes increasingly a field of contention in the battle for Europe. No matter what their proclivity or strategy in other matters, both salafists and the UOIF consider it imperative that veiling be allowed in schools. Veiling marks the perpetuation of community control over their flocks and mental separation from the values of an environment suspected of corrupting Islam. For salafists, all Europe is a land of unbelief, and they are obsessed by the threat of "Christianization" and other deviations that might affect their offspring, such as singing, dancing, coed schooling, sports, or even biology textbooks that contradict divine revelation. The salafists see women in terms that defy any form of legal equality: this is clear from their declarations in favor of women's seclusion and their predilection for violence against women as a means of imposing correct behavior. (Women, on the other hand, are not allowed to beat men for the same reasons.)

The UOIF defends the right to wear the veil at school in public by recourse to universalist, not communalist, arguments. In this way, they are able to muster support outside the community, while avoiding the question of legal equality between men and women, which contravenes sharia—a position that is unlikely to win the support of environmentalists, anti-globalization activists, and leftists, even those who champion "authenticity."

In statements targeting the media and mass audiences, demands for the right to veil at school are phrased essentially in terms of multiculturalism, which its advocates present as a core value of modernity. In contrast, secularism is disparaged as oppressive Jacobinism imposed by a declining nation-state. From this perspective, the veiled cybernaut in Aubervilliers who sent an email to her favorite salafist sheikh in Saudi Arabia to find out whether she could take the pill while living in "the land of unbelief" embodies the values of a new globalized individualism and personifies a universal democracy where communalist seclusion is transcended by the reach of the Internet.

This vision was taken up during the February 2004 demonstrations by young women who draped themselves in the French flag and chanted, "Not my husband, not my father, I'm the one who chose to veil." Yet the Islamist network in the workers' cities exerts pressure on women to conform, and the preachers call for the implementation of "minority sharia." One salafist sheikh told the media that Islam authorizes beating one's wife severely. Even a charismatic preacher like Tariq Ramadan, who claims to be a very modern universalist, comes up short on the question of legal equality between men and women for fear of antagonizing those in his constituency who believe that stoning an adulterous wife is part and parcel of the doctrine of Islam.

The atmosphere of a nation is troubled when community identities, whatever their origin—ethnic or religious, Muslim, Jewish, or Christian, African, Arab, Asian, or Gallic—become the overriding issue in schools. Demonstrations of hatred between young Muslims and Jews are on the rise, and they become especially acute on the playground the morning after Al Jazeera reports on Israeli repression of Palestinians, showing tanks and bulldozers mowing down Palestinian homes and the funerals of Palestinian victims or "martyrs" killed in suicide operations. Citizens are worried when French educators are reduced to grouping students of a given faith together in a single school, to prevent the persecution they endure when they are isolated.

Between July and December 2003, these concerns prompted President Chirac to convene a commission responsible for deliberating the implementation of secularism—or *laïcité*—in twenty-first-century France. Named the Stasi Commission after its president, it was responsible for redefining this secular pact guaranteeing the separation of church and state in France. When this public policy was instituted in 1905, France was predominantly rural and was not the target of significant immigration. These laws were passed at a time when *laïcité* was defined as a "disconnection" from the Catholic Church, which influenced every domain of social organization with papal bulls rather than democratic debate. A century later, France, like all countries of Western Europe, was undergoing important demographic transformations as millions of people flowed in, most from across the Mediterranean or from the Indian subcontinent. In this context, *laïcité* took on an entirely different meaning. Its goal was no longer to defend freedom of conscience against a dominant Catholic Church, which has lost its arrogance and its powers of constraint, but to bring together populations of diverse origins by establishing rules of coexistence that allowed each individual to express that same freedom of conscience.

Such freedom, however, is undermined by closed community identities that keep a tight rein on liberty or pit the different components of Europe's new pluralistic society against one other on ethnic, racial, or religious grounds. In the early twentieth century, the Vatican brought the weight of the Index and excommunication to bear on the souls of its flocks in Catholic countries. Today, in much the same way, salafism, Hasidic Jewish communalism, and some charismatic or evangelical Christian movements—as well as various hybrid sects—endeavor to wedge their congregations into enclosures where indoctrination undermines the basic foundations of individual citizens' freedom of conscience.

While it is an exaggeration to claim, as the Islamists do, that in twenty-first-century Europe the underprivileged classes are essentially "Muslim," the fact remains that populations of immigrant Muslim descent—like all migratory waves in history—are mostly disenfranchised groups. Many obstacles hinder their upward social mobility, and not all of these obstacles arise from xenophobia or racism, still less from Islamophobia (a term invented by the Islamist movement to deflect any criticism directed against it). But discriminatory attitudes play a large part.

In the twentieth century, communism or socialism secured the dialectical integration of Europe's underprivileged classes into the political debate. That integration was institutionalized through participation in elections and even access to government. Today, these ideologies are irremediably obsolete, as the collapse of the Berlin Wall confirmed. European political space no longer contains a party or organization with which those who believe they have been classified unjustly in the social hierarchy can identify. From time to time, in Vienna or Amsterdam, Rome or Paris, the far right has managed to capture the malcontents' vote, but this is a xenophobic reflex. Its essential target is the "indigenous" European population, defined to the detriment of those with immigrant origins—even if some of the latter are starting to perceive far-right ideology as a means of achieving inclusion and putting forward their own social demands.

It would be naive to imagine that dispossessed young people from the southern and eastern Mediterranean region could integrate seamlessly into European society. That society itself is fragmented by conflict: social groups struggle against one another, conclude alliances to improve their relative positions, conquer power or grab market share. The recent history of immigration, like that of the lower classes in general, shows clearly that upward social mobility comes about only through political struggle— through radical challenge to the foundations of the social order. It is unsurprising that this conflictual dimension should manifest itself today in discontent among Europeans from Muslim backgrounds, or that religious leaders should take advantage of their plight to advance their own agenda, be it Islamist, salafist, or whatever.

But it would also be illusory to believe that religious leaders are necessarily the only possible representatives of this population—or that this population will be content to define itself exclusively as

"Young Muslims" whose consciousness must be expressed through Islamist militancy. The battle for Europe is larger than the one that religious leaders would have these young Muslims fight. It is a battle over the right of self-definition. The war for Muslim minds around the world may turn on the outcome of this struggle.

Conclusion

For the past fourteen centuries, Muslim societies have been pulled between two poles that have influenced the ebb and flow of Islamic civilizations—*jihad* and *fitna*.

The first of these terms is well known, and within traditional Islamic culture it has a positive connotation. It designates the effort required of each believer to extend the influence of Islamic faith and values outward, to the larger world, and to tighten their grip not only on the unruly passions of individuals but also on the extended social organization. Jihad is the instrument that restores harmonious order to the world by submitting a reluctant humanity to the Quran's unchanging laws. At its extreme, that endeavor expresses itself in holy war, either for purposes of conquest or for defense. But the concept also inspires, less ostentatiously, the everyday proselytism aimed at making Muslims "better believers" and the intense activity directed at converting nonbelievers through nonviolent means. In its largest sense, jihad is the moving force behind the propagation of the faith, which takes place "by the sword and the holy book."

The second word, fitna, is less known by those who are not conversant with Islam. It has an opposite and negative connotation from jihad. It signifies sedition, war in the heart of Islam, a centrif-

ugal force that threatens the faithful with community fragmentation, disintegration, and ruin. Whereas jihad sublimates internal
tensions and projects them outward, toward the land of unbelief,
fitna undermines Muslim society from within. This danger preys
on the conscience of the ulema and scholars of religion, motivat-
ing them to remain vigilant and prudent so that fitna can be
avoided.

The responsibility to avoid fitna explains why only the ulema
can legally declare jihad in its extreme form as armed struggle.
Only they are qualified, through learning and experience, to weigh
the hoped-for gains against the risk that jihad might devolve into
fitna. This question must be considered carefully in times of mobilization, whether to defend the *umma* against the attacks of unbelievers—the faraway enemy—or to go on the offensive against
them. But judgment is even more critical when jihad is contemplated within the realm of Islam itself, against the nearby enemy—
corrupt regimes suspected of violating sharia. Suspended like the
sword of Damocles, jihad threatens not just the ruler's power but
the larger social order. If jihad is declared inappropriately, there is
a danger that anarchy and chaos may follow.

The 9/11 attack on the United States, according to its perpetrators, was the ultimate expression of jihad striking at the heart of the
faithless Western enemy. It delivered the initial blow in a battle
that was expected eventually to conquer first Europe and then
America, leading ultimately to the West's submission to the one
true faith. This would bring to its apotheosis a process that had
eaten away at Byzantium for centuries, gradually taking over its
empire and ending its civilization. While awaiting this radiant
future—evoked in messianic tones by online sheikhs issuing
fatwas—the holy war, as envisioned by radical Islamists, took as its
first goal the destruction of the nearby enemy through a ricochet

effect. Attacks on the West would topple evil regimes in Islamic countries that drew their power and protection from Western hegemony.

Beyond the circle of Bin Laden and Zawahiri and their supporters and admirers, however, the majority of Islamists and salafists, let alone most of the world's Muslims, no longer see the commando action carried out by the *"umma's* blessed vanguard" against the twin towers and the Pentagon as fulfilling the promise of jihad. On the contrary, after the first few seconds of enthusiasm for this blow to America's "arrogance," most Muslims saw the massacre of innocents on September 11 as opening the door to disorder and devastation within the house of Islam. Not only did the U.S. military promptly destroy the regimes of the Taliban and Saddam Hussein, not only were American troops camped on Islam's soil from Baghdad to Kabul, but the holy war that was supposed to flare up and "burn the hands" of the infidel West, as Zawahiri put it, brought about only ruin and destruction in the Middle East, at least for the near term. The uprising of the faithful that was expected to seize power and reverse the decline of Islamist political movements in the 1990s did not materialize.

The ulema have lost control over the declaration of jihad and no longer have a means of warning believers against fitna. Militant activists have overridden them, laughing at their circumspection and turning their backs on the rich histories of Muslim cultures. These masters of postmodern technologies surf the Web and pilot airplanes, while nurturing a totally closed, salafist vision of the world. To resolve the tension underlying this dissociation of consciousness, they embark on a quest for martyrdom. Convinced that their death will trigger a cataclysm which can save the community of believers and that they will be transported immediately to Paradise, they eagerly volunteer for suicide operations, without stopping to consider whether the violence they deploy in order to quit life will leave fitna in its wake.

Fitna is precisely the condition that one finds today in the Middle East. The situation in Palestine is worse than it has been at any time since the *nakba*, the "catastrophe" or defeat of 1948. Hamas and Islamic Jihad consume their energy in an unending series of suicide attacks that have not weakened Israel's resolve. Meanwhile, Ariel Sharon, his position made more secure by the threat of terror in the United States, is implementing a policy of harsh repression, which, besides annihilating Islamist leaders and activists, has crushed Palestinian society, pulverized its political structures, and shredded its economy. As a result, Judeophobia has never been so intense, or so widespread, as it is in the Muslim world today.

The opportunistic invasion and occupation of Iraq by the United States and its allies opened a Pandora's box of ethnic strife and hostility. Despite the official handover of power to an indigenous government on June 28, 2004, the nation's future as a unified state is highly uncertain. Insurgent attacks claim victims almost every day. Iraqi citizens, whether Arabs or Kurds, Sunnis or Shiites, are bearing the brunt of the killing and maiming as the country sinks deeper into fitna. Since 2003, on jihadist websites, Iraq has been declared a new battleground for an all-out holy war. Bin Laden's imitators are calling for the massacre of foreign soldiers, Shiites, Kurds, and "collaborators," while ordering women to veil and demanding the strict application of sharia.

From the moment that U.S. troops triumphantly entered Baghdad, the kingdom of Saudi Arabia, which Bin Laden and most of the September 11 hijackers once called home, has experienced an increase in terrorist activities. Through hostage-taking, murder, and bombing operations, terrorists have targeted expats who are essential to the petro-monarchy's survival, thus jeopardizing the kingdom's economic equilibrium as the world's main supplier of oil. This downward spiral into political instability portends dire consequences for the nation and the region. The Muslim world itself could not survive such a turn of events: destabilization would threaten the security of the holy sites and the pilgrimage to Mecca. Fitna would engulf Islam's symbolic center, the heart of the community of believers—the *qibla* toward which every Muslim in the world turns in prayer.

The Western powers, heavily dependent on the eight or ten million barrels of oil the kingdom produces every day, would have no choice but to secure the oil zone of Hasa in the kingdom's Eastern Province with armed forces. Such a project—an item that has been on the neoconservatives' agenda for over a decade—becomes more easily defended when Western lives are threatened, as was the case when jihadists slit the throats of foreigners (including one American) in Khobar on May 29, 2004, and when another American was kidnapped and beheaded in Riyadh fifteen days later. The horrifying images were online in a matter of minutes; militants have now annexed cyberspace to Dar al-Harb—the land of war— making the Internet jihad's newest frontier.

Since September 11, the world has been trapped in a vicious dialectic of jihad and fitna. By provoking a massive reaction from the United States, in the form of the Bush administration's war on terror, Bin Laden and his followers succeeded at stirring up unprecedented hatred for America throughout the Muslim world. Even if Arab public opinion, which has displayed its versatile, sentimental character in the past, shows a capacity for change, this reversal of emotion will take time. Things might have gone differently if the Muslim middle class could have identified with a positive project instigated by Washington for the region. Ironically, that is precisely what the democratization of the New Middle East was intended to be, in the minds of the neocons and those they influenced in the White House: democracy was touted as a cure for the corruption and authoritarianism of ruling elites and as insurance against terrorism, which the neocons saw as merely a reaction to despotism and despair.

But these bearers of the discourse of democratization and modernization are associated, in the Muslim imagination at large, with the Bush administration's favoritism toward Sharon. The moral fiber of America's democratic project was further frayed by images of U.S. military police engaging in the sexual abuse and torture of Iraqi prisoners at Abu Ghraib. As a result, today, the word "democracy," preceded by the adjective "Western," has negative connotations for a large swathe of the educated Muslim middle class—although that class was the potential beneficiary of democratization. The Arabic word *damakrata*, which designates the democratization process, is frequently used pejoratively, signifying a change imposed from without.

This disillusionment is of course highly beneficial to the region's authoritarian governments. Rulers go from one international venue to another, insisting that they are favorable to reforms but that change cannot be imposed externally, especially if it violates a people's traditions and culture. Posing as the champions of nationalism, they wage facile battles against foreign imperialism while postponing any meaningful reform until an unspecified future date. The Bush administration's ineptness in the region could not have led to a more complete dead end.

Beyond the seemingly bottomless chaos of war—both the United States' war on terror and the Islamist jihad—the most notable development in the aftermath of September 11 is the breakdown of social and political projects throughout the Middle East. Future directions must now be sought elsewhere—in the quest for "Andalusia Lost" that pervades Muslim consciousness. But for such a quest to succeed in pulling the Muslim world out of its post-9/11 stagnation, Andalusia must be reconceived in a new way. Rather than representing a bastion of jihad on European soil, as the militants who organized the bombing of Madrid intended, Andalusia must come to symbolize a place where the hybridization and flowering of two distinct cultures can produce extraordinary progress in civilization. The advent of a new Andalusia is the only way out of the passions and impediments that Osama bin Laden's jihad and George W. Bush's war on terror have produced.

The effort is already under way to define and structure contemporary Islam in Europe. Today's new Andalusia is in gestation in Europe's outer cities, inhabited by young people of Muslim background from the south and east of the Mediterranean. But in contrast with medieval Spain, where intellectual influence came from the Muslim Orient and political power was in the hands of Muslim rulers, this is an Andalusia in reverse: intellectual creativity and innovation emanate from the West, and elites from Pacific Asia are integrated into its cultural sphere.

In Westminster, the European Parliament, the Bundestag, and in regional and municipal councils throughout Western Europe, the democratic political system that emerged from the European Enlightenment is starting to absorb men and women born in a Muslim tradition, for the first time in history. A promising generation of young Muslims now have opportunities to exercise democratic rights that are forbidden—or so restricted as to be emptied of significance—in countries where Islam represents the majority religion. Their political participation has its roots in local organizations, where many of these entrepreneurs, activists, professionals, and civil servants got their start. Such grassroots political activity requires a separation of mosque and state, as Islam settles into the

European milieu. This separation of the secular and religious domains is the prerequisite for liberating the forces of reform in the Muslim world.

Overturning the conditions under which European Islam is created and maintained opens the possibility that a new generation of Muslim thinkers will emerge—men and women with a universalist perspective, freed from the straitjacket of authoritarianism and corruption, emancipated from subservience toward their rulers and from the rage of a rebellion that endorses jihad, excommunication, and violence. The prospect that European Muslims may transcend both jihad and fitna pleases neither radical activists nor salafists and Islamists—even if the Islamists themselves, once they are actors in the European political arena, find their own rigid principles giving way to the compromises of democracy.

The crucial importance of the battle for Islam in Europe has not escaped the attention of those who wish to build an internal citadel on European soil, where the articles of faith are frozen in the heart of the "land of unbelief." Against this option, it is imperative to work toward full democratic participation for young people of Muslim background, through institutions—especially those of education and culture—that encourage upward social mobility and the emergence of new elites. Moving beyond the ideological constraints of jihad and fitna and, indeed, beyond Europe's geographical borders, these young men and women will present a new face of Islam—reconciled with modernity—to the larger world.

Sources

1. The Failure of the Oslo Peace

Books

Brown, Nathan J. *Palestinian Politics after the Oslo Accords: Resuming Arab Palestine.* Berkeley: University of California Press, 2003.

Dieckhoff, Alain, and Rémy Leveau, eds. *Israéliens et Palestiniens: la guerre en partage.* Paris: Balland, 2003.

Laurens, Henry. *L'Orient arabe à l'heure américaine: de la guerre du Golfe à la guerre d'Irak.* Paris: Colin, 2004.

Little, Douglas. *American Orientalism: The United States and the Middle East since 1945.* Chapel Hill: University of North California Press, 2002.

Parsons, Nigel Craig. *From Oslo to Al-Aqsa: The Politics of the Palestinian Authority.* London: Routledge, 2003.

Quandt, William B. *Peace Process: American Diplomacy and the Arab-Israeli Conflict since 1967.* Washington, DC: Brookings Institution Press; Berkeley: University of California Press, 2001.

Ross, Dennis. *The Missing Peace: The Inside Story of the Fight for Middle East Peace.* New York: Farrar, Straus, & Giroux, 2004.

Rothstein, Robert L., Moshé Ma'oz, and Khalil Shiqaqi. *The Israeli-Palestinian Peace Process: Oslo and the Lessons of Failure: Perspectives, Predicaments and Prospects.* Studies in Peace Politics in the Middle East. Brighton: Sussex Academic Press, 2002.

Said, Edward W. *The End of the Peace Process: Oslo and After.* New York: Pantheon, 2000.

Usher, Graham. *Dispatches from Palestine: The Rise and Fall of the Oslo Peace Process.* London: Pluto Press, 1999.

Articles, Papers, Documents

Celso, Anthony N. "The Death of the Oslo Accords: Israeli Security Options in the Post-Arafat Era." *Mediterranean Quarterly* 14, no. 1 (Winter 2003): 67–84.

Dieckhoff, Alain. "Israël-Palestine: du processus de paix au processus de guerre (1991–2003)." *Questions internationales* 1 (May–June 2003): 24–34.

Halkin, Hillel. "Does Sharon Have a Plan?" *Commentary* 117, no. 6 (June 2004).

"The Israeli-Palestinian Conflict." *International Affairs* 80, no. 2 (March 2004): 191–255.

Kristol, William. "A New Approach to the Middle East." *Daily Standard* 22 (May 2002).

"Proche-Orient: le naufrage." *Critique internationale* 16 (July 2002): 31–56.

Schattner, Marius. "De la paix manquée d'Oslo à la marche vers l'abîme." *Politique étrangère* 3 (July–September 2002): 587–600.

Zunes, Stephen. "The United States and the Breakdown of the Israeli–Palestinian Peace Process." *Middle East Policy* 8, no. 4 (December 2001): 66–85.

2. THE NEOCONSERVATIVE REVOLUTION

Books

DeMuth, Christopher C., and William Kristol. *The Neoconservative Imagination: Essays in Honor of Irving Kristol.* Washington, DC: AEI Press, 1995.

Dorrien, Gary J. *The Neoconservative Mind: Politics, Culture, and the War of Ideology.* Philadelphia: Temple University Press, 1993.

Ehrman, John. *The Rise of Neoconservatism: Intellectuals and Foreign Affairs, 1945–1994.* New Haven: Yale University Press, 1995.

Gerson, Mark. *The Neoconservative Vision: From the Cold War to the Culture Wars.* Lanham: Madison Books, 1996.

Kagan, Robert, and William Kristol. *Present Dangers: Crisis and Opportunity in American Foreign and Defense Policy.* San Francisco: Encounter Books, 2000.

Kristol, Irving. *Neoconservatism: The Autobiography of an Idea*. New York: Free Press, 1995.

——— *Reflections of a Neoconservative: Looking Back, Looking Ahead*. New York: Basic Books, 1983.

Podhoretz, Norman. *My Love Affair with America: The Cautionary Tale of a Cheerful Conservative*. New York: Free Press, 2000.

Steinfels, Peter. *The Neoconservatives: The Men Who Are Changing America's Politics*. New York: Simon & Schuster, 1979.

Articles, Papers, Documents

Boot, Max. "Neocons." *Foreign Policy* 140 (January–February 2004): 20–28.

Kristol, Irving. "The Neoconservative Persuasion." *Weekly Standard* 8, no. 47 (August 25, 2003).

Kristol, William, and Steven Lenzner. "What Was Leo Strauss Up To?" *Daily Standard*, September 9, 2003.

Muravchik, Joshua. "The Neoconservative Cabal." *Commentary* 116, no. 2 (September 2003).

Perle, Richard, et al. "A Clean Break: A New Strategy for Securing the Realm." Jerusalem and Washington, DC: Institute for Advanced Strategic and Political Studies, 1996.

Podhoretz, Norman. "Neoconservatism: A Eulogy." *Commentary* 101, no. 3 (March 1996): 19–27.

Wolfowitz, Paul. Interview with Sam Tannenhaus. *Vanity Fair*, May 9, 2003.

3. Striking at the Faraway Enemy

Books

Abd al-Rahim, Ali. *Hilf al-Irhab [The Pact of Terror]: Abdallah Azzam, Ayman al-Zawahiri, Osama bin Laden*. 3 vols. (documents). Cairo: Dar Mahroussa, 2004.

Anonymous. *Through Our Enemies' Eyes: Osama bin Laden, Radical Islam, and the Future of America*. Washington, DC: Brassey's, 2002.

Bergen, Peter L. *Holy War, Inc.: Inside the Secret World of Osama bin Laden*. London: Weidenfeld & Nicolson, 2001.

Burke, Jason. *Al-Qaeda: Casting a Shadow of Terror*. London: Tauris, 2003.

Clark, Wesley K. *Winning Modern Wars: Iraq, Terrorism, and the American Empire*. New York: Public Affairs, 2003.

Fouda, Yosri, and Nick Fielding. *Masterminds of Terror*. New York: Arcade, 2003.

Gunaratna, Rohan. *Inside Al Qaeda: Global Network of Terror*. London: Hurst, 2002.

Levitt, Matthew. *Targeting Terror: US Policy toward Middle Eastern State Sponsors and Terrorist Organizations Post-September 11*. Washington, DC: Washington Institute for Near East Policy, 2002.

Moore, Robin. *The Hunt for Bin Laden*. New York: Random House, 2003.

Articles, Papers, Documents

Bergen, Peter L. "The Bin Laden Trial: What Did We Learn?" *Studies in Conflict and Terrorism* 24, no. 6 (November–December 2001): 429–434.

Doran, Michael. "The Pragmatic Fanaticism of Al Qaeda: An Anatomy of Extremism." *Middle East Policy, Political Science Quarterly* 117, no. 2 (2002).

"Interrogation of al-Zawahiri's Deputy Revealed the Jihad and Al-Qaeda Secrets." *Al-Hayat*, March 18, 1999.

Ismail, Jamal, ed. "Al-Jazeera, Bin Ladin, and I" (interview with Ayman al-Zawahiri). *Al Zaman*, July 2000.

Kepel, Gilles. "Les stratégies islamistes de légitimation de la violence." *Raisons politiques* 9 (February–April 2003): 81–95.

Raafat, Amir. "The World's Second Most Wanted Man." *The Star* (Amman), November 22, 2001.

Raphaeli, Nimrod. "Ayman Muhammad Rabi' Al-Zawahiri: The Making of an Arch Terrorist." *Terrorism and Political Violence* 14, no. 4 (Winter 2002): 1–22.

Tourabi, Abdellah. *Les attentats du 16 mai 2003 à Casablanca: anatomie d'un suicide collectif*. Paper for the Diplôme d'études approfondies. Paris: Sciences Po, 2003.

Wiktorowicz, Quintan, and John Kaltner. "Killing in the Name of Islam: Al-Qaeda's Justification for September 11." *Middle East Policy* 10, no. 2 (Summer 2003).

Wright, Lawrence. "The Man behind Bin Laden: How an Egyptian Doctor Became a Master of Terror." *New Yorker*, September 2002.

al-Zayyat, Montasser. *The Road to Al-Qaeda: The Story of Osama bin Laden's Right-hand Man*. London: Pluto, 2003.

4. AL QAEDA'S RESILIENCE

Books

The 9/11 Commission Report: Final Report of the National Commission on Terrorist Attacks upon the United States. New York: Norton, 2004.

Buckley, Mary, and Rick Fawn. *Global Responses to Terrorism: 9/11, the War in Afghanistan and Beyond.* London: Routledge, 2003.

Clarke, Richard A. *Against All Enemies: Inside America's War on Terror.* New York: Free Press, 2004.

Crotty, William. *The Politics of Terror: The U.S. Response to 9/11.* Boston: Northeastern University Press, 2004.

Frum, David, and Richard Perle. *An End to Evil: How to Win the War on Terror.* New York: Random House, 2003.

Hayden, Patrick, Tom Lansford, and Robert P. Watson. *America's War on Terror.* Aldershot, Burlington: Ashgate, 2003.

Kellner, Douglas. *From 9/11 to Terror War: The Dangers of the Bush Legacy.* Lanham, MD: Rowman & Littlefield, 2003.

Kepel, Gilles. *Jihad: The Trail of Political Islam.* Cambridge: Harvard University Press, 2002.

Lewis, Bernard. *The Crisis of Islam: Holy War and Unholy Terror.* London: Weidenfeld & Nicolson, 2003.

Lewis, William Hubert. "The War on Terror: A Retrospective." *Mediterranean Quarterly* 13, no. 4 (Fall 2003): 21–37.

Mann, James. *Rise of the Vulcans: The History of Bush's War Cabinet.* New York: Viking Books, 2004.

Murtha, John P. *From Vietnam to 9/11: On the Front Lines of National Security.* University Park: Pennsylvania State University Press, 2002.

Articles, Papers, Documents

"9/11 and After." *Foreign Affairs* 80, no. 6 (November–December 2001): 2–58.

Burke, Anthony. "Just War or Ethical Peace? Moral Discourses of Strategic Violence after 9/11." *International Affairs* 80, no. 2 (March 2003): 329–353.

Joint Inquiry into Intelligence Community Activities before and after the Terrorist Attacks of September 11, 2001. Report of the U.S. Senate Select

Committee on Intelligence & U.S. House Permanent Select Committee on Intelligence, December 2002.

Kagan, Robert, and William Kristol. "The Bush Doctrine Unfolds." *Weekly Standard*, March 4, 2002.

———"The Bush Era." *Weekly Standard*, February 11, 2002.

Leffler, Melvyn P. "9/11 and the Past and Future of American Foreign Policy." *International Affairs* 79, no. 5 (October 2003): 1045–1063.

Lombardi, Ben. "The 'Bush Doctrine': Anticipatory Self-Defence and the New US National Security Strategy." *International Spectator*, April 2002.

Stein, Kenneth W. "La doctrine Bush de l'engagement sélectif ou la continuité de la politique étrangère au Moyen-Orient." *Politique étrangère*, January 2002.

"The 'War on Terror.'" *Intelligence and National Security* 17, no. 4 (Winter 2002): 31–76.

5. SAUDI ARABIA IN THE EYE OF THE STORM

Books

Benthall, Jonathan, and Jérôme Bellion-Jourdan. *The Charitable Crescent: Politics of Aid in the Muslim World*. London: Tauris, 2003.

Champion, Daryl. *The Paradoxical Kingdom: Saudi Arabia and the Momentum of Reform*. London: Hurst, 2003.

Cordesman, Anthony H. *Saudi Arabia: Guarding the Desert Kingdom*. Boulder: Westview, 1997.

———*Saudi Arabia Enters the Twenty-first Century: The Military and International Security Dimensions*. New York: Praeger, 2003.

———*Saudi Arabia Enters the Twenty-first Century: The Political, Foreign Policy, Economic, and Energy Dimensions*. New York: Praeger, 2003.

Fandy, Mamoun. *Saudi Arabia and the Politics of Dissent*. Basingstoke: Macmillan, 1999.

Gause, Gregory F. *Oil Monarchies: Domestic and Security Challenges in the Arab Gulf States*. New York: Council on Foreign Relations Press, 1994.

Heller, Mark A., and Nadav Safran. *The New Middle Class and Regime Stability in Saudi Arabia*. Cambridge: Center for Middle Eastern Studies (Harvard University), 1985.

Helms, Christine Moss. *The Cohesion of Saudi Arabia: Evolution of Political Identity*. London: Croom Helm, 1981.

Kechichian, Joseph Albert. *Succession in Saudi Arabia.* New York: Palgrave, 2001.

Kostiner, Joseph. *The Making of Saudi Arabia: 1916–1936, from Chieftaincy to Monarchical State.* New York: Oxford University Press, 1993.

———*Middle East Monarchies: The Challenge of Modernity.* Boulder: Rienner, 2000.

Lacroix, Stéphane. *Le champ intellectuel saoudien après le 11 septembre.* Paper for the Diplôme d'études approfondies. Paris: Sciences Po, 2003.

Peterson, J. E. *Saudi Arabia and the Illusion of Security.* Adelphi Paper 348, International Institute for Strategic Studies. Oxford: Oxford University Press, 2002.

al-Rasheed, Madawi. *A History of Saudi Arabia.* New York: Cambridge University Press, 2002.

Vassiliev, Alexei. *The History of Saudi Arabia.* London: Saqi Books, 2000.

Articles, Papers, Documents

Abou el Fadl, Khaled. "The Orphans of Modernity and the Clash of Civilizations." *Global Dialogue* 4, no. 2 (Spring 2002): 1–16.

Ahrari, Ehsan. "Political Succession in Saudi Arabia: Systemic Stability and Security Implications." *Comparative Strategy* 18, no. 1 (January–March 1999): 13–29.

"L'Arabie saoudite et la péninsule après le 11 septembre: défis et enjeux d'une région en crise." *Maghreb-Machrek* 174 (October–December 2001): 3–74.

Azzam, Maha. "Al-Qaeda: The Misunderstood Wahhabi Connection and the Ideology of Violence." Royal Institute of International Affairs, Middle East program, Briefing Paper 1 (February 2003).

Bradley, John R. "Are the Saudis Sunk? The Wahhabi–Saud Pact Has Held the Desert Kingdom Together since the 1920s; Now It's Pulling Apart." *Prospect Magazine*, September 2003.

Bromley, Simon. "Oil and the Middle East: The End of US Hegemony?" *Middle East Report* 208 (Fall 1998): 19–22.

Byman, Daniel L., and Jerrold D. Green. "The Enigma of Political Stability in the Persian Gulf Monarchies." *MERIA Journal*, September 1999.

Dekmejian, Richard H. "The Liberal Impulse in Saudi Arabia." *Middle East Journal* 75, no. 3 (Summer 2003): 400–413.

Gause, Gregory F., III. "Be Careful What You Wish For: The Future of US–
Saudi Relations." *World Policy Journal*, Spring 2002.

———"The Persistence of Monarchy in the Arabian Peninsula: A Comparative Analysis." In Joseph Kostiner, ed., *Middle East Monarchies: The
Challenge of Modernity*. London: Westview, 2000.

al-Hawali, Safar bin Abd al-Rahman. "Zahirat al-Irja' fi al-Fikr al-Islami
[The Phenomenon of Irja in Islamic Thought]." Doctoral diss., Umm
al-Qura University, Mecca, 1986.

Jehl, Douglas. "Holy War Lured Saudis as Rulers Looked Away." *New York
Times*, December 27, 2001.

Jones, Toby. "Seeking a 'Social Contract' for Saudi Arabia." *Middle East Report* 228 (Fall 2003): 42–48.

Judis, John B. "Who Will Control Iraq's Oil? Over a Barrel." *New Republic*,
January 20, 2003.

Kechichian, Joseph Albert. "Testing the Saudi 'Will to Power': Challenges
Confronting Prince Abdallah." *Middle East Policy* 10, no. 4 (Winter
2003): 100–115.

McMillan, Joseph, Anthony H. Cordesman, Mamoun Fandy, and Fareed
Mohamed. "Symposium: The United States and Saudi Arabia: Ameri-
can Interests and Challenges to the Kingdom in 2002." *Middle East
Policy* 9, no. 1 (March 2002): 1–32.

Morse, Edward L. "Is the Energy Map Next on the Neo-Conservative Car-
tography Agenda?" *Middle East Economic Digest* 46, no. 33 (August 18,
2003).

Nonneman, Gerd. "Saudi-European Relations, 1902–2001: A Pragmatic
Quest for Relative Autonomy." *International Affairs* 77, no. 3 (2001):
631–661.

Okruhlik, Gwenn. "Dissidence et réforme en Arabie Saoudite: de la religion, de l'Etat et de la famille." *La pensée* 335 (July–September 2003):
21–33.

Pollack, Josh. "Saudi Arabia and the United States, 1931–2002." *MERIA Journal*, September 2002.

Russell, James A. "'In Defense of the Nation': Terror and Reform in Saudi
Arabia." *Strategic Insights*, October 3, 2003.

Sennott, Charles M. "Driving a Wedge: Bin Laden, the US and Saudi Arabia." *Boston Globe* series, March 2002.

Seznec, Jean-François. "Stirrings in Saudi Arabia." *Journal of Democracy* 13, no. 4 (October 2002): 33–40.

Teitelbaum, Joshua. "The 'Desert Democracy.'" *Jerusalem Report*, December 15, 2003.

Tucker, Robert. "Oil: The Issue of American Intervention." *Commentary*, January 1995.

Unger, Craig. "Saving the Saudis." *Vanity Fair*, October 2003.

Vitalis, Robert. "Black Gold, White Crude: An Essay on American Exceptionalism, Hierarchy, and Hegemony in the Gulf." *Diplomatic History* 26, no. 2 (Spring 2002): 185–213.

6. THE CALAMITY OF NATION-BUILDING IN IRAQ

Books

Baram, Amatzia, and Barry M. Rubin. *Iraq's Road to War.* New York: St. Martin's Press, 1993.

Braude, Joseph. *The New Iraq: Rebuilding the Country for Its People, the Middle East, and the World.* New York: Basic Books, 2003.

Clawson, Patrick. *How to Build a New Iraq after Saddam.* Washington, DC: Washington Institute for Near East Policy, 2002.

Cordesman, Anthony H. *The Iraq War: Strategy, Tactics, and Military Lessons.* New York: Praeger, 2003.

Dodge, Toby. *Inventing Iraq: The Failure of Nation-building and a History Denied.* New York: Columbia University Press, 2003.

Dodge, Toby, and Steven Simon, eds. *Iraq at the Crossroads: State and Society in the Shadow of Regime Change.* Adelphi Paper 354, International Institute for Strategic Studies. Oxford: Oxford University Press, 2003.

Jabar, Faleh A. *The Shi'ite Movement in Iraq.* London: Saqi Books, 2003.

Kaplan, Lawrence F., and William Kristol. *The War over Iraq: Saddam's - Tyranny and America's Mission.* San Francisco: Encounter Books, 2003.

Luizard, Pierre-Jean. *La formation de l'Irak contemporain: le rôle politique des ulémas chiites à la fin de la domination ottomane et au moment de la création de l'Etat irakien.* Paris: Editions du Centre national de la recherche scientifique, 1991.

———*La question irakienne.* Paris: Fayard, 2002.

Murray, William, and Robert H. Scales, Jr. *The Iraq War: A Military History.* Cambridge: Harvard University Press, 2003.

Nakash, Yitzhak. *The Shi'is of Iraq.* Princeton: Princeton University Press, 2003.

Simons, Geoffrey Leslie. *Future Iraq: US Policy in Reshaping the Middle East.* London: Saqi Books, 2003.

Articles, Papers, Documents

Ajami, Fouad. "Iraq and the Arabs' Future." *Foreign Affairs* 82, no. 4 (January–February 2003): 2–18.

Ayoob, Mohammed. "The War against Iraq: Normative and Strategic Implications." *Middle East Policy* 10, no. 2 (Summer 2003).

Barnett, Jon, Beth Eggleston, and Michael Webber. "Peace and Development in Post-War Iraq." *Middle East Policy* 10, no. 3 (Autumn 2003).

Byman, Daniel. "After the Storm: U.S. Policy toward Iraq since 1991." *Political Science Quarterly* 115, no. 4 (January 2001).

Cirincione, Joseph. "Why We Are in Iraq." Speech at the American University, Washington, DC, March 23, 2003.

Cirincione, Joseph, Jessica T. Mathews, and George Perkovich. "Iraq: What Next?" Carnegie Endowment for International Peace, January 2003.

Dawisha, Adeed, and Karen Dawisha. "How to Build a Democratic Iraq." *Foreign Affairs* 82, no. 3 (May 2003): 36–50.

"From Victory to Success: Afterwar Policy in Iraq." *Foreign Policy*, July 2003.

Gerecht, Reuel Marc. "Why We Need a Democratic Iraq." *Weekly Standard*, March 24, 2003.

Hayes, Stephen F. "Saddam's Al-Qaeda Connection." *Weekly Standard* 8, no. 48 (September 2003).

Isherwood, Michael W. "U.S. Strategic Options for Iraq: Easier Said than Done." *Washington Quarterly*, Spring 2002.

Kagan, Robert, and William Kristol. "Why We Went to War." *Weekly Standard*, October 20, 2003.

Kristol, William. "The Iraq–al Qaeda Connection." *Daily Standard*, December 12, 2002.

Luizard, Pierre-Jean. "Les fatwas 'politiques' de l'ayatollah Al-Sistâni (Septembre 2002–Octobre 2003)." *Maghreb-Machrek* 178 (Winter 2004): 109–122.

———"Irak: comment éviter la partition?" *Politique internationale* 103 (Spring 2004): 141–160.

Marr, Phebe. "Iraq 'the Day After': Internal Dynamics in Post-Saddam Iraq." *Naval War College Review* 56, no. 1 (Winter 2003): 13–29.

"The Middle East after Saddam." *Washington Quarterly* 26, no. 3 (Summer 2003): 117–203.

Nakash, Yitzhak. "The Shi'ites and the Future of Iraq." *Foreign Affairs* 82, no. 4 (July–August 2003): 17–26.

Nye, Joseph S. "U.S. Power and Strategy after Iraq." *Foreign Affairs* 82, no. 4 (July–August 2003).

"Origins of Regime Change in Iraq." *Proliferation Brief* 6, no. 5 (March 19, 2003).

Ottaway, Marina, and Judith Yaphe. "Political Reconstruction in Iraq: A Reality Check." Carnegie Endowment for International Peace, March 2003.

Samii, Abbas William. "Shia Political Alternatives in Postwar Iraq." *Middle East Policy* 10, no. 2 (Summer 2003): 93–101.

Schanzer, Jonathan. *Ansar Al-Islam: Iraq's Al-Qaeda Connection.* Washington, DC: Washington Institute for Near East Policy, 2003.

Vulliamy, Ed, and Kate Connolly. "The Iraqi Connection." *Guardian Unlimited*, 2003.

Wimmer, Andreas. "Democracy and Ethno-religious Conflict in Iraq." *Survival* 45, no. 4 (Winter 2004): 111–133.

7. THE BATTLE FOR EUROPE

Books

Abd al Malik. *Qu'Allah bénisse la France.* Paris: Albin Michel, 2004.

Abdelkrim, Farid. *Na'al bou la France?!* La Courneuve: Gedis, 2002.

Adjir, Dalila, and Baghezza Addelaali. *Entrée interdite aux animaux et aux femmes voilées: lettre ouverte aux nouveaux hussards noirs de la République.* Foreword by F. Burgat. Valenciennes: Akhira, 2004.

Babès, Leila, and Tareq Oubrou. *Loi d'Allah, loi des hommes: liberté, égalité et femmes en islam.* Paris: Albin Michel, 2003.

Ben Halima, Abderraouk. *Le Tabligh: étape IV.* Saint-Etienne: Le Figuier, 2000.

Benzine, Rachid. *Les nouveaux penseurs de l'islam.* Paris: Albin Michel, 2004.

Bouzar, Dounia, and Saïda Kada. *L'une voilée, l'autre pas*. Paris: Albin Michel, 2003.

Ibn Baz, Abd al Aziz, Nasr al Din Albani, and Mohammed Ibn Uthaimin. *Fatawa al 'ulama al akabir: fima ahdira min dima' fi-l jaza'ir [Fatwas of the Greatest Ulema: On the Blood Spilled Uselessly in Algeria]*. Ajman: Maktabat al furqan, 1422 h.

Nordmann, Charlotte, ed. *Le foulard islamique en questions*. Paris: Amsterdam, 2004.

Ramadan, Tariq. *Arabes et musulmans face à la mondialisation: le défi du pluralisme*. Lyon: Tawhid, 2003.

———*De l'islam*. Lyon: Tawhid, 2002.

———*Globalisation: muslim resistances = La mondialisation: résistances musulmanes = La globalizacion: resistencias musulmanas*. Lyon: Tawhid, 2003.

———*Jihad, violence, guerre et paix en Islam*. Lyon: Tawhid, 2002.

———*Musulmans d'Occident: construire et contribuer*. Lyon: Tawhid, 2002.

———*Les musulmans d'Occident et l'avenir de l'islam*. Paris: Sindbad, 2003.

Ramadan, Tariq, and Alain Gresh. *L'islam en questions*. Arles: Actes Sud, 2002.

Ramadan, Tariq, and Jacques Neirynck. *Peut-on vivre avec l'islam?* Lausanne: Favre, 2004.

Venel, Nancy. *Musulmanes françaises: des pratiquantes voilées à l'université*. Paris: L'Harmattan, 1999.

———*Musulmans et citoyens*. Paris: PUF, 2004.

Weibel, Nadine B. *Par-delà le voile: femmes d'islam en Europe*, Brussels: Complexe, 2000.

Wieviorka, Michel, ed. *L'avenir de l'islam en France et en Europe*. Entretiens d'Auxerre. Paris: Balland, 2003.

Articles, Papers, Documents

Kechat, Larbi. "Pour un islam humaniste." *Esprit* 239 (January 1998): 77–98.

Khedimmellah, Moussa. "La carrière religieuse des jeunes prédicateurs de la Tabligh Jama'at en France: de la galère des banlieues à la dignité retrouvée par la Jet-society." *Islam* 1 (January–March 2002).

Malek, Abdel. *Le face à face des cœurs*. Rap recording with a bonus track titled "Que dieu bénisse la France [existentiel]." 2004.

Oubrou, Tareq. "Introduction théorique à la shari'a de minorité." *Islam de
France* 2 (May–June 1998): 27–41.

Ramadan, Tariq. "Islam et démocratie." *Pouvoirs* 204 (2003): 5–142.

Acknowledgments

Writing a book is a solitary process, but one that could not take place if the author did not benefit from the cooperation of all the talented people he met and by whom he was inspired, as well as the generosity of friends. This work is the result of the exceptional circumstances the Middle East has experienced since September 11 and of the imperative need to understand the region at a time when it is undergoing incredible upheavals. That imperative found its initial expression in constant travels, which provide the substratum, and I am glad to thank those who welcomed me, especially in the Arabian peninsula. In the United Arab Emirates, Ambassador François Gouyette, an eminent Arabist, exerted every effort to ensure that the "EuroGolfe network," which provided me access to a wealth of data and unparalleled analysis, came to fruition. I am infinitely indebted to the general coordinator of the EuroGulf network, and the main reason for its success, Bernard El Ghoul; he offered assistance when this book was still in the preparatory stages, and we shared many questions. I am also glad to thank France's diplomatic missions in the region, which always welcomed me handsomely, as well as the Abu Dhabi Cultural Foundation, the King Faisal Foundation in Riyadh, the Qatar Foundation, and my colleagues at Kuwait University's Faculty of Social Sciences, as well as all the friends who shared their knowledge of the Gulf.

In the United States, I benefited from considerable assistance in deciphering the neoconservative universe. My gratitude goes to Hillel Fradkin, as well as to all those who, within that circle, agreed to participate in contentious but always stimulating debates. Pierre Thénard, the perfect host on my many visits to Washington, DC, offered me his exacting, faithful friendship throughout this research project.

At the Institute of "Sciences Politiques" in Paris, I am grateful to President Richard Descoings, for the trust he showed me by granting me the chair of Middle Eastern and Mediterranean studies. We are fortunate in being able to offer a remarkable group of students, who register every year from all over the world, research conditions that measure up to their potential. When the author of a book is an academic, his first debt is toward his students, for the constant stimulation they provide and the pertinent impertinence their youth permits. This work was "tested" for two semesters in a spoken framework, during a course on the "Middle East crisis": thanks to those who participated and helped me think by asking questions. Among the students specializing in Middle Eastern studies, I would like to express my particular gratitude to Youssef Belal, Coralie Chambon, Thomas Heghammer, Stéphane Lacroix, Omar Saghi, and Abdellah Tourabi, as well as Myriam Benraad, who was a talented, efficient, and demanding research assistant. I benefited directly from their exceptional knowledge of the field and the sources. All of them were enrolled in Science Po's Muslim World Ph.D. program, which was set up in 1985 and has now been subsumed by an administrative reorganization. I am glad to pay homage to that exceptional hothouse, where a young generation of university professors and many regional experts in various professions received their training.

I would like to express my profound gratitude to Pascale Ghazaleh for her excellent work and the exceptional diligence she showed in translating my French text. In the preparation of this English-language edition, which differs somewhat from the French publication, I have benefited from the editorial advice of Joyce Seltzer and Susan Wallace Boehmer at Harvard University Press.

Finally, Ianis Augustin graciously accepted the fact that this paper twin would receive part of his father's daily devotion. I would like him to know that without his affection, and that of Yasmina, Charlotte, Nicolas, and Milan, nothing would have been possible.

Index

Friedman, Milton, 53
Fukuyama, Francis: *The End of History*, 68–69

Gamaa Islamiya, 82, 89
Gaulle, Charles de, 27–28, 33
Germany, 143, 208, 241–242, 249, 250
Ghamdi, Ahmad al-Haznawi al-, 132–133, 190
GIA (Groupe Islamique Armé [Armed Islamic Group]), 90, 91, 96, 125, 157–158, 242, 243, 273
Glucksman, André, 277
Gorbachev, Mikhail, 52, 55
Gore, Al, 16–17
Guantanamo Bay, 148, 243
Gulf Cooperation Council, 218
Gulf War of 1991, 23–24, 37–40, 44, 211, 219; Saudi Arabia during, 25–26, 87, 92, 180–181, 184, 218; and George H. W. Bush, 38–40, 55–56, 60, 63, 87, 230–231

Hadith, 159, 165–166
Hakim, Mohammad Baqir al-, 227, 230, 233–234, 236
Hakim, Muhsin al-, 228
Hakim, Abd al-Aziz al-, 236
Hamas, 12, 14, 16, 19–20, 24, 25, 43, 46, 101, 150, 219, 237, 291
Haram Sharif, 10–11, 14
Harbi, Khaled al-, 109
Hashemite dynasty, 162, 214–215
Hawala system, 89
Hawali, Safar al-, 175–176, 178, 182–184, 185, 188–190, 193, 195, 196
Hezbollah, 66; and Israeli withdrawal from Lebanon, 13, 15, 19; suicide attacks by, 13, 19, 35, 100–101; and Iran, 100–101
Hostages, 34, 100, 240, 247
Huda, Bint al-, 229
Huntington, Samuel: *Clash of Civilizations*, 61–62, 68, 94

Hussein, Imam, 34, 224, 225, 226
Hussein, Saddam, 3, 6–7, 17, 20, 65–69, 114, 138, 150; and weapons of mass destruction, 7, 67–68, 203–205, 208; Kuwait invaded by, 23–24, 25–26, 37–39, 55–56, 87, 92, 116, 167, 180–181, 184, 214, 218–219, 230; Iran invaded by, 33–34, 36, 37, 52, 116, 167, 180, 210–211, 214, 217–218, 224, 229–230; alleged relations with Al Qaeda, 111, 115–116, 197–198, 205–208, 240; policies toward Shia, 198, 201, 217, 225, 226, 227, 229, 230, 232–233; policies toward Sunnis, 200, 218–220; capture of, 201–202; policies toward Kurds, 210–211, 212; rise to power, 215–216, 227

Ibn Saud, King, 25–26, 153, 155, 161–163, 165, 171, 181, 186
Ibn Taymiyya, 137, 157–158, 159, 193, 239, 280
Ikhwan, 161–163, 165, 192
Indonesia: Islamist attack on Bali discotheque, 130, 185
International Atomic Energy Commission (IAEA), 203–204
International Federation of Islamic Student Organizations, 173
Internet, 35, 189, 199, 247, 251–253; use by Islamist movement, 1, 6, 7–8, 94, 110, 117, 122, 126–132, 156, 158, 160, 174, 177, 184, 191, 238, 247, 255–256, 260, 273, 277, 280–281, 283, 289, 290, 291, 292
Iran: attitudes of neoconservatives toward, 3, 66, 111, 198; relations with U.S., 30, 33, 36, 51–52, 84, 111, 167, 179, 198, 202, 203, 211; under the Shah, 30, 72, 180, 210; war with Iraq, 33–34, 36, 37, 52, 116, 167, 180, 210–211, 214, 217–218, 224, 229–230; relations with Iraq, 33–34, 36, 37, 52, 180, 210–211, 212, 214, 217–218, 223–224, 229–230; Khomeini and Islamic revolution, 33–34, 36–37, 52, 72, 84, 100, 151, 164, 167, 179, 180, 217, 218,